Counseling Theories

Practical Applications with Children and Adolescents in School Settings

Ann Vernon

Terry Kottman

LOVE PUBLISHING COMPANY®

Denver • London • Sydney

 Published by Love Publishing Company
P.O. Box 22353
Denver, Colorado 80222
www.lovepublishing.com

Library of Congress Catalog Card Number 2007941558

Copyright © 2009 by Love Publishing Company
Printed in the United States of America
ISBN 978-0-89108-335-1

Dedications

For Ann Vernon

This book is dedicated to my mother for inspiring me to be an educator.

For Terry Kottman

This book is dedicated to Jacob and Rick for always believing in me.

CONTENTS

3 *Multimodal Child Counseling in School Settings*   85

Matt Englar-Carlson and Alison Englar-Carlson

4 *Brief Counseling: Problem Solving and Solution Focused*   123

John M. Littrell

PREFACE

As counselor educators, we challenged our graduate students to "find their theory," stressing the importance of being congruent in theory and in practice. As we expected, this proved difficult for many students, because while they liked bits and pieces of many theories, sifting through them in order to adopt a basic set of theoretical assumptions was confusing and frustrating. Their impatience with the process reminded us of wanting to read the end of a good novel first so we could skip through the chapters because we knew the outcome. Our analogy was that they would find it difficult to build a tower without starting at the bottom.

And so they continued to read and sort through various constructs. They interviewed practitioners about how they selected and applied their theory, reporting back that their interviewees were basically eclectic. "If that works for them, why can't that work for us?" they questioned. "It's like driving a car," we explained … "You get much better performance if you have four matching tires. Your car may still run with mismatched tires, but not as well." That seemed to make some sense and motivated them to continue their search.

We certainly empathasized with our students' struggle but remained convinced that their job performance would be significantly enhanced if they could "practice what they preached." We suggested that being authentic by living their theory would make it much easier to help clients, because they would know from experience how the theory worked in real life. We were confident that they would find this integration of knowledge with the "real world" to be a far superior approach to counseling.

At the same time, we realized that, because our students were going to be working primarily with children and adolescents, it was even more difficult for them to do this. Most theory texts do not address specific applications with young populations, nor do they emphasize application of concepts to group and classroom settings. This book addresses that void.

In order to provide the most practical and informative material, we contacted leading experts in their respective fields to contribute to this publication, directing them to specifically describe how counseling professionals could apply this theory with young clients. We expect that after reading this book, you will have a more thorough understanding of the key constructs of each theory, as well as a clear picture of how to integrate theory with practice. Individual, group, and classroom applications are addressed, as well as how to work with parents and teachers. Each chapter concludes with a discussion of two case studies, one with a child and the other with an adolescent, to illustrate how to address the same problems from multiple theoretical perspectives.

Authors of each chapter no doubt engaged in the same soul-searching process as we encourage our readers to do. We think that this publication will be helpful to current practitioners who are still "searching" for a theory, as well as for future school counselors. We anticipate that the practical applications described in this book will help counseling professionals and future counselors know how to apply "a theory" with young clients.

Ann Vernon, PhD
Terry Kottman, PhD

Meet the Editors

Ann Vernon, PhD, NCC, LMHC, is Professor Emeritus, University of Northern Iowa, where she served as Professor and Coordinator of the School and Mental Health Counseling Programs for many years. Prior to being a counselor educator, Dr. Vernon was an elementary counselor and a middle school English teacher. Dr. Vernon has published extensively on counseling children and adolescents, developmental counseling, and applications of REBT with children and adolescents. Dr. Vernon is the former director of the Midwest Center for Rational Emotive Behavior Therapy, Vice President of the Albert Ellis Board of Trustees, and is considered one of the few leading experts on applications of REBT with children and adolescents. She currently conducts REBT training programs in Romania at the University of Oradea, the RINO Mental Health Center in Amsterdam, throughout Australia for the Australian Center for Cognitive-Behavioral Therapy, and has been an active presenter throughout the United States, Canada, and South America.

Terry Kottman, PhD, NCC, LMHC is a registered play therapist-supervisor who founded The Encouragement Zone, a center where she provides play therapy training, counseling, coaching, and "playshops" for adults. Dr. Kottman was a faculty member at The University of North Texas and The University of Northern Iowa prior to establishing her training center. She is the author of numerous books, book chapters, and journal articles on school counseling; play therapy; practical applications of Adlerian theory with children, teachers, and parents; and perfectionism. Dr. Kottman developed Adlerian play therapy, an approach to counseling children that combines the ideas and techniques of Individual Psychology and play therapy.

Meet the Authors

Jen Alexander, M.A.E., has worked as an elementary school counselor in Iowa for nearly ten years. She has extensive experience working with children with severe emotional and behavioral disorders both as a teacher and counselor. She trained with Dr. Kottman and uses Adlerian play therapy and sand tray therapy in her work with children and families.

Jill Bryant, PhD, is an Assistant Professor in Counseling and Human Services at Indiana University South Bend. She has used Adlerian theory in her practice for 15 years, first as a school counselor and more recently as a mental health counselor.

Andrea Christopher taught fifth grade in Colorado and is now an elementary guidance counselor at Lincoln Elementary in Cedar Falls, IA. A majority of the staff at Lincoln has been trained in or is familiar with Perceptual Control Theory. Andrea is now an ACT I Practicum Facilitator for the International Association for Applied Control Theory (IAACT).

Alison Englar-Carlson, PhD, is a school psychologist in the Garden Grove Unified School District in Garden Grove, CA. She has worked as a certified school counselor and school psychologist in Pennsylvania, Washington, and California where she applied multimodal theory in her practice.

Matt Englar-Carlson, PhD, is an associate professor of counseling at the California State University at Fullerton. Prior to receiving his PhD in counseling psychology from the Pennsylvania State University, he was an elementary school counselor in the San Francisco Bay Area. He was mentored at the Pennsylvania State University by the grandfather of multimodal child counseling, Donald D. Keat, PhD. Matt has lectured and taught about the application of multimodal therapy at national and international conferences. Clinically, Matt has applied the multimodal model in school settings with children and families across individual, group, and classroom settings. Matt's current research focuses on counseling boys and men. Recent publications include books *In the Room with Men* and *Counseling Troubled Boys.*

Perry Good is a popular speaker, trainer, and counselor. A senior faculty member of the International Association for Applied Control Theory (IAACT), she has conducted more than 4,000 workshops in the United States and throughout the world—Australia, Canada, Croatia, Indonesia, Norway, and Slovenia. Perry has written four books and co-authored a fifth with Jeff Grumley and Shelley Roy.

Susan Kroger, MA, NCC, is a mental health counselor specializing in early childhood development. She uses Adlerian play therapy in her work with elementary aged children and their families at the Center for Mental Health in Great Falls, MT.

Dr. John M. Littrell has been a counselor educator for 33 years. He has published extensively and produced six counseling videotapes for professional audiences. He has served on the editorial boards of *Professional School Counseling* and *Counselor Education and Supervision*. His specialty is the topic of brief, solution-focused counseling.

Dee Ray, PhD, P\LPC-S, NCC, RPT-S, is an Associate Professor in the Counseling Program and Director of the Child and Family Resource Clinic at the university of North Texas. Dr. Ray specializes in the areas of Child-Centered Play Therapy and school counseling. She is the past editor of the International Journal of Play Therapy, author of over 30 publications, and a frequent professional speaker at national and international conferences. She has 20 years of experience as a clinician and school counselor, has served as a counselor educator for ten years, and has been on faculty at UNT for six years.

Shelley A. W. Roy holds a master's degree in education from Hamline University in St. Paul, MN. She is a recognized leader in human resource development. She has served as Chair of the Board of Directors and is a trainer for the International Association for Applied Control Theory. Shelley has provided training across the United States, Canada, Australia, and China.

April Schottelkorb, M.Ed., LPCI, is a doctoral candidate in the counselor education program at the University of North Texas. April worked as an elementary and middle school counselor in Montana for several years where she utilized a child-centered approach in her counseling with students, and as a doctoral student she employs this theory with individuals in a clinical setting.

Case Study Contributor

Laurie Kirkpatrick, M.A.E, is a former high school English teacher. For several years Laurie worked as a secondary school counselor where she employed REBT with adolescents clients. Currently she is an admissions counselor at Upper Iowa University in Fayette, Iowa.

CHAPTER 1

PRACTICAL PERSON-CENTERED THEORY APPLICATION IN THE SCHOOLS

● ●

Dee C. Ray and April A. Schottelkorb

● ●

Overview

Person-centered theory, also referred to as client-centered theory, was developed by Carl Rogers (1902–1987), who is cited as being the most influential counselor and psychotherapist in American history (Kirschenbaum, 2004). He made a significant impact on the counseling profession by transforming the perception of the client, the counselor, and the therapeutic relationship. Through an extensive body of research, exemplary cases, and writings, Rogers demonstrated the need for and success of client-centered theory. Rogers promoted the basic principle of trust that individuals and groups can set their own goals and monitor their own progress in counseling (Raskin & Rogers, 2005).

Person-centered theory is based on 19 propositions listed in *Client-Centered Therapy* (Rogers, 1951) that describe personality and development. These 19 propositions show the personality to evolve naturally through a subjective perception of reality. As people experience life through their own lenses and understanding, they create a self that is a culmination of internal processes consisting of emotions and insights, or *self-created values*, combined with external processes consisting of the influence of parental values and cultural norms, or *introjected values*. Emotions and behavior are then based on this perception, which leads to *self-directed goals*. When a child encounters experiences that are consistent with his or her concept of the self, there is no problem. However, when a child begins to encounter messages that differ from the self-concept, these inconsistent messages must be assimilated to form a new self-concept, or psychological maladjustment will result. A child who learns to accept those experiences that are consistent and assimilate the ones that are inconsistent will evolve toward *self-actualization*, which leads to a deeper understanding and acceptance of self and others. Hence, human nature is positive, forward-moving, constructive, realistic, and trustworthy (Rogers, 1957). Rogers was a firm believer in the wholeness of the individual. One part of the being does not act without an impact on all others. For significant growth, all parts of the being must move together.

Virginia Axline (1947), who was a student and colleague of Rogers, fully applied the philosophy and concepts of person-centered theory to her work in counseling children. Axline applied person-centered theory in a developmentally responsive manner in her work with children by providing an environment conducive to their natural way of communicating. This environment consisted of a playroom of specific toys that allowed children to express their inner selves through play. The relationship that developed in the context of the playroom provided children a safe environment in which to express themselves verbally and nonverbally.

Child-centered counselors have a unique philosophy regarding the understanding of children. Children are seen as people who are capable of positive self-direction; metaphorically, as flowers to bloom, not clay to be shaped. Flowers require ideal conditions to bloom beautifully: sun, food, water, etc. When these conditions are lacking, the flower wilts and dies. In contrast, clay is poked, prodded, scraped, and molded until the creator produces a desired image. The image is a projection of the creator, not a quality of the clay. When school counselors adopt the "flower" metaphor of children, a focus on the needs of the children will begin to permeate the overall guidance program.

Landreth (2002) offered ten basic tenets about children that serve as a framework for child-centered counselors. They are:

1. Children are not miniature adults. As explained by developmental theory, children think and act differently than adults.

2. Children are people. They are capable of intense emotions and complicated thoughts.
3. Children are unique and worthy of respect. Each child possesses an individual personality and will.
4. Children are resilient. Although children experience some unfathomable situations, they are able to persevere beyond adult understanding.
5. Children have an inherent tendency toward growth and maturity. They are endowed with the will to strive for self-actualization.
6. Children are capable of positive self-direction. On their own, children are creative and able to develop ways to work positively in their world.
7. Children's natural language is play. Play is their safest and most comfortable way to express themselves.
8. Children have a right to remain silent. Because children operate most expressively in a nonverbal world, the child-centered counselor does not force them to communicate in an adult verbal world.
9. Children will take the therapeutic experience to where they need to be. The counselor need not direct the experience.
10. Children's growth cannot be accelerated. Children operate on their own developmental time schedule that an adult cannot direct.

These 10 beliefs offer a different way to understand children than the school system usually espouses. Traditional school systems generally apply a behavioral model that externally stimulates children to perform or not perform certain behaviors. This perspective emphasizes compliance over the specificity of the child as an individual, unique being.

Major Constructs of Person-Centered Theory

Goals of Counseling

In his own words, Rogers (1942) very clearly summarized the goal of counseling:

> It aims directly toward the greater independence and integration of the individual rather than hoping that such results will accrue if the counselor assists in solving the problem. The indi-

vidual and not the problem is the focus. The aim is not to solve one particular problem, but to assist the individual to grow, so that he can cope with the present problem and with later problems in a better-integrated fashion. (p.28)

The goal of person-centered counseling is to establish conditions so that the child can experience growth and integration. Raskin and Rogers (2005) postulated that if the counselor is successful in conveying genuineness, unconditional positive regard, and empathy, then the client will respond with a changed personality organization. Person-centered counselors believe that a child's experience within the counseling relationship is the factor that is most meaningful and helpful in creating lasting, positive change.

Although this goal of person-centered counseling may seem to differ from the usual goals of school counseling, in actuality, they fit together very well. The American School Counselor Association (ASCA) (2004) stated that the role of the professional school counselor is to assist all students' academic, personal, social, and career development needs with the goal of maximizing student achievement. ASCA further stated that student achievement can be maximized when school counselors help provide a safe learning environment along with guidance curriculum, responsive services, individual planning, and system support. All of these school counselor responsibilities require that school counselors foster an environment conducive to learning. Thus, when school counselors provide the core conditions of person-centered counseling—unconditional positive regard, empathy, and genuineness—they maximize students' growth potential.

Role of the Counselor and the Counseling Relationship

As previously stated, the counselor must provide specific core conditions to create an environment for change (Raskin & Rogers, 2005):

- *Empathy*—the counselor must get within the child's world and seek to live the attitudes expressed.
- *Unconditional positive regard*—the counselor must demonstrate a warmth and acceptance of the child.
- *Congruence*—the counselor must be willing to express any personal feelings that exist in the relationship.

■ *Implied conditions*—these may include psychological contact between the counselor and the child, the child experiencing incongruence, and the child experiencing conditions offered by the counselor.

The cornerstone of person-centered counseling is the therapeutic relationship. Rogers (1942) described four aspects of the therapeutic relationship.

1. The counselor provides warmth and responsiveness that makes rapport possible and gradually develops into a deeper emotional relationship.
2. The counselor establishes permissiveness in regard to the expression of feeling. When the child recognizes the counselor's acceptance of statements, the child will express all feelings and attitudes.
3. The counselor sets therapeutic limitations. Setting a structure for counseling, regarding timing and behavior, enables the older child to gain insight and the younger child to experience social reality.
4. The counselor eschews pressure or coercion. The counselor does not offer advice, suggestion, or pressure to follow one course of action over another.

Building on her developmental understanding of children, Axline (1947) identified eight basic principles that guide the counselor in child-centered play therapy. These basic principles are consistent with a person-centered emphasis on the primacy of the counseling relationship. These principles require the counselor to

1. develop a warm, friendly relationship with the child;
2. accept the child unconditionally, without wishing the child were different in some way;
3. establish a feeling of permissiveness in the relationship so that the child feels free to express him- or herself;
4. recognize and reflect the feelings of the child to create understanding for the child;
5. respect the child's innate ability to solve his or her own problems and offer the opportunity to return responsibility to the child;

6. not attempt to direct the child's actions or conversation, but instead allow the child to lead the way;
7. recognize the gradual nature of the child's process and to not try to rush counseling; and
8. impose only those limitations that are necessary to anchor the child's counseling to the world of reality.

These eight principles can provide guidance for school counselors who maintain a person-centered philosophy. Although specifically written with young children in mind, Axline's principles are applicable to people of all ages. For example, if a 16-year-old student came to a high school counseling office because of a fight she had with her teacher, a child-centered counselor would offer her the core conditions of empathy, genuineness, and unconditional positive regard. This student would be free to say what she needed to say within the confines of this school counseling office. This student would lead the conversation, and the school counselor would follow by making reflections of feeling, content, and meaning, which would allow her to discover what she wanted to do next. Although the school counselor may have some helpful ideas and suggestions to give her, telling her what to do would deny her innate abilities to problem solve. The person-centered school counselor's role is to act like a magnifying glass: to help reflect a clearer picture of the person that the student is. This clearer vision will allow her to move, grow, and change.

A school counselor's child-centered philosophy does not change as children reach new developmental levels or when one leaves the counseling office—it is a philosophy to be applied to all aspects of a school counseling role. Besides offering the core conditions within the confines of the counseling office, school counselors have opportunities to help create positive conditions of change when teaching guidance curriculum, leading groups, facilitating faculty meetings, and conferencing with parents. Child-centered school counselors believe that this attitude of providing specific conditions will facilitate change and growth for all who receive it.

Process of Change

According to Rychlak (1981), if a person's perception of experiences is incongruent with the perception of self, so that he or she holds to a self-concept that is not reflective of underlying organic feelings, then increasing tension comes to bear upon the personality structure. More simply stated, Rogers found that clients with this degree of incongruence suffer from low self-esteem (Raskin & Rogers, 2005). The incongruence between self-concept and self-ideal causes a noticeable lack of self-regard.

Rogers (1942) clearly delineated the therapeutic process that was necessary to facilitate substantive personality reorganization. The process begins when the child comes for help. The helping situation is defined as one in which the counselor does not have the answers, but will provide a place where the child can work out his or her own solutions. The counselor encourages free expression and accepts, recognizes, and clarifies negative feelings. When the child is able to fully express negative feelings, small movement toward the expression of positive impulses will occur. The counselor accepts and recognizes positive feelings as well. The child gains understanding and acceptance of self, followed by an awareness of possible decisions or courses of action. The child will follow with small but significant positive actions and with broader understanding, leading to further positive action. As a result, the child experiences a decreasing need for help and a recognition that the counseling relationship will end.

This therapeutic process may take many different forms in the school setting. In the case of individual or group counseling, the school counselor may meet with students referred by parents, teachers, and/or administrators. Once children come to the counseling room, they learn that this is a special time set aside for them, and they can use their time in many of the ways that they determine. The therapeutic relationship may also take place during guidance curriculum lessons. The school counselor provides a place for all students in the classroom where they can voice their authentic thoughts and feelings, and where these opinions are valued, accepted, and reflected back to them. Limits on actions that harm others or themselves are set, but the school counselor continues to accept and respect the underlying genuine feelings and thoughts of the students. Regardless of the setting in which they interact, the school counselor will encourage the therapeutic process, which will create more growth and change within the student.

Multicultural Applications

Because the acceptance of the child as a holistic organism negates any preconceived labels or designations, child-centered school counselors have the opportunity to serve all students while embracing their cultural and ethnic backgrounds. As the school counselor seeks to fully know and understand each child, it is imperative to recognize the significance of the child's cultural environment. Person-centered philosophy is sometimes criticized because its individual focus potentially ignores the contextual nature of some cultures (Kirschenbaum, 2004). However, a well-trained child-centered school counselor will recognize the impact of culture and embrace it along with the individual. Colbert and Colbert (2003) suggested that school counselors move from an individual student approach to a systems advocate approach in order to increase multicultural competency. The action-oriented child-centered approach allows, and even encourages, the counselor to work within the system of the school to train adults to work congruently with children, thereby creating a safer, more enhancing environment for all.

Child-Centered Research

As schools move toward evidenced-based practice, it becomes imperative for school counselors to cite research and literature on any approach that they implement within their schools. Kirschenbaum and Jourdan (2005) reported that more person-centered literature had been published in the 17 years since Rogers' death than in the previous 40 years. They noted that this is one method of determining the level of impact and current practice of person-centered counseling. In the largest meta-analysis to date on humanistic therapy outcome, Elliott (2001) found that clients who participated in humanistic therapies showed

- substantial change over time,
- stable post-therapy gains, and
- amounts of change equivalent to clients in non-humanistic therapies, including cognitive-behavioral therapies.

One area of increasing research has focused on child-centered play therapy in the schools. In a meta-analysis of play therapy outcome research, Ray, Bratton, Rhine, and Jones (2001) found that play therapy is an effective treatment. Treatment groups receiving play therapy performed .80 standard deviations better than nontreatment groups, placing them in the large effect size category. The meta-analysis included 94 studies spanning six decades, of which 73 were identified as investigations into humanistic/nondirective play therapy and 36 were conducted in school settings. Fall, Balvanz, Johnson, and Nelson (1999) compared 31 children who received 6 child-centered play therapy sessions facilitated by school counselors to 31 children not receiving services. They found that self-efficacy increased significantly for those children participating in play therapy. Johnson, McLeod, and Fall (1997) studied children who had received an educational label in the schools and found that, with one exception, all the subjects displayed both feelings and control through language and actions in the child-centered play therapy sessions. Over the course of the study, the children's skills in coping with the issues of their lives were observed to increase.

Post (1999) found that with a mean of four sessions, 77 at-risk 4th, 5th, and 6th grade students participating in play therapy significantly differed from their 91 control group peers. The results indicated that, although participating in child-centered play therapy did not enhance at-risk students' overall self-esteem, the students not participating in play therapy demonstrated a significant decrease in self-esteem over the course of the school year. Additionally, findings indicated that the experimental group developed an internalized locus of control over the course of the school year, while the control group remained the same. Flahive & Ray (2007) found that after 10 sessions of a child-centered approach to sand-tray therapy for preadolescents in upper elementary school, their teachers reported that the students significantly improved their internalizing and externalizing problem behaviors. Likewise, parents reported significant improvement in externalizing problem behaviors. The wait-list control group continued to experience increased behavioral problems, both internalizing and externalizing. Garza and Bratton (2005) found that, in comparison to a curriculum-based small group intervention, 15 child-centered play therapy sessions for Hispanic elementary students significantly decreased parental reports of externalizing behavioral problems, with the greatest decreases in conduct problems.

Past and recent research on person-centered verbal counseling and child-centered play counseling clearly supports the use of these methodologies with students in all grade levels, K–12. The research cited suggests that at the elementary level, school counselors choose child-centered play counseling because of the developmental age of their clients. At the middle and high school levels, person-centered talk and expressive arts counseling approaches become more developmentally appropriate. Regardless of the developmental level, person-centered counseling employs the core conditions of empathy, genuineness, and unconditional positive regard. As a school counselor demonstrates these conditions, students can grow and develop.

Interventions

Because of its reliance on basic counseling skills of active listening, reflective responding, and relational alignment, child-centered theory offers the school counselor a way of being. This way of being is a genuine style that the school counselor uses therapeutically to work with individual students, to work with small groups of students, to work in classroom guidance, to train teachers and parents, and to consult with staff.

A successful child-centered approach requires that the counselor meet consistently with students who are in need. Offering a consistent, safe counseling relationship in the school setting increases the likelihood of progress in counseling. Therefore, a school counselor should provide a consistent time and place for both individual and group counseling sessions.

Notably, it may not be feasible for a school counselor to be ready to have a child-centered session with a student at any time. Although a brief five minute child-centered intervention of reflecting a child's feelings and content can help the child move on to the next class period, more time may be necessary in order for this intervention to be effective. Sometimes a more directive approach will suffice for a short time period. However, the child-centered school counselor believes that a directive approach is a "quick-fix" method that will not result in significant, long-term change for the child. For example, if David has continual behavioral problems with his teacher and is sent to the office for a behavioral referral at least once a week, as a child-centered school counselor sees it, David will only cease his negative behaviors and increase positive behaviors when he feels that he is fully understood and accepted, thereby enabling him to accept himself. This requires that the counselor provide David regular child-centered sessions on a weekly basis. However, if he or she normally sees David on Tuesday, and he is sent to the office for behavioral disturbance on

Monday, the counselor might take five minutes to set up a plan with David regarding other coping mechanisms for his situation so that he will function without a major incident between Monday and Tuesday. This five-minute intervention will not help David in the long run, but it will help him through the next few hours until he continues to make deeper changes and progress through regularly scheduled counseling sessions.

An advantage of child-centered theory includes that the school counselor creates an environment where he or she can find out what is really happening with a student. Because a child-centered school counselor focuses on the child, rather than the identified problem, the child is free to express profound concerns that might be leading to his or her behavioral problems. Children are rarely concerned about their behavioral problems in schools or with teachers. Instead, when given the opportunity to express what is really going on with them, children almost inevitably express concerns about issues at home or with personal relationships.

The next two scenarios illustrate how behavioral problems in school often reflect student issues outside of school. The child-centered school counselor provides an environment where these underlying issues can be explored and worked through, as these examples demonstrate.

Scenario #1

Robert was referred by his homeroom teacher, who reported that he was failing the seventh grade because he refused to turn in homework and study for his tests. The first time I (Dee Ray) saw Robert, he walked into my office and dropped his head face down on my table. I reflected, "You feel bad." "You really don't want to be here." "You just wish you were somewhere else." "You seem kinda down." Robert never responded verbally. I continued to reflect throughout the 30 minute session. The next week, when I saw Robert, he drew a picture of his family in which he presented his stepfather as separated from the rest of the family on the paper, his mother with her back to the family, and he was competing against his dad in a game. He told a story about his mother coming home each night after work and going straight to her computer to talk with her friends. He spoke of an incident where his mother refused to read a bedtime story to his younger sister, even after he asked her to do so. He then further shared that he hated living with his mother and stepfather and wanted to live with his father.

After this session, Robert's affect was completely different. He was talkative, and we role-played interactions with his teacher at his request. Within a few weeks, Robert approached his teacher and talked with her about why he was failing and what he needed to do to raise his grades. Robert immediately began to turn in his homework and to pass his classes. Although this was the school's main concern, this resolution was secondary to Robert's priorities.

Following his assertive talk with his teacher, Robert and I began to talk about his relationship with his mom and dad. Robert clearly wanted to live with his dad and had many well thought out reasons for making the change. He also wanted his mom to pay more attention to him and do more with him. At his request, Robert and I role-played possible discussions with his mom. For several weeks, he came to sessions excited about a new way to talk to his mom. When he finally approached his mom, he shared his feelings with her and his plans. She quickly opposed his decision to move in with his father and was coolly receptive to his need for her to spend more time with him.

Although her response was not warm, Robert sought me out before school the next day to express his enthusiasm. He was excited that he had bravely talked with his mother, and he was undaunted by her reaction. Robert continued to try to talk his mom into allowing him to move in with his father. She never complied, but she did allow him to spend more time with his father. Robert also continued to complete his schoolwork and moved on to 8th grade the following year. Robert was presented to me as a student who was failing classes. If I had only focused on the problem of homework and tests, I would have missed the deeper level of pain that Robert felt, which was the reason for his behavioral symptoms. Through providing an environment of freedom and understanding, Robert was able to break through his depression and low self-esteem to seek behaviors that were more positive.

Scenario #2

Jacob was a second grade student when I (Dee Ray) met him. Jacob had shown tendencies to be violent toward his teacher and the principal. By October of the school year, he was being sent to the office for behavioral discipline referrals approximately 3 times a week. Generally, he was sent from the classroom for cursing, yelling, hitting others, and threatening the teacher. On the first day I saw Jacob, he had been sent to the principal's office for threatening his teacher. Only after exhausting all disciplinary actions and in spite of her doubts as to the usefulness of a counseling intervention, the principal agreed to allow me to see him. The school social worker was worried when I insisted on taking Jacob to the play-room, which was located in an outside portable building. As we headed to the playroom, Jacob was yelling about how much he hated his teacher, the principal, and the school. I simply reflected his anger and never attempted to contain him. He did not physically threaten me, although he said he wanted to "kill all of you" as we walked.

When we arrived in the playroom, Jacob began to throw things around the room. He threw all of the toys on the floor or against the wall. Interestingly, after we entered the playroom, he never mentioned his teacher or principal again. He did yell obscenities quite loudly. The following is a short transcript of the session:

Counselor:	You're so angry you want to say the worst things you can think of.
Jacob:	I don't care what you say. I hate all of you.
Counselor:	You're so mad, you hate us all.
Jacob:	(picks up a plastic dish) I'm gonna throw this at you.
Counselor:	You're so mad you want to hurt me, but I'm not for throwing things at. You can throw it over there.
Jacob:	(throws it to counselor's side)
Counselor:	You felt that you had to throw it, but you made sure it didn't hit me.
Jacob:	I hate you. I hate my whole family. I hate my whole faggot family.
Counselor:	You don't just hate me, you hate your whole family right now.
Jacob:	(still throwing toys against wall) They're liars! They're stupid! I hate them.
Counselor:	They've really hurt you.
Jacob:	(goes to bop bag) No, I'm gonna hurt them (begins to kick, punch, and scream at the bop bag).
Counselor:	You're going to really get them back. You get to hurt them now.

Jacob: (continues to beat up bop bag for 20 minutes until absolutely exhausted, sits down out of breath)
Counselor: You really got them and now you're tired.
Jacob: (a satisfied sigh) Yeah.

This ended our session, and Jacob and I continued to see each other weekly for the rest of the year. I learned that his mother had abandoned him and that his uncle had sexually abused him within the last two years. He had already been initiated into gang activity and was engaging in criminal acts. The abuse was reported, and I worked with his grandmother (his legal guardian) on ways to reflect his feelings and limit his behavior.

Our sessions continued in a very similar manner to the one described. He used the child-centered play therapy sessions to express an intense amount of anger and frustration. Although his aggression remained high in session, his behavioral discipline referrals ceased, and he was not sent to the office the remainder of the school year. His relationship with his teacher and principal improved, despite continued problems at home.

Both of these scenarios illustrate the effectiveness of a child-centered counseling approach. Children innately know what they need to work on to make their lives better. When child-centered counselors respect this self-actualizing tendency, they will see changes in children.

Selling the Child-Centered Approach to School Personnel

Teachers and administrators often experience difficulty in understanding how a person-centered approach can be helpful for the problems that they experience in the classroom. They might sometimes complain when a child visits the counselor that, "they're not actually doing anything, just getting out of class," or "letting him play is just giving him a reward for his bad behavior."

These kinds of misunderstandings between teachers and counselors can be improved by educating the school staff. In order to help school personnel understand the value of the child-centered approach, they need to understand how it works and recognize its success. School counselors should offer in-service trainings on their counseling and guidance approach. They should share examples, within the limits of confidentiality of course, and allow teachers and administrators to question their methodology. Possibly even more than other school counselors, person-centered school counselors must advocate for their approach and must form a supportive rhetoric for how they operate.

Another consideration in applying the person-centered theoretical approach in schools is the selection of students to receive services. When coordinating a comprehensive developmental guidance program, elementary school counselors must recognize their personal limitations. It is not possible for a school counselor to provide counseling to every student who is in need. In fact, if possible, most students should be referred to outside resources for help. Referral helps to balance the counseling load. When making referrals, a school counselor should maintain a current list of competent person-centered adolescent and play counselors.

When referring a child to another counselor is not an option, the counselor should look at certain factors to determine appropriate intervention:

- Severity of problem
- Appropriateness for group counseling
- Level of confidentiality that can be assured
- Developmental level

This prioritization of students may be difficult for many person-centered school counselors. However, when a counselor's caseload ranges from 300–800 students, prioritization becomes a necessary evil. An example of prioritizing is for the school counselor to start seeing children who are acting out severely. After six weeks of regular sessions, the counselor should re-evaluate each student's behavior to check for progress. If behavioral progress has occurred, the counselor will properly terminate with the student and move on to the next student. The difficulty in this approach is that a person-centered school counselor, as discussed, is concerned more with the child than the child's behavioral problems. A school counselor might see that the child is no longer behaving problematically in the classroom but in session notes the internal struggle still taking place in the child. At this point, the counselor must use therapeutic judgment to decide whether this child is in more need than the child who is next in line. Although this is an agonizing decision for most school counselors, one advantage of counseling in schools is the opportunity to continue observing the student after termination. If the student's behavioral problems resurface immediately, the school counselor will know that the relationship ended prematurely and can resume the counseling relationship.

Counseling Applications with Young Children

INDIVIDUAL COUNSELING APPLICATIONS

From a child-centered approach, play therapy is the most appropriate modality of individual counseling. The use of play therapy is based on children's developmental stages. Piaget (1962) offered his theory of cognitive development, which distinguishes the way that children understand and process information from the way that adults function. Most children on the elementary level function at the two stages identified as preoperational (2–7 years) and concrete operational (8–11 years). These stages are approximately identified with chronological ages, but development is specific to the individual. At the preoperational stage, a child is acquiring the skill of language where symbols are used to mentally represent objects. Also, in this stage, a child's thinking is rigid and limited to how things appear at the time. This is the stage of magical thinking, in which children create implausible explanations for things they do not understand. A child's play behaviors become increasingly imaginary but the complexity of make-believe play increases to encompass emerging cognitive patterns. Internally, the child is amassing understanding and knowledge, but externally, the child still lacks the ability to communicate this enhanced way of working within the world. Play is the child's most natural way of communicating this internal awareness of self and others.

The concrete operational stage offers children the ability to reason logically and organize thoughts coherently. They are able to manipulate ideas and accept logical social rules. However, they can only think about actual physical objects; they still cannot maneuver abstract reasoning. They are unable to express certain complicated emotions, such as guilt or resentment, because understanding such emotions requires abstract thought. For those children operating in the concrete stage, play helps to bridge the gap between concrete experience and abstract thought.

In summary, play is an important medium for children for several reasons:

- Play is the natural language of children (Landreth, 2002).
- Developmentally, play bridges the gap between concrete experience and abstract thought.

- Play offers children the opportunity to organize real-life experiences that are often complicated and abstract in nature.
- Children gain a sense of control through play and learn coping skills.

Play therapy applies this understanding of children by offering them a therapeutic environment for their play.

When elementary school counselors have a solid developmental understanding of children, it seems natural that they would then embrace the use of play therapy with their students. Landreth (2002) promoted the use of play therapy in the schools by explaining the objective of play therapy in a school is to help children become ready to profit from what teachers have to offer.

Although play therapy is the most developmentally appropriate form of counseling young children, some school counselors do not receive training in play therapy during their master's education. As a child-centered school counselor, it is important to seek out play therapy training and supervision at conferences and workshops. To find training near you, check with the Association for Play Therapy (www.a4pt.org) and the Center for Play Therapy (www.centerforplaytherapy.com). In addition, most states have a play therapy organization that offers an annual conference with opportunities to learn play therapy procedures.

After receiving adequate training in play therapy procedures, a school counselor will be prepared to set up a playroom in his or her school. In a school environment, it is preferable to locate the playroom away from heavy traffic or administrative offices. Because play therapy allows for the child's full expression, play sessions may be loud or involve verbal or nonverbal interaction that teachers or administrators do not understand. Landreth (2002) suggested that dimensions of a playroom be 12 by 15 feet. However, an open space of most sizes will suffice. In schools, janitorial closets, old bookrooms, or portable buildings can be used for a playroom. If a school counselor is very limited on space, he or she can develop a traveling playroom by maintaining a box or bag of materials that can be used in an empty classroom or behind the stage in the auditorium. The appendix to this chapter provides a list of materials that can be used for a playroom serving children of ages 5–12 (the usual range of ages served by an elementary school counselor). A detailed list of materials needed for a playroom or traveling bag can be found in Landreth (2002).

The following counselor skills are considered to be essential to the play therapy process. These are specific skills expected to be demonstrated in most play therapy sessions. The extent to which they will be used depends on the needs of the child and the relationship. Further detail on these skills can be found in Ray (2004).

Nonverbal skills   Play therapy is heavily reliant on nonverbal skills. Because play counselors believe that play is the language of children, the verbal world becomes less important in a play therapy session. Nonverbal skills are critical to any person-centered approach, but especially to play therapy. Nonverbal skills include leaning forward toward the child, being physically directed toward the child at all times, and appearing interested in and comfortable with the child throughout session. When responding to a child, the counselor's tone will be congruent with the child's affect by matching the level of affect displayed by child. As with counseling adults, the counselor should strive to be congruent with the manner in which the child expresses him- or herself. The counselor should not only match the child's affect but should also convey a sense of genuineness. The skill of matching verbal response with nonverbal response is representative of the counselor's level of genuineness with the child. Specifically speaking, the counselor would not flatly respond, "You're excited about the house you drew." but will match the emotional content of the child's words by adding excitement to his or her intonation. However, the counselor is careful to not animate his or her tone of voice so much that it overwhelms the child.

Verbal skills   The delivery of verbal responses by a play counselor to the child is almost as impactful as the words chosen. Effective delivery of responses includes a focus on succinct, interactive responses and rate of responses. Because play therapy is offered to young children and because play therapy recognizes the limited language ability of these children, therapeutic responses must be short. A maximum of ten words is a good general rule. Lengthy responses lose the interest of the child quickly, confuse the child, and often convey a lack of understanding on the part of the counselor. Addressing the rate of responses indicates the counselor is matching his or her level of interaction to that of the child. If the child is quiet and reserved, then the play counselor will slow his or her responses. If the child is highly interactive and talkative, the play counselor will want to match this level of energy with an increased number of responses.

Verbal responses in child-centered play therapy can be structured into categories that help facilitate growth in the child. The following are several relevant categories of verbal responses.

1. *Tracking behavior.* The counselor verbally responds to the child's behavior simply by stating what he or she observes. Tracking behavior allows the child to know that the counselor is interested in and accepting of the child. It also helps the counselor immerse him- or herself into the child's world. For example, (as a child picks up the scissors) "You're picking that up" or (as child jumps up and down) "You're jumping up and down."

2. *Reflecting content.* Reflecting content in play therapy is identical to reflecting content in talk therapy. To reflect content, the play counselor paraphrases the verbal interaction of the child. Reflecting content validates children's perceptions of their experience and helps to clarify children's understanding of themselves (Landreth, 2002). For example, the counselor responds to the child's detailed story of going to amusement park with his grandparents, by saying, "You got to do something really special to you with your grandparents."

3. *Reflecting feeling.* Reflecting feeling is the verbal response to emotions expressed by children in play therapy. The reflection of feeling can sometimes be threatening to a child and should be presented carefully. Reflecting feeling helps a child become aware of emotions, thereby leading to the appropriate acceptance and expression of such emotions. For example,the child throws a toy soldier across the room while saying, "He killed everyone. I hate him." The counselor responds, "You are really angry with that guy." Or, the child tries to take the top off of the glue unsuccessfully and then throws it on the floor. The counselor says, "You're frustrated with that."

4. *Facilitating decision-making/returning responsibility.* One of the play counselor's goals is to help the child experience a sense of his or her own capability and to take responsibility for his or her expression of capability. Responses that facilitate decision-making or return responsibility help a child experience him- or herself as able and empowered. For examples, the child wants to draw a picture and asks, "What color should the flower be?" The counselor responds, "In here, you can decide what color you want it to be." Or, before making an attempt, the child hands the

counselor the marker and asks, "Can you take the top off for me?" The counselor responds, "That looks like something you can do."

5. *Facilitating creativity/spontaneity.* Helping children experience their own sense of creativity and freedom is another benefit of play therapy. Acceptance and encouragement of creativity sends a message to children that they are unique and special in their own way. Experiencing freedom of expression allows them to develop flexibility in thought and action. For example, the child asks, "What do I make with these blocks?" The counselor says, "You can create whatever you want with those." Or, the child moves from one project to another in play session. The counselor acknowledges, "You changed to do just what you want."

6. *Esteem building/encouraging.* Encouraging children to feel better about themselves is a constant objective for the play counselor. The use of esteem building statements helps children experience themselves as capable. For example, the child tries a few ways to reach the top shelf. The counselor says, "You're trying again. You're not giving up." The child tries and tries to reach the top shelf, and after a few attempts, she succeeds. The counselor encourages, "You did it. You found a way to do it."

A word about praise and encouragement: Because praise is highly promoted in teacher education, school counselors often struggle with the difference between praising and esteem-building responses. A praise response, such as, "That's a pretty picture." or "I like the way you did that." encourages the child to perform for the counselor, and continue to seek external reinforcement, thereby eroding a sense of self. An esteem-building response, such as, "You're really proud of your picture" or "You made that just the way you wanted" encourages children to develop an internal sense of evaluation leading to an internal sense of responsibility.

7. *Facilitating relationship.* Because the counseling relationship serves as a model for all intimate relationships, the counselor should respond to any attempt by the child to address the relationship. Relational responses help the child learn effective communication patterns and express the counselor's care for the child. For example, the child is creating a scene in the dollhouse and stops to look up at the counselor but says nothing. "You're wondering what I think about that." Or, the child brushes the counselor's hair into a ponytail and says, "Now yours is like mine." The counselor might say, "You want us to look just alike." Finally, after the counselor sets the limit, the child responds, "You're stupid." The

counselor reflects, "You're really angry with me." Relationship responses should always include a reference to the child and a reference to self as counselor.

8. *Limit-setting.* Minimal limits help to provide an environment that fosters self-direction and self-responsibility. The goal is to help the child move toward the ability to self-limit. The philosophy of a permissive environment is sometimes antithetical to the beliefs of many schools. Hence, school counselors struggle with their own belief systems regarding limit-setting. Typically, limits are set when children attempt to damage themselves, another person, and expensive or irreplaceable toys, or if their behavior impedes counselor acceptance.

Landreth (2002) proposed the A-C-T model for setting limits in play therapy:

Acknowledge the feeling
Communicate the limit
Target an alternative

This method has been widely adopted by play counselors as the initial response to setting a limit in the playroom. In this model, the play counselor recognizes and addresses the child's feelings in the moment, "You're really excited about the paint." Secondly, the counselor sets a short, concrete, definitive limit, "But it's not for throwing on the walls." Finally, the counselor provides an alternative to the action, "You may use it on the paper." When children have directed energy in the moment, it is important to provide them an alternative outlet for that energy so that they do not feel the need to act on impulse. Although there are other methods for setting limits, the A-C-T model is short, direct, and works effectively.

GROUP COUNSELING APPLICATIONS

The skills used in child-centered individual play therapy are the same skills used in child-centered group play therapy. As in child-centered individual play therapy, a child-centered school counselor recognizes the group members' ability to develop their own potential to move in a positive direction (Landreth & Sweeney, 1999). Ginott (1961) recognized a child's "social hunger" as a need to interact with and develop relationships with other children. Group play therapy feeds this social hunger by placing children together in an environment that provides for freedom of expression and understanding of multiple worldviews. White and Flynt (1999) advocated the use of child-centered group play therapy in the schools due to its focus on

- developmental appropriateness,
- variation of function (applicable for preventive, remedial, or crisis intervention counseling),
- vicarious learning and cathartic effect,
- positive socialization, and
- growth through insight.

The practicality of using child-centered group play therapy in a school environment is limited by space and scheduling. Generally, the school counselor is provided very limited space for the use of play therapy. In response to this limitation, the school counselor may be able to serve only 2–3 children in a group setting. This number allows for comfortable movement in the space provided, while still providing the benefits of a social environment. Also, it is sometimes difficult for a play counselor to attend effectively to each group member if the number exceeds three.

An additional consideration for school counselors is the scheduling of students. School counselors will need to work with teachers to find the least restrictive time for students to attend counseling. Choosing multiple children from the same classroom sometimes helps with this problem.

Counseling Applications with Adolescents

INDIVIDUAL COUNSELING APPLICATIONS

Because child-centered play therapy is based in person-centered theory, any and all concepts regarding play therapy from this chapter are applicable to verbal person-centered counseling. Thus, just as it is important to reflect feelings in child counseling sessions, it is also important in working with adolescents. As preadolescents and adolescents advance through the verbal stage of communication, person-centered theory can provide for this development through two modalities, verbal counseling or expressive arts.

A child at the pre-adolescent or adolescent stage might often choose to communicate to the counselor in a verbal format. The school counselor then uses *verbal counseling* through the person-centered approach to reach the goal of providing a safe environment for the student while he or she moves toward self-integration and greater self-regard. Thompson and Rudolph (2000) conceptualized effective person-centered counseling with children by using the analogy of student and teacher. Children take on the role of teaching counselors about their problems. The counselor moves to the role of student, who lets the teacher (child) know how well the subject matter is understood through reflection and summary. By teaching the counselor, children learn about themselves and their lives. Counselors will typically use the provision of the three necessary conditions of empathy, unconditional positive regard, and genuineness through the techniques of active listening, reflection, clarification, and summarization. Although categories such as returning responsibility, esteem-building, facilitating creativity and spontaneity, and limit-setting were introduced through play therapy, these types of responses are also quite helpful in working verbally with adolescents.

Beyond verbal counseling, school counselors can also utilize *expressive arts*. Expressive arts counseling facilitates, for older children and adolescents, a process of creative self-development by providing them with inner resources to cope with internal and external struggles (Bratton & Ferebee, 1999). Expressive arts therapies include, but are not limited to, the presentation of paint, clay, photography, sandtray, and play activities. Newsome (2003) suggested that creative outlets allow students to communicate emotions that cannot be assessed through rational language.

Expressive arts counseling is sometimes presented in a very structured way so that the counselor determines the direction of the activity. From a child-centered perspective, the use of expressive arts would be explored merely through the presentation of the materials. For example, a high school counselor might regularly keep a sandtray and shelf of figurines in his or her office open for use by students. When a student arrived in the office, the counselor would merely present the counseling structure as, "This is a place where you can talk or use any of the materials in my office." Upon this presentation, the student would choose whether to enter a nonverbal world of communication or a verbal world of communication. This is especially helpful for resistant adolescent students. If the student chooses to place figures in the sand, the counselor would merely use his or her child-centered skills by reflecting and clarifying the student's nonverbal and verbal responses. A similar structure would be used for all child-centered expressive arts. A counselor could offer a shelf of art materials including variations of paper, markers, paints, chalks, magazine pictures and words, a digital camera with a one-step printer, ribbons, cotton balls, pipe cleaners, scrapbook materials and the like. The counselor would then leave these materials open for use by students who wish to create a project during a session. Sometimes these materials will be used by anxious students to keep their hands busy while they are talking about something of importance to them. This offers a nonthreatening environment to approach threatening areas of content.

GROUP COUNSELING APPLICATIONS

Group counseling is the modality of choice when serving adolescents in a middle and high school settings (Azima & Richmond, 1989). Adolescents are highly socially attuned at their particular developmental level and appear to respond more readily to peers than to adults. Studer (2005) summarized the benefits of group counseling in schools as

- being more time-effective than individual counseling,
- offering ease of sharing with peers versus an adult counselor,
- establishing a sense of belonging, and
- gaining new information from personal sharing and feedback.

The literature clearly establishes the ideal number of group participants at approximately eight members, especially for adolescents and adults (Davis, 2005; Gazda, 1989; Schmidt, 1999). However, in the school environment, unless the group is held before or after school, scheduling eight students can be difficult. Typically, 5–6 members will suffice to provide needed group dynamics.

Toward the end of his career, Rogers worked almost exclusively within the context of group counseling and group dynamics. Rogers found the encounter group to be a powerful tool in therapy because of its illustration of the growth process. Rogers (1970/1976) explained the process of encounter groups by describing the pattern found in most groups. The process begins with (a) milling around because of an absence of directional responsibility in the group, then (b) an initial resistance to personal expression or exploration, followed by (c) surface description of past feelings, moving into (d) the expression of negative feelings toward other group members that establishes safety for (e) expression and exploration of personally meaningful material, leading to (f) expression of immediate interpersonal feelings in the group which develops (g) a healing capacity in the group and fosters (h) self-acceptance and the beginning of change delving into (i) the cracking of facades that invites (j) individual feedback that leads to (k) confrontation that forms (l) helping relationships outside of the group sessions and then (m) the basic encounter (true experiencing of another person) occurs, encouraging (n) expression of positive feelings and closeness to develop the final step of (o) behavior changes in the group.

This pattern can be generalized to most groups and certainly to verbally oriented adolescent groups in the schools. School counselors who run person-centered groups in the school employ many of the same skills as they use in individual sessions. However, the school counselor additionally reflects upon the dynamics among the individual adolescent members in the person-centered groups.

Classroom Guidance Applications and Interventions

Guidance programs will also benefit from a comprehensive integration of the basic philosophy behind child-centered play therapy. This philosophy includes recognition of the value of play as the natural medium of expression along with a trust in the child as a capable person. In addition, basic to this philosophy is the need for adults in the child's life to offer an environment conducive for growth. Based on these guidelines, the school counselor can introduce play as part and parcel of each program component. For the secondary school counselor, emphasis on providing an environment to meet the needs of individual students within a larger context will help to focus the guidance curriculum.

Guidance curriculum is the educational component of the whole guidance program. School counselors must take into account the academic and emotional needs of all students, and they must attempt to provide students with the necessary tools to cope with difficult situations. Using basic child-centered philosophy, the school counselor would initially assess the needs of the children being served. The counselor can assess needs by talking with classes and groups of children to determine the types of situations that most of them experience. The counselor might provide a survey for children that can be administered by the teacher either orally or in writing. A survey should include questions regarding home life situations as well as academic situations.

Once the counselor is aware of typical situations for the student population, he or she can create or choose guidance curricula accordingly. For example, many guidance curricula are directed at increasing self-esteem or enhancing self-concept. Yet many students are concerned with making and keeping friends, a more concrete concept than self-esteem. Students will respond to guidance programs that that directly relate to their concerns.

After a school counselor has identified the guidance curricula most relevant to his or her students, the task then becomes how to deliver the guidance in a manner that will be well received. Considering knowledge of play and children, guidance at the elementary level should be delivered in a way that actively involves children. Guidance should be kinesthetic and participatory in delivery. For young children, kinesthetic activities can involve art, puppets, and other play materials. For example, if a counselor is delivering a puppet show about caring for others, the students should be allowed to interact verbally with the puppets and touch the puppets. Following the counselor, the students could make up their own puppet show on the subject. Presenting a puppet show with no interaction ignores the developmental need of children to learn and experience through play. Older elementary students can participate in guidance by role-playing and creating dramas. They also respond to expressive arts and music. In addition, older elementary students have the ability to deliver guidance in peer form. This keeps them actively involved and learning through experience.

For adolescents, recognizing their developmental needs provides a basis for a person-centered application. Middle school and high school students are capable and self-aware enough to identify their own needs for guidance information. They should be surveyed regarding their needs and preferences for guidance material. In addition, it is developmentally appropriate to train adolescents in basic person-centered skills and in guidance delivery in the group format. Peer-led group facilitation will help adolescents respond more openly and beneficially to meet their own personal goals.

Working with Parents and Teachers

Children spend the majority of their time with their parents and teachers. It is therefore crucial for school counselors to help these important people learn skills to interact more effectively with children. One key element of ASCA's system support for the guidance program is parent education. At the early elementary level, many parents are still quite interested in parent education. After seeing significant changes in their school-age child, parents will seek help through the transitions. A school counselor who provides child-centered play therapy will naturally work to teach parents the skills that seem to be working in counseling.

The most effective method for this education is *filial training*. Filial training is based on the model developed by Bernard and Louise Guerney in the 1960s (Guerney, 2000). Filial training uses play as a means of facilitating the relationship between parent and child. In addition, filial training teaches parents basic parenting skills that help them to communicate more effectively with their children. Filial training allows the school counselor to educate parents regarding not only their children, but also regarding the benefits of play and child-centered play therapy.

Landreth (2002) modified the filial therapy training model to a ten-week psychoeducational and support format in which the counselor instructs parents in a group setting on principles of child-centered play therapy. The parents then conduct 30-minute play sessions with their children on a weekly basis. The counselor supervises parents in developing their relationship skills with their child. Filial therapy helps parents to strengthen their relationships with their children, create understanding and acceptance of their child, develop warm memories, and rediscover the joy of parenting (Guerney & Stover, 1971; Landreth, 2002; VanFleet, 1994). In addition, strong outcome research supports the efficacy of the filial model (Ray, Bratton, Rhine, & Jones, 2001). Recently, the filial therapy model has been applied to teachers in the school setting. Ray, Muro, and Schumann (2004) explored the use of the filial model with teachers trained to facilitate play sessions with a student of focus. Post, McAllister, Sheely, Hess, and Flowers (2004) and White, Flynt, and Draper (1997) have successfully researched the use of a modified filial model with teachers.

Operating from a child-centered perspective, a school counselor may want to involve teachers and staff in the guidance program. By teaching reflective listening, returning responsibility, and choice giving to school adults, the school counselor can create an environment conducive to effective individual decision-making.

Reflective listening involves active listening by the adult and then the presentation of a reflective statement to the child. If a child spends several minutes telling the teacher about dinosaurs, the teacher can respond with a simple statement, such as "You sure know a lot about dinosaurs." Reflective statements serve a few purposes. The child is sent the message that someone is listening and someone cares. Also, the adult is sending the message that the child is important and counts in some way. Reflective statements build self-esteem in children.

Returning responsibility addresses the value that children are capable people. Ginott (1965) referred to returning responsibility as freedom phrases. These are phrases that adults can use to send the message that we trust the child and the child's ability to make positive decisions. Freedom phrases include, "It's up to you," "You can decide," and "That's your choice." Returning responsibility to children allows them to experience making decisions and the consequences of those decisions, which is key to academic success. In addition, returning responsibility increases self-esteem by sending the message the child is trusted.

Finally, *choice giving* is an integral part of helping children move into the realm of making life decisions. Adults in schools can give choices in almost any arena. Simple choices like "John, would you like to use a pencil or a pen today?" help children feel empowered in their daily decision-making. Bigger choices like, "John, do you choose to go to the office for throwing the rock or to sit outside in the hallway?" allow the child to determine and experience consequences. These are just a few of the skills that help create a climate in which a child learns to make individual academic decisions that will affect the development of personal self-regard.

•••

CASE STUDY: MANUEL

The child-centered approach to Manuel's case would take a different strategic pattern than that evident in his history within the school system. As presented, many adults have taken on the responsibility of identifying Manuel's problem and creating a plan for him. From the history, it appears that Manuel has interacted with his mother, father, 1st grade teacher, psychiatrist, school psychologist, 3rd grade teacher, unidentified administrators, and now, his school counselor. All of these adults have had his best interest at heart and have created multiple "solutions" to his "problems."

Thus far, the solutions included medical referral, concentration techniques, praise, and redirection. Thus far, none of these adult-initiated solutions have been successful. This type of problem–solution orientation to children's issues is typical in the school environment. Often, school personnel and parents will spend extensive amounts of time and energy working to figure out what the problem is and then attempting to find solutions. However, from a child-centered perspective, what appears to be missing in the equation is the child.

As professionals, we can make many assumptions regarding Manuel based on his history and the behavior reported by parents and teachers. He might be resistant to following the same patterns as his siblings in order to find his own identity, he might suffer from low self-esteem because of pressure from his parents, he might be acting helpless to gain attention from adults in his life, or he might be highly extraverted and active, and thereby feels restrictively confined by the school environment. Any of these hypotheses might be accurate, along with many more. Whatever the hypothesis, Manuel is not sharing his reason verbally, but he is "behaving" it. Hence, he is demonstrating what most elementary age children would do in his situation. He expresses himself more through his actions than through his words. A child-centered school counselor would respond to this case by offering play therapy so that Manuel can truly express how he sees his world and be understood and accepted in his expression.

Initial Preparation for Child-Centered Play Therapy Intervention

In initially approaching this case, the child-centered school counselor would begin by surveying the best methods for bringing Manuel's perspective into the intervention. The first appropriate intervention would be to observe Manuel in the school environment. Observation, prior to initialization of counseling, allows the counselor to see Manuel's response to the learning environment, as well as his interaction in his social environment. Because diagnosis is discouraged in child-centered theory because of its tendency to influence the counselor's relationship with the child by focusing on the problem (Rogers, 1951), observation serves the narrow purpose of giving the counselor a sense of how the child experiences his or her world in context. The school counselor would want to observe Manuel during an instructional period and during a more social period, such as lunch or recess. These observations give the counselor an idea of how

Manuel responds to school and social expectations. After observation, the counselor would set up a time with the teacher to pull him out of class for 30 minutes at the same time each week.

If permission has been obtained for Manuel to participate in counseling, initial interviews with teachers and parents are not necessary at this point in the relationship. Initial interviews tend to focus on the problems that Manuel is experiencing and might deter the counselor from focusing on him as a person. However, it is recommended that the counselor discuss with his parents and teachers how play therapy will help Manuel with their concerns. For example a counselor may say to a teacher, "I can see that you're really frustrated in dealing with Manuel. You've tried many different solutions, and it just seems that they are not working. I believe that if Manuel participates in play therapy, he will convey through his play why it is that he feels anxious and bad about himself. I think if he can express this understanding, he will be able to break through his negative self-concept and learn to view himself more positively, and thereby act in a more positive manner. I certainly can't promise this will be the case, but it is what we're working toward. I'll let you know how things are going periodically, and you can keep me informed of your experiences, too."

Child-Centered Play Therapy Intervention

In school child-centered play therapy, it can be helpful to pick up a child directly from the classroom instead of allowing him or her to come and go independently from the counselor's office. This approach allows the counselor to see the transition from the class and allows the child to chat on the way to the counselor's playroom. The counselor should avoid talking with the teacher when picking up the child. Sometimes teachers use this opportunity to share problems that occurred during the day, and this is not an appropriate time. Redirection in this case is usually helpful: "That sounds like something we can talk about during your preparation period. I'll come by then."

Upon arriving in the playroom, which had been set up according to the guidelines identified earlier in the chapter, the counselor introduced the room to Manuel. Here is an excerpt from the first session.

CO: In here is the playroom, and you can play with the toys in lots of the ways you like. (Conveying the permissiveness of the environment)

Manuel: All of these are yours!?

CO: You are amazed that all of these toys are in here. (Reflecting his feeling and intent in order to provide understanding.)

Manuel: (wanders around room) Yeah. I wish I had all of these toys.

CO: You would like to have this many toys.

Manuel: (looks at dollhouse and says with disdain) These are girl toys.

CO: You don't like girl toys. (Reflecting feeling)

Manuel: (pushes dollhouse and throws girl figures out of dollhouse) Girl toys are stupid.

CO: (pointing to girl figures) They're stupid, and you don't want them in there. (Reflecting Manuel's negative feelings so that he will feel a sense of acceptance)

Manuel: (looking at easel) Hey! Can I paint?

CO: Sounds like you want to paint. In here, that's up to you. (Reflecting child's intent and returning responsibility to Manuel so that he will learn to operate from an internal sense of self, not external.)

For the rest of the session, Manuel painted 2 pictures: one of himself playing basketball, and one of himself playing soccer. He talked about how good he was at both sports. The counselor reflected with responses such as "You're really proud of how well you play basketball." and "You think you're really good at soccer." These statements help Manuel become aware of his feelings and thoughts about his sports experiences. The following is an excerpt from the last few statements of the first session.

CO: Manuel, our time is up in the playroom today. (Setting the structure of the session.)

Manuel: (working quickly on painting) I just need a few more minutes to finish this picture.

CO: You really want to finish that picture, but our time is up in the playroom today. You can finish it next week. (Using the A-C-T model to set limits).

Manuel: Okay, okay, I'm giving this picture to you.

CO: You really want me to have the picture of you playing soccer. (Again, counselor is reflecting intent. If counselor responded with "Thank you, it's beautiful." the focus would be taken off of Manuel and moved to his desire to impress or please the counselor.)

The counselor walked Manuel back to the playroom. It is recommended that the counselor always walk a child back to the classroom following a play session. Walking back with the child helps the counselor discern whether the child is ready for the classroom or whether the counselor and child should walk around the school for a few minutes to reorient the child back to the school structure.

In three subsequent sessions, Manuel continued to concentrate on either painting or acting out his sports moves in the playroom. He purposefully avoided the dollhouse, often kicking or moving it out of his way. In the fifth session, the following interaction occurred following Manuel's account of how he threw the winning basket in last night's basketball game.

CO: So, because of you, the team won the basketball game.
Manuel: I was the best!
CO: Basketball is something you are really good at.
Manuel: Not like school.
CO: You're good at basketball, but not so good at school.
Manuel: (moves toward dollhouse, sits down, and picks up figures) School is stupid.
CO: You're not good at school because it is stupid.

Manuel does not respond verbally. He begins to move the figures around. He places all of the female figures together in the kitchen area. He places the boy figure in the furthest room from kitchen by himself. He places the father figure outside of the house.

CO: (pointing to girl figures, then to boy figure): They all go in there, but he goes over here.
Manuel: They're always together. They're laughing. (Pointing to each figure individually). She is cooking dinner, she is doing her math homework, and she is writing her paper.
CO: So, they are all very busy.
Manuel: (pointing to boy figure) He's not. He's just by himself.
CO: He's a little lonely sitting by himself. (This response is not based on interpretation, but on the sound of Manuel's voice as he explained the boy.)
Manuel: Yep. He's always by himself.

CO: So, he's lonely a lot.
Manuel: (noticeably changes to more positive affect) But he's going outside to play basketball with his friends.
CO: When he plays basketball, he doesn't feel so lonely.
Manuel: No, 'cause he's the best.

Manuel then moved away from the dollhouse and acted out his previous basketball moves.

In the following sessions, Manuel continued to play out scenes in the dollhouse. A few scenes included the girl figures calling the boy figure "stupid," a girl figure babying the boy figure by feeding him and tucking him in bed, and the father figure was always absent outside of the house. As sessions progressed, Manuel moved the boy figure closer to the girl figures and in the 10th session, Manuel moved the boy in the kitchen with the girl figures to do homework. At the end of the 10th session, based on in-session and out-of-session occurrences, the counselor decided to terminate play therapy with Manuel. The counselor told Manuel in the 11th session that they would only have two more play sessions. The counselor let Manuel know that after they finished their play sessions that he could come by to see her if he ever needed to talk with her.

Out of the Playroom

PARENTS

Following the first session, the counselor contacted Manuel's parents over the phone. The counselor informed them about play therapy, how it works, and how she thought it would help Manuel. The counselor explained the process in a similar way as she explained it to the teacher. She told the parents that she would contact them periodically to let them know how Manuel was doing. Following the sixth session, the counselor set up a meeting with the parents. In the parent meeting, the counselor explained that based on their play sessions, Manuel appeared to find most of his self-confidence in his sports achievements. She additionally explained that because Manuel concentrated on sports and not on schoolwork, he appeared to sometimes feel left out of the family. This was a simplistic explanation, yet it is one that parents could understand and could respond to in a helpful, rather than a defensive, way. The counselor listened to the parents' perspective and reflected back her understanding. After the parents felt understood, the counselor recommended that the father set up a regularly scheduled play appointment with Manuel where they play basketball or any sport of the child's choice for 30 minutes each week. She also recommended that the mother initiate sports talk with Manuel and/or read his sports magazines so that she could talk about the things that he was interested in. Although Manuel's mother was initially resistant, not seeing the benefit of sports talk when he was doing poorly in school, the counselor reflected this concern back to her and asked her to try it as an experiment, not making any guarantees that it would work. In making these recommendations, the counselor attempted to help Manuel's parents develop a positive relationship based on what was important to the child; she did not attempt to solve his "problem."

After the 9th session, the counselor called Manuel's parents to check on progress. His mother reported that she really enjoyed having her sports talks with Manuel. She reported that she did not know how well he could read until they read a magazine together, and she reported how she felt closer to him because of these talks. She also reported that, although Manuel was not making As in school, he was passing, and the teacher told her that he had been less frustrated with schoolwork. She was disappointed that the father had only had his playtime with Manuel once since beginning, but she said his work had been busy and he intended to set this up again. After the 10th session, the counselor called the mother again to tell her that because the teacher and she had reported progress in Manuel's schoolwork, the play sessions would be ending in two weeks. However, the counselor reassured her that she could contact the counselor at any time if she had concerns.

TEACHER

The counselor remained in consistent contact with the teacher throughout Manuel's play sessions. The counselor could not share specifics from the sessions with the teacher because of the limits of confidentiality. Within this limitation, the counselor shared progress with the teacher by making the following kinds of statements. "Manuel appears to feel like his only worth is through his achievements in sports. I think this really discourages his ability to learn in school. I wonder if there is some way to tie some of his school work, like reading assignments and math examples, to sports questions." When given this suggestion, not direction, the teacher was able to help Manuel pick out reading books that were related to sports and to develop questions related to sports. Another example of giving feedback to the teacher was, "Manuel seems to be a child who really likes to interact with others. He also seems to feel that he does not get to make a lot of his own decisions when it comes to school. I wonder if it would work to sometimes give him a choice of either doing his schoolwork in an individual carrel or doing it in a team with a few other children." This kind of feedback also helps to empower the teacher to collaborate with the school counselor to make decisions instead of being told what would work best. With this kind of feedback, the teacher immediately began to use the child-centered skills of choice-giving, returning responsibility, and reflection. After several weeks of these kinds of responses, the teacher began to notice a change in Manuel. Around the sixth week, he demonstrated less frustration with work he did not understand. He also showed more joy in the classroom. By the 10th week, the teacher reported that Manuel was turning in all of his schoolwork, and that, although he was not an straight-A student, she was really enjoying him in the classroom.

The child-centered counselor concentrated on the individual nature of the child and the importance of the child's relationships. Through experiencing an accepting relationship in play session, Manuel was able to express his loneliness and frustration. Through providing his parents with relational tools, instead of solutions, the counselor helped them break through the problem barriers and re-establish contact with their son. The counselor's constant support and basic child-centered techniques helped the teacher establish a more personal relationship with Manuel as well. Finally, the increase in his self-concept provided through an environment of genuineness, acceptance, and unconditional positive regard helped Manuel improve his behavior.

• •

CASE STUDY: AMY

Initial Preparation for Person-Centered Group Counseling Intervention

Amy is an adolescent experiencing some typical and some atypical types of problems. Typical issues related to her developmental level of adolescence include conflicts with parents, not feeling understood by anyone, oversensitization to personal events (such as arguments or not reaching an achievement goal), and conflicts with peers. What appears to be atypical is a high level of depression and an overdependence on specific teachers. Because the school counselor has already ruled out the threat of suicide, the intervention may address more of Amy's typical adolescent problems. The group modality appears to be the most effective intervention for Amy. Many of her peers experience some level of distress tied to the similar issues. It has also been shown that the adults in Amy's life, her parents, her 8th grade teacher, and her current English teacher, have been unable to help Amy with her issues of concern. Many developmentalists (Elkind, 2001; Gilligan, 1993; Greenspan & Salmon, 1993; Loevinger, 1976) have recognized the primacy of peers during the adolescent phase of development. Hence, it seems that group counseling would be the intervention of choice for this particular child and this particular case.

Prior to placing Amy in a group, the counselor would need to prepare for group by going through steps to ensure the effectiveness of the intervention. As in an individual student case, observation is a key component to a person-centered counseling intervention. Observing a student in a high school class is not likely to be a feasible, practical option. However, observing the student in the lunchroom, hallways, or after-school activities is helpful if it can be accomplished in a noninvasive manner. As Amy's counselor, I would find out where her locker is and casually walk through that hallway during breaks. It helps to observe Amy's social status and interaction with others, which helps the counselor understand Amy's reality, rather than her parents' or teachers' perception of her situation.

Following observation, the counselor would need to determine appropriate members for the group. Because of the gender specificity of adolescent development (Gilligan, 1993), it is recommended that the counselor seek an all-girl group for Amy. This will help to provide Amy and other members with a group that can more universally relate to them and their struggles. The counselor would seek girls who are the same age and experiencing similar difficulties as Amy, but who may be in different places on their journey. The counselor would need to set up a consistent weekly closed group that would last 6 weeks, since this is the grading period time schedule. Working within the grading structure of the school is often helpful when scheduling counseling interventions. A closed group will ensure that the group can develop trust and cohesiveness as soon as possible. In this case, because the counselor was only able to schedule the group for 45 minutes each week, membership was limited to four freshman girls so that each girl would have ample time to participate.

Group Counseling Intervention

The group met at 9:30 on Tuesday mornings. Members consisted of Amy, Joelle, Mary, and Lauren. Amy, Mary, and Lauren are Caucasian and Joelle is African-American. All of the girls were from the same socioeconomic level. The counselor's office was designed with a small roundtable that seats six and a small sandtray in the corner with a shelf of figurines beside it. In open cabinets, the counselor kept a supply of art materials consistent with the list provided earlier in this chapter under expressive arts. The counselor introduced the session by asking each girl to share her name, grade, and homeroom teacher. The following is an excerpt from the first counseling session after introductions were made.

CO: We have started this group because the four of you have many things in common. In this group, you may choose to talk to each other or use any of the materials in this room. We will be meeting for 6 weeks at the same time each week. (Counselor has provided some structure to ease the discomfort common among older students regarding the counseling situation. However, permissiveness is emphasized in the introduction.)

(A long period of silence ensues.)

CO: It seems you're a little uncomfortable getting started.
Mary: (to Lauren) You're new here.
Lauren: Yeah, I moved from Colorado.
Mary: Cool, do you ski?
Lauren: We skied all the time there.
Joelle: We went skiing last year on vacation, but we went to New Mexico.
Amy: I've been skiing, but I suck at it.
CO: So, it seems you are all interested in skiing, but Amy, you don't feel like you're too good at it.

Amy: I spent the whole time falling down. Even my little sister was better than I was.

Mary: My little sister is better at everything than I am.

Lauren: Skiing is not so hard. You just have to practice a lot.

CO: Lauren, it sounds like you're trying to encourage Mary and Amy.

Lauren: Yeah, they can't be that bad at it.

Amy: Believe me, I am.

CO: You just don't buy it, Amy.

(More silence.)

Joelle: (Looks around room. Points to shelves with art materials) Can we use that stuff over there?

CO: That's up to you.

Joelle: (gets up and heads to shelves starts looking at materials)

Amy: (gets up and heads to sandtray; she runs her fingers through the sand).

CO: (To Amy) It looks like you like the way that feels.

Amy: It feels like the beach.

Mary: I love the beach!

Lauren: Me too!

Joelle: Me too!

CO: It looks like that's another thing all of you have in common.

As the session continued, Joelle pulled out some construction paper, magazine pictures, and markers. She brought them back to the table where all the girls looked at the pictures and talked about what the girls in the pictures were wearing. Joelle began to draw a picture of a house, and all the girls commented on how good she was at drawing. Session ended.

In the two subsequent sessions, the girls began to talk more frequently and interactively regarding their favorite movie stars, movies, television shows, and the like. As Joelle demonstrated her skills in drawing, both Amy and Lauren emphasized that they were in honors classes, and Mary talked about being on the volleyball team. The counselor felt that the girls were attempting to demonstrate their strengths to each other before they could show their weaknesses. Amy and Mary often made self-derogatory comments. In the fourth session, the girls had picked out their favorite pictures and began to glue them on to construction paper, when the following interaction occurred:

Amy: (holding up a picture of a model) I'll never look like her.

Lauren: She's not that great. Look how big her nose is.

Amy: But look how skinny she is.

Joelle: I think she's too skinny.

CO: (to Amy and Joelle) The two of you have a different idea of what's skinny.

Amy: She's not too skinny. I wish I could look like that. I'll always be fat.

Mary: Amy, you are always putting yourself down.

Joelle: Yeah, why do you do that?

Lauren: Yeah, it's really annoying.

Amy: Well, Mary you think you're bad at everything too.

Mary: Not like you.

Joelle: Yeah, Mary you do say a lot of mean things about yourself too.

Mary: No, I don't.

Lauren: You really do.

Mary: (yelling) No, I don't.

CO: Mary, you're angry about being told that you put yourself down, and, Amy, you sound kinda angry too.

Amy: Well, it's true.

Joelle: (sarcastically) Well, it's annoying.

CO: So, Joelle, when you hear Amy and Mary put themselves down you think it's annoying, and you don't like it.

Lauren: Me, too.

Joelle: It's way more fun when they talk about being good at classes or volleyball. Plus, when Amy says she's fat and stupid, nobody believes her. She's just trying to get attention.

Amy: (indignantly and raising her voice) I am not!

Lauren: Amy, you wear a size small and you are in honors classes.

Amy: So?

Joelle: So, you're not stupid, and you're not fat. You just want everyone to tell you that you're not.

Amy: (begins to cry)

CO: You really feel alone right now.

Amy: (through tears) Nobody understands me. I do feel fat and stupid.

CO: It seems like nobody can understand how bad you feel about
           yourself.

Mary: I do. I always feel like that too.

Joelle: I feel ugly too. I don't have any friends, but my mom says,
           "You don't go around talking about it" so I don't.

Lauren: I'm your friend Joelle.

Amy: I'm your friend too.

Mary: Me too.

This interaction demonstrated that as trust developed in the group, the girls were able to confront each other genuinely. The counselor facilitated their emotions by reflecting their pain and providing commonalities. Also, by reflecting the views of some group members in a less harsh manner, the counselor is able to break through the defensiveness of individual group members but still communicate the message that the group was trying to send. In this specific interaction, Amy experienced that the group was not okay with her social behaviors, but they were in full understanding of her emotional state. All four girls experienced common support for each other and common understanding. In the remaining two sessions, the girls continued to explore their support of each other and made plans to go out on the weekends together.

Outside of the Counseling Sessions

Because of system changes in high school and the belief that adolescents have the ability to construct their own environment conducive to their growth, a person-centered high school counselor works less closely with parents and teachers than an elementary child-centered school counselor would. In this case, the school counselor contacted Amy's mother at the beginning of the group to provide her with details regarding the group's structure. At that time, the school counselor offered to meet with Amy's mother if she desired, and Amy's mother did not believe it was necessary to meet at that time. The school counselor contacted Amy's mother again at the end of the six-week group to let her know that she thought Amy had made good progress in her positive feelings and in her social supports. Amy's mother reported that Amy was not "complaining as much as she usually does." Again, the school counselor offered to meet with the mother if she ever wanted to consult with her in the future. The school counselor also checked with Amy's English teacher at the fourth week of sessions. The English teacher reported that Amy was no longer coming by her house. By the end of the six weeks, the English teacher reported that Amy had decreased her contact with her even at school.

Amy's "problems" were difficulties that she had the ability to struggle through, given an operational environment. The success of the intervention did not result so much from the counselor's insightful reflections as from the counselor's identification of the most effective modality. Offering a group modality implemented the person-centered philosophy that the environment would provide understanding and acceptance. The counselor helped facilitate this environment by providing structure to the sessions, reflecting the group members, and accepting emotions and perceptions.

Conclusion

Currently many graduate level school counseling programs focus less often on person-centered theory in its applicability to the school environment. Although school counselors learn the core conditions of person-centered theory as part of their basic training, they are often directed to implement more directive approaches in their work in the schools. The focus in person-centered theory on relationship variables, therapeutic alliance, and active listening offers school counselors a structured and productive method from which to provide counseling to students at all grade levels.

This chapter has reviewed how the school counselor can practically apply person-centered theory to the school setting. Although person-centered theory may not appear compatible with the behavioral focus of many school systems, this way of working provides the school counselor a solid theoretical base from which to facilitate change in children and adolescents. A person-centered school counselor is able to maintain a humanistic philosophy if he or she is also willing to educate parents, teachers, school staff, and administrators about how this philosophy works and how it is beneficial to the school's overall goals of educating students. When a student, as any human, feels understood, accepted, and valued as a person, the innate tendency to move toward becoming a better person is activated and put into action. Such action in the school environment is expectantly translated into progress in education and learning, better relationships with teachers, and improved social skills.

References

ASCA (2004, June). *The role of the professional school counselor.* Retrieved August 5, 2006, from http://www.schoolcounselor.org

Axline, V. (1947). *Play therapy.* New York: Ballantine Books.

Azima, F. J., & Richmond, L. H. (Eds.) (1989). *Adolescent group psychotherapy.* American Group Psychotherapy Association Monograph 4. Madison, WI: International Universities Press.

Bratton, S. C., & Ferebee, K. W. (1999). Structured expressive art activities with preadolescents. In D. S. Sweeney & L. E. Homeyer (Eds.), *Group play therapy: How to do it, how it works, and whom it's best for* (pp. 192–214). San Francisco: Jossey-Bass.

Colbert, R., & Colbert, M. (2003). School counselor involvement in culture-centered education reform. In P. Pedersen & J. Carey (Eds.), *Multicultural counseling in schools: A practical handbook* (2nd ed.) (pp. 3–26). Boston: Pearson Education.

Davis, T. (2005). *Exploring school counseling: Professional practices and perspectives.* Boston: Lahaska Press.

Elkind, D. (2001). *The hurried child: Growing up too fast too soon* (3rd ed.). Cambridge, MA: Perseus.

Elliott, R. (2001). The effectiveness of humanistic therapies: A meta-analysis. In D. Cain & J. Seeman (Eds.), *Humanistic psychotherapies: Handbook of research and practice* (pp. 57–81). Washington, DC: American Psychological Association.

Fall, M., Balvanz, J., Johnson, L., & Nelson, L. (1999). A play therapy intervention and its relationship to self-efficacy and learning behaviors. *Professional School Counseling, 2*(3), 194–204.

Flahive, M., & Ray, D. (2007). Effect of group sandtray therapy with preadolescents in a school setting. *Journal for Specialists in Group Work, 32,* 362–382.

Garza, Y., & Bratton, S. (2005). School-based child centered play therapy with Hispanic children: Outcomes and cultural considerations. *International Journal of Play Therapy, 14*(1), 51–80.

Gazda, G. (1989). *Group counseling: A developmental approach* (4th ed.). Boston: Allyn & Bacon.

Gilligan, C. (1993). *In a different voice: Psychological theory and women's development.* Cambridge, MA: Harvard University Press.

Ginott, H. (1961). *Group psychotherapy with children: The theory and practice of play therapy.* New York: McGraw-Hill.

Ginott, H. (1965). *Between parent and child.* New York: Macmillan.

Greenspan, S., & Salmon, J. (1993). *Playground politics: Understanding the emotional life of your school-age child.* Reading, MA: Addison-Wesley.

Guerney, L. (2000). Filial therapy into the 21st century. *International Journal of Play Therapy, 9*(2), 1–17.

Guerney, B.G., Jr., & Stover, L. (1971). *Filial therapy* (Final report on MH 18254-01). Unpublished manuscript, Pennsylvania State University.

Johnson, L., McLeod, E., & Fall, M. (1997). Play therapy with labeled children in the schools. *Professional School Counseling, 1*, 31–34.

Kirschenbaum, H. (2004). Carl Rogers's life and work: An assessment on the 100th anniversary of his birth. *Journal of Counseling and Development, 82*, 116–124.

Kirschenbaum, H., & Jourdan, A. (2005). The current status of Carl Rogers and the person-centered approach. *Psychotherapy: Theory, Research, Practice, Training, 42*, 37–51.

Landreth, G. (2002). *Play therapy: The art of the relationship* (2nd ed.). New York: Brunner-Routledge.

Landreth, G., & Sweeney, D. (1999). The freedom to be: Child-centered group play therapy. In D. Sweeney & L. Homeyer, (Eds.), *Handbook of group play therapy: How to do it, how it works, whom it's best for* (pp. 39–64). San Francisco: Jossey-Bass.

Loevinger, J. (1976). *Ego development*. San Francisco: Jossey-Bass.

Newsome, D. (2003). Counseling interventions using expressive arts. In B. Erford (Ed.), *Transforming the school counseling profession* (pp. 231–247). Upper Saddle River, NJ: Merrill Prentice Hall.

Piaget, J. (1962). *Play, dreams, and imitation in childhood*. New York: Routledge.

Post, P. (1999). Impact of child-centered play therapy on the self-esteem, locus of control, and anxiety of at-risk 4th, 5th, and 6th grade students. *International Journal of Play Therapy, 8*(2), 1–18.

Post, P., McAllister, M., Sheely, A., Hess, B., & Flowers, C. (2004). Child centered kinder training for teachers of pre-school children deemed at-risk. *International Journal of Play Therapy, 13*, 53–74.

Raskin, N., & Rogers, C. (2005). Person-centered therapy. In R. Corsini and D. Wedding, (Eds.), *Current psychotherapies* (7th ed.) (pp. 130–165). Belmont, CA: Brooks/Cole.

Ray, D. (2004). Supervision of basic and advanced skills in play therapy. *Journal of Professional Counseling: Practice, Theory, and Research, 32*(2), 28–41.

Ray, D., Bratton, S., Rhine, T., & Jones, L. (2001). The effectiveness of play therapy: Responding to the critics. *International Journal of Play Therapy, 10*, 85–108.

Ray, D., Muro, J., & Schumann, B. (2004). Play therapy in the schools: Lessons learned. *International Journal of Play Therapy, 13*, 79–100.

Rogers, C. (1942). *Counseling and psychotherapy*. Boston: Houghton Mifflin.

Rogers, C. (1951). *Client-centered therapy*. Boston: Houghton Mifflin.

Rogers, C. (1957). The necessary and sufficient conditions of therapeutic personality change. *Journal of Consulting Psychology, 21*, 95–103.

Rogers, C. (1976). Encounter and intimacy versus alienation and detachment. In J. Ehrenwald (Ed.), *The history of psychotherapy* (pp. 542–554). New York: Jason Aronson. (Reprinted from *Carl Rogers on encounter groups*, by C. Rogers, 1970, New York: Harper and Row.)

Rychlak, J. (1981). *Introduction to personality and psychotherapy* (2nd ed.). Boston: Houghton Mifflin.

Schmidt, J. (1999). *Counseling in schools: Essential services and comprehensive programs* (3rd ed.). Boston: Allyn & Bacon.

Studer, J. (2005). *The professional school counselor: An advocate for students*. Belmont, CΛ: Brooks/Cole.

Thompson, C., & Rudolph, L. (2000). *Counseling children* (5th ed.). Belmont, CA: Brooks/Cole.

VanFleet, R. (1994). *Filial therapy: Strengthening parent-child relationships through play*. Sarasota, FL: Professional Resource Press.

White, J., & Flynt, M. (1999). Play groups in elementary school. In D. Sweeney and L. Homeyer, (Eds.), *Handbook of group play therapy: How to do it, how it works, and whom it's best for* (pp. 336–358). San Francisco: Jossey-Bass.

White, J., Flynt, M., & Draper, K. (1997). Kinder therapy: Teachers as therapeutic agents. *International Journal of Play Therapy, 6*, 33–49.

APPENDIX

Suggested Materials for Traveling or School Playroom

Ring toss game
Football
Basketball
Jenga
Legos
Soldiers (2 colors)
Aggressive People Figures
    (Wrestlers, etc.)
Barbie Doll
Family figures
Plastic knife
Baton
Police helmet
Handcuffs
Rope
2 plastic dart guns (if allowed)
Clay
Paper plates
Glitter glue
Markers
Magazines
Sewing materials
Ribbons
Beads
Cotton

Glue
Scissors
Yarn
Masks
Buttons
Construction paper
Aggressive puppet
Non-aggressive puppet
Animal figures (domestic & wild)
Cell phone
Planes/Cars/Rescue
Vehicles
School Bus
Snake
Spider

If Stationary:
Sand in large plastic bin
Small figures
Spray bottle with water
Paints
Easel/table-top easel
Large/clear table
Dollhouse

CHAPTER 2

PARTNERS IN THE SCHOOLS:
ADLERIAN SCHOOL COUNSELING

••

Terry Kottman, Jill Bryant, Jennifer Alexander, and Susan Kroger

••

Overview

The theory of Individual Psychology (otherwise known as Adlerian Psychology) was introduced by Alfred Adler early in the 20th century. Adlerian theory contains ideas about the nature of human beings (how their personalities form, what motivates them, how they develop difficulties, how they resolve problems, what happens when they are maladjusted) and about the nature of the counseling process (goals of counseling, role of the counselor, methods of facilitating change, stages of counseling, and intervention strategies) (Ansbacher & Ansbacher, 1956; Carlson & Slavik, 1997; Kottman, 2003b; Oberst & Stewart, 2003; Watts, 1999). The counseling literature offers much support for adopting Adlerian theory as the most effective approach to school counseling (Brigman & Molina, 1999; Campbell, 2003; Clark, 1994; Dustin & Ehly, 1992; Edwards, 2004; Edwards & Gfroerer, 2001; Fallon, 2004; Gilbert & Morawski, 2005; Herring & Runion, 1994; Muro & Kottman, 1995; Nicoll, 1994; Pryor & Tollerud, 1999; Otwell & Mullis, 1997; Schmidt, 1999; Sciarra, 2004; Thompson & Rudolph, 2000). As Pryor and Tollerud (1999) suggested:

> Adlerian principles have served as a basis for working in schools since Alfred Adler first introduced them in the early 1900s, and they still have useful applications today. (p. 299)

Adlerians believe that people are socially embedded, goal-directed, creative, decision-making beings who have subjective views of their experiences (Adler, 1956; Carlson & Slavik, 1997; Dinkmeyer, Dinkmeyer, & Sperry, 1987; Kottman, 2003b). According to Adlerian theory, individuals are best understood holistically as total beings "whose thoughts, feelings, and beliefs are present in a consistent and unified pattern of actions" (Carlson & Slavik, 1997, p. xi). Children, based on their observations of the interactions in their families and with other people, develop a *lifestyle*, a pattern of behavior based on their beliefs about themselves, others, and the world (Kottman, 2003b; Thompson & Rudolph, 2000).

The concept of social embeddedness is based on the premise that human beings are born with a need to belong—in their families, in their classrooms, in their workplace, in their neighborhoods, in other collections of people (Adler, 1956, 1931/1958; Thompson & Rudolph, 2000; Watts, 1999). Adler believed that people are born with the capacity to learn how to connect with other people but "social interest"—this striving toward connection and cooperation with others—does not happen without being fostered by the significant adults in a child's life (Adler, 1937, 1956, 1931/1958; Ansbacher, 1991).

As another basic tenet of Adlerian theory, all behavior is goal-directed. Adler believed that every human behavior, including emotions, has a purpose. In Adlerian theory

> the issue is not the cause of the behavior but determining what children want to accomplish, either in the real world or in their own minds. Behaviors do not continue over time unless they "work" for children." (Thompson & Rudolph, 2000, p. 277)

In looking at children's problem behaviors, Adlerians use a model developed by Dreikurs and Soltz (1964), who posited that children's misbehavior has four basic goals: attention, power, revenge, and proving inadequacy. The counselor can identify children's goals by

1. observing their behavior in the playroom and listening to parents and teachers describe behaviors that are upsetting to them,
2. using questions and observation to explore the emotional reactions of adults when confronted with the child's inappropriate behavior,

3. using self-examination to explore his or her own reactions to the child's behavior, and

4. asking questions about and observing the child's reaction to correction or discipline.

Lew and Bettner (1996, 2000) suggested that counselors, teachers, and parents can foster more positive, constructive goals—the "Crucial Cs": feeling *connected*, feeling *capable*, believing that they *count*, and demonstrating *courage*.

The Adlerian view emphasizes that a person is a creative, decision-making being who takes the "givens" of life (heredity and environment) and interprets, modifies, and expresses them in singularly personal and unique ways (Beames, 1992; Kottman, 2003b). "The individual is both the picture and the artist. He [sic] is the artist of his own personality" (Ansbacher & Ansbacher, 1956, p. 177).

According to Adlerian theory, each person expresses this capacity for creativity through self-determinism by making choices. Because of the "individual" nature of each person, in Adlerian psychology the counselor has to understand and celebrate the special qualities inherent in that person. This is done in a holistic way by exploring the expression of uniqueness across five life tasks (Mosak, 1977):

1. Work or school
2. Relationships with friends and relatives (Adler, 1931/1958)
3. Intimate relationships (Adler, 1931/1958)
4. Finding meaning in life (spirituality/existential)
5. Coming to terms with self and self-regulation

Adlerians take a phenomenological perspective, based on their belief that reality is subjective, created by individuals. Adler believed that human beings develop "fictions as conscious and non-conscious ideas that do not necessarily have a correspondence with reality, but that serve the purpose to guide us to cope better with reality" (Oberst & Stewart, 2003, p. 13). Therefore, what actually happens in any given situation is not as important as how people interpret what happens. These interpretations are filtered through their previously formed perceptions and convictions, resulting in people finding confirmation of what they already believe about themselves, others, and the world (Kottman, 2003b).

Because this subjective filtering is so pervasive, the counselor must examine and understand clients' perceptions and convictions and the thoughts, feelings, and behaviors connected to those perceptions and convictions—the lifestyle. Lifestyle is the person's unique, creative approach to life and belonging. As the person's basic orientation to life (Adler, 1956, 1931/1958; Carlson & Slavik, 1997; Kottman, 2003b), lifestyle

> organizes and simplifies coping with the world by assigning rules and values; it selects, predicts, anticipates; its perceptions are guided by its own "private logic"; it selects what information it allows to enter, what it will attend to, what affects will be aroused and what its response will be. (Watts, 1999, p. 3)

According to Adlerian theory, children usually develop their lifestyle before the age of 8. By observing others and their reactions in relationships and various situations in life, children come to conclusions about themselves, others, and the world. Children's thoughts, feelings, and behaviors organically evolve from these conclusions because they act as if their perceptions and conclusions are true and real. Although children are usually keen observers, they often lack the abstract reasoning skills and experience to be able to accurately evaluate and interpret situations and relationships, so inevitably some of their conclusions about how life and relationships work are inaccurate.

Many of these faulty or self-defeating convictions become the foundation for people's lifestyles, which often undermine their ability to sustain positive self-images, develop successful relationship skills, learn to express their feelings in constructive ways, and exhibit socially appropriate behavior. Thus, individuals may need help to discover these self-defeating patterns and change them.

Major Constructs of Adlerian Theory

In considering the application of a counseling theory to a specific setting such as school counseling, several elements come into play—the nature of the counseling relationship, stages of counseling, goals of counseling, the counselor's role, and implications for working with a diverse multicultural population.

Nature of the Counseling Relationship

In Adlerian counseling the relationship between the counselor and the client is a collaborative and respectful alliance, in which the counselor and the client work together. The relationship is egalitarian, with the counselor acting as a partner, a "friendly guide—willing to see the truth—to point out mistakes and to suggest better ways" (Manaster & Corsini, 1982, p. 152). A key factor in the relationship in Adlerian counseling is a sense of shared power and responsibility for helping the client make lasting changes in perceptions, attitudes, thinking patterns, and behaviors.

The counselor is the expert on the change process and on developmental patterns, and the client is the expert on his or her own life experiences. By combining these two areas of expertise, the counselor and the client can move forward together. A major factor in the Adlerian counseling relationship is the combination of the client's ability to express his or her subjective experiencing of life with the counselor's ability to bring an objective, outside perspective that can help the client examine and reexamine his or her perceptions, interpretations, and behavioral patterns.

Stages of Counseling

The four stages in Adlerian counseling are (Ansbacher & Ansbacher, 1956; Kottman, 2003b; Manaster & Corsini, 1982):

1. building an egalitarian relationship with the client,
2. exploring the client's lifestyle,
3. helping the client gain insight into his or her lifestyle, and
4. providing reorientation and reeducation for the client when necessary

These stages may overlap. For instance, the counselor continues to build the relationship while beginning to gather information about the client's lifestyle, helping the client shift his or her beliefs about self, others, and the world, and learning new skills for interaction with others.

When the counselor is working with a school child or adolescent, he or she should simultaneously consult with the adults in the child's life (parents and teachers, when appropriate) (Kottman, 2005a, 2003b). This consultation follows the same four stages, with the emphasis on the adult and his or her lifestyle and on the interaction between the lifestyles of the adult and the child.

Goals of Counseling Process and Role of the Counselor

The major goals of Adlerian counseling are to help clients (Mosak, 1995)

1. increase their social interest;
2. reduce their feelings of inferiority;
3. learn positive ways of dealing with remaining feelings of inferiority;
4. make changes in their self-defeating beliefs about themselves, others, and the world;
5. change negative motivation;
6. gain a sense of equality with others; and
7. become contributing, cooperating members of society.

In focusing on work with children, Kottman (2003b) suggested that the goals of counseling are to

> move the child from destructive goals and misbehavior toward constructive goals, enhance attainment of the Crucial Cs; increase the child's social interest; adjust self-defeating per-ceptions in the child's beliefs about self, others, and the world; reduce discouragement; and help the child to understand and "own" his or her personal assets. (p. 28)

Applying these goals to school counseling, the counselor must also consider ways to enhance student development across the academic domain, the career domain, and the personal/social domain (ASCA, 2005). This could involve helping children develop positive attitudes toward school, improve their behaviors in school, formulate appropriate academic and career goals, enhance academic achievement, build and maintain positive relationships with peers and authority figures, and learn to appreciate their own strengths.

Depending on the phase of counseling, the goals of the counseling process and the role of the Adlerian counselor shift somewhat (Kottman, 1999b, 2001, 2003b). In the first phase of counseling, the goal is to build the relationship. The counselor's role is that of partner and encourager. In this phase the counselor is almost always relatively nondirective, allowing the child to lead the process most of the time. Power is shared by giving the child choices about what to do in the sessions so he or she will begin to trust the counselor, creating a sense of teamwork and cooperation.

During the second phase of counseling, the counselor is an active, directive explorer. He or she must obtain information about the child's attitudes, perceptions, thinking processes, feelings, and so forth.

In the third phase the Adlerian counselor is relatively directive, conveying essential information about lifestyles, mistaken beliefs, goals of misbehavior, Crucial Cs, assets, and so forth to the child, the parents, and the teacher. The counselor's role during this phase is rather dichotomous. Sometimes the counselor is nondirective and empathically supportive, especially when trying to gently move the child (and parents and/or teachers) to a new understanding of situations and relationships. At other times the counselor is directive and confrontational—challenging long-held self-defeating beliefs about self, others, and the world and pointing out discrepancies between what is said and what is done between the verbal and nonverbal communication.

In the fourth phase (reorientation/reeducation) the Adlerian counselor is an active teacher and encourager. The counselor uses intervention strategies designed to help the child adopt more positive attitudes and perceptions, and to help the child learn and practice new skills for interacting positively with others and coping with difficult situations and relationships. The counselor may also employ teaching skills and encouragement when working with parents and teachers.

Multicultural Applications

Given the evolving multicultural composition of the United States, it behooves school counselors to find counseling theories that they can apply appropriately across a wide spectrum of children from various cultures and ethnic groups (Canino & Spurlock, 2000; Gil & Drewes, 2005; Holmgren, 1996; McGoldrick, 1998; Thompson & Rudolph, 2000; Vargas & Koss-Chioino, 1992). According to Fallon (2004), Herring and Runion (1994) and Thompson and Rudolph (2000), Individual Psychology is just such a theory.

Herring and Runion (1994) suggested that Adlerian theory is particularly applicable to counseling children and youth with diverse ethnicities because of several of its theoretical constructs and techniques. According

to those authors, Adlerians believe that each person is creative, responsible, and can be understood only in his or her social context. These beliefs
help to keep Adlerians from "forcing all children into generic categories"
(p. 215).

Other concepts that make an Adlerian approach with a multicultural
population desirable, in their opinion, is the focus on relationships, equality, and cooperation.

> Adlerian concepts are congruent with the values of many ethnic
> and cultural groups. This congruence exists primarily due to the
> considerable flexibility of Adlerian cognitive and action-ori-
> ented techniques. The Adlerian emphasis on the individuals'
> subjective view and interpretation of his or her world leads to
> respect as well for ethnic values and perceptions. (Herring &
> Runion, 1994, pp. 218 219)

Interventions

Adlerian theory can help school counselors, teachers, and other school
personnel understand children and their issues clearly, enabling the design
of effective strategies for helping children learn to cope with problem situations both at school and at home. By helping children feel valued, learn
skills for connecting with others, increase their sense of belonging, learn
socially appropriate ways to express their feelings, decrease their feelings
of discouragement, and learn skills for dealing with problems, the
Adlerian school counselor can optimize children's learning and social
development.

> Adlerian theory has been used for decades to help counselors
> and educators to understand the inner world of the student. By
> exploring how a student understands and experiences the
> world, the professional school counselor can develop effective
> interventions that teach the child how to adapt to and cope with
> life's difficulties in a cooperative and socially appropriate man-
> ner. Misbehavior is seen as a learning issue and all students are
> seen as desiring to belong and to interact in a healthy and ben-
> eficial way with others. Adlerian interventions seek to help the
> student understand his behavior and to learn how to develop
> greater self-control. (Fallon, 2004, p. 113)

Individual Counseling Applications and Interventions With Children

The stages of individual counseling with children involve building a relationship, exploring the child's lifestyle, helping the child gain insight, and reorienting/reeducating the child.

BUILDING A RELATIONSHIP

The first stage involves building an egalitarian partnership with the child. The school counselor uses a variety of basic counseling skills to make a connection with the student, including reflecting feelings, paraphrasing, summarizing, encouraging, and metacommunicating. In Adlerian counseling, encouragement is especially helpful when the counselor points out the individual's assets, highlights his or her progress and efforts, and models the "courage to be imperfect."

Metacommunication (Kottman, 2003b) is a skill that can be used at all age levels. The counselor metacommunicates by guessing or commenting about (a) the meaning of the child's nonverbal communication, (b) the child's reaction to questions or interpretations, and (c) patterns in the child's behavior.

With younger elementary school students, the counselor may want to use play therapy techniques such as tracking behavior and returning responsibility to the child to facilitate the communication, using the "language" of children—play (Kottman, 2001, 2003b; Kottman & Johnson, 1993). In play therapy, tracking behavior means pointing out what the child is doing in play. This communicates that the counselor is "with" the client, paying attention to what he or she is doing with the toys. The counselor returns responsibility to the child by not doing things (such as tying the child's shoes or making decisions for the child) that he or she can do.

With older elementary school children, some combination of talking, doing art activities (Kottman, 2003b; Langarten, 1993; Malchiodi, 1998; Riley, 1999), doing sand tray therapy (Homeyer & Sweeney, 1998; Kestly, 2005), and playing active games (Ashby, Kottman, & DeGraaf, 2008; Kottman, Ashby, & DeGraaf, 2001) seems to be the most effective way to communicate through language, and at the same time acknowledging that play and activities may be necessary to engage many children in the counseling process. It also allows them to communicate through metaphor rather than directly.

EXPLORING THE CHILD'S LIFESTYLE

In the second stage the school counselor begins to collaborate with the child in examining his or her lifestyle—gathering information from the child, parents, and teachers. The counselor uses questioning strategies, play therapy and art techniques, reports from significant adults in the child's life, and observation of the child's behaviors in the counseling session and other situations, as vehicles for gathering information about the child's assets, goals of misbehavior, Crucial Cs, personality priorities, mistaken beliefs, and patterns of behavior.

The counselor also gathers information about psychological birth-order, family atmosphere, and classroom/school atmosphere, and how these factors impact the child and how he or she perceives self, others, and the world (Kottman, 2003b; Gilbert & Morawski, 2005). With some children, especially older elementary children, asking for early recollections can be helpful (Clark, 1994; Kottman, 2003b; Myer & James, 1991; Thompson & Rudolph, 2000).

As the counselor gathers this information, he or she conceptualizes the child's lifestyle and the lifestyles of significant adults. Based on these conceptualizations, the counselor plans strategies for intervention with the student and for consultation with parents and teachers. This plan begins with an emphasis on helping all parties involved develop insight into their own lifestyles and into the interaction of their own lifestyles with the lifestyles of the other people involved. Then the counselor helps clients generate ideas for developing and practicing new or revised patterns of thinking and feeling, and learning new behaviors.

HELPING THE CHILD GAIN INSIGHT

In the third stage the Adlerian school counselor begins to help the student better understand his or her lifestyle. The counselor uses interpretations, metacommunication, tentative hypotheses about goals of behavior, storytelling, and metaphors (Kottman & Stiles, 1990; Kottman, 2003a), bibliotherapy, role playing, and art activities to hold a mirror up to the client. The counselor also "spits in the client's soup"—an Adlerian technique designed to gently point out situations in which the child is sabotaging himself or herself. As this insight develops, the counselor challenges the student to make some decisions about whether to begin shifting his or her attitudes, thinking patterns, relationships, and/or behaviors.

REORIENTING AND REEDUCATING THE CHILD

During the fourth phase the counselor works with the child to consolidate changes in attitudes and perceptions by helping him or her translate new ways of thinking and feeling into behavioral changes. The counselor teaches the student new skills, such as anger management, assertiveness, negotiation, relationship building, and problem solving, and helps the child practice these skills in the safe environment of the counseling sessions and then transfer these skills to other situations and relationships. The counselor uses teaching techniques such as brainstorming, modeling, sharing metaphors, role-playing, and playing games. As the child progresses, the counselor uses encouragement focused on effort put out by the child and on positive shifts in behavior, attitudes, and relationship skills.

Individual Counseling Applications and Interventions With Adolescents

Individual counseling with adolescents involves the same steps previously described, but geared to an older student.

BUILDING A RELATIONSHIP

Adolescents have unique needs in forming therapeutic relationships. At a time when teens hold peer perceptions of them in high regard while withdrawing from family relationships, other adults, such as a school counselor, may offer a "grounded voice" among many conflicting opinions. In addition, school counselors afford the possibility of encouragement, exploration of issues, and insight into difficulties.

Basic counseling skills are used to establish rapport. Teens usually appreciate reflection of content and feelings, particularly when they are feeling upset and discouraged and desire clarity to reduce confusion. A highly egalitarian style will minimize defensiveness. The school counselor must also send a strong message to teens that the counselor is interested in their perspective and is not simply an extension of the agenda of other adults such as parents or teachers. Because the primary developmental task of adolescence is identity achievement, teens may be highly sensitive to the expectations of important adults in their life. Therefore, the counselor must tread softly.

EXPLORING THE ADOLESCENT'S LIFESTYLE

In the second phase of counseling, school counselors employ questioning techniques to explore the areas of school, family, friendships, and possibly romantic relationships. The partnership continues to develop as the student shares his or her subjective view and meaning-making with the counselor while the counselor offers hope through his or her counseling skills and expertise in the area of behavioral change.

Assessment continues as the counselor gathers specific information from the student, the parents, and teachers about psychological birth order, personality priorities, and the goals of misbehavior. Early recollections are often valuable during this assessment phase, as adolescents are more likely than younger children to provide detailed information.

In addition to talk therapy, some teens benefit from paper-and-pencil activities that explore aspects of their current status. A teen struggling with self-concept could complete a Likert-scale assessing self-perceptions in a number of areas. These questionnaires can deliver valuable insight into the adolescent's mind and assist in suggesting clinical hypotheses regarding lifestyle and mistaken beliefs. They can also offer a springboard for further discussion and exploration. Some adolescents enjoy art techniques, adventure therapy strategies, or sand tray therapy. Because performance anxiety is more prevalent in this age group than with younger children, however, the counselor must present these techniques in a non-threatening, casual way.

HELPING THE ADOLESCENT GAIN INSIGHT

In the third phase the school counselor must help students explore their lifestyles, mistaken beliefs, private logic, and goals of misbehavior, and compare them with alternative possibilities. To accomplish this, counselors may utilize advanced helping skills. At this stage, interpretations, confrontation, and sand tray therapy can be helpful to illuminate both problems and solutions. Many teens enjoy role playing and are often amenable to gaining insight into their own behavioral, attitudinal, and emotional patterns, especially if the counselor "plays" them and they "play" someone else.

If counselors are trained in Adlerian applications of sand tray therapy (Kottman, 2005b), they may make a sand tray that illustrates their perception of the teen's situation. With resistant students, using a metaphor or story to address an issue indirectly may work, providing them insight without their having to acknowledge the problem directly (Breen, 2005).

REORIENTATION AND REEDUCATION

During the final phase the school counselor encourages students to begin incorporating their new goals, beliefs, and behaviors into their lives. Counselors may use information-giving skills based on their expertise to support adolescents' efforts to change. These skills include advising, instructing, directing, suggesting, problem solving, evaluating, and immediacy (Poorman, 2003).

Information-giving based on reactions, experience, or perceptions can also be useful in counseling adolescents at this stage. And carefully planned self-disclosure can promote students' goals for change. Similarly, offering feedback can help students as they role-play or attempt new behaviors in the session before trying them outside the confines of the school counselor's office. All of the advanced skills noted above should be used in conjunction with encouragement, to promote change and diminish discouragement and apprehension.

Group Counseling Applications and Interventions

Adlerian theory, with its focus on the social embededness of behavior, lends itself to group methods (Kottman, 1999a). The tenets and constructs inherent in Adlerian theory are addressed easily, and in some cases more appropriately, in groups. Groups offer school counselors the opportunity to assess and address interpersonal issues more effectively because groups in time will "develop into a social microcosm of the participant members" (Yalom, 1995, p. 28). As Sonstegard (1998) suggested

> Recognizing that the problems of individuals are essentially social give group counseling a special significance—both in terms of diagnosis and remediation. In the action and interaction within each group, individuals express their goals, their sense of belonging, their intentions and social connectedness. (p. 167)

BUILDING A RELATIONSHIP

Just as in individual counseling, building a therapeutic relationship is paramount in Adlerian group counseling. Establishing group rules and group norms, as well as individual and group goals, can facilitate the creation of a collaborative environment.

Children and adolescents alike respond well to community-building activities. Using energizers or other experiential activities (Ashby, Kottman, & DeGraaf, 2008; Kottman, Ashby, & DeGraaf, 2001; Riviere, 2005) assists group members in building a sense of belonging. Yalom (1995) asserted that group cohesion is a basic property of groups in general and is also a therapeutic factor in the group counseling process. School counselors can take this opportunity to model the egalitarian nature of Adlerian counseling and begin the process of encouragement at both the individual and the group level.

Elementary school children often respond well to some initial structure provided by the counselor. Because of their developmental limitations, younger children cannot establish some of the rules and norms necessary to make a counseling group successful. The school counselor may wish to provide some initial rules regarding confidentiality, taking turns, and other procedural issues to start the group process. Because of the limited verbal abilities of elementary aged children, structured activities are helpful in the beginning stages, to give preliminary focus to the group's task. In addition to energizers and ice-breakers, school counselors may wish to include sentence starters, art activities, or paper-and-pencil activities. These activities should incorporate some form of group sharing or disclosure, to address the goal of community-building and group cohesion.

Adolescents tend to want to take an active part in the initial stages of group formation. They are capable of creating rules and norms and developing goals, and they may feel a strong sense of ownership in the beginning. Allowing group members to take on responsibility communicates a democratic, therapeutic relationship to them and eliminates concerns about authoritarian rule. Although adolescents are, in some ways, more capable than younger children in the early stage of group formation, they are also sometimes wary and suspicious. Therefore, school counselors will have to plan some structured community-building activities to reduce any anxiety or trepidation. Along with ice-breakers, adolescents usually respond positively to activity-based experiences, expressive therapeutic activities, and discussion and exploration of individual goals.

EXPLORING LIFESTYLE

In the second stage of group counseling, the goal is to explore each group members' lifestyle using Adlerian assessment techniques, including discussions of personality priorities, the Crucial Cs, and goals of misbehavior. In addition, school counselors will wish to examine the impact of each member's lifestyle on the focus of the group (anger management, study skills, etc.). A number of Adlerian techniques mentioned earlier in the chapter (e.g., early recollections, birth order, and family/school atmosphere) are equally appropriate in a group setting. Other group counseling activities that are appropriate to the students' developmental level and germane to the group's topic can also be included in this stage of group work, as long as the emphasis of these activities is congruent with the exploration of lifestyle (Sonstegard & Bitter, 1998). As in individual counseling, the group counselor analyzes the information and creates a hypothesis of the each member's lifestyle.

HELPING THE STUDENT GAIN INSIGHT

In contrast to individual counseling, group counseling affords the school counselor the opportunity to observe individuals in a social setting. Although individual goals may be embedded in life outside the group, the here-and-now orientation of group counseling is what may illuminate mistaken beliefs for group members (Corey, 2004; Yalom, 1995). The social interactions in group afford opportunities to observe how an individual's lifestyle is played out in everyday life. Children and adolescents benefit from this "mirror" and receive feedback not only from the school counselor but from other members of the group as well.

Further, group members may benefit from universality (Yalom, 1995) as they discover that they are not alone in their struggles, perceptions, relationships, or feelings. Whenever possible, the school counselor should encourage group members to offer their interpretations and insight, and step in only when the group fails to provide accurate feedback to a group member (Sonstegard & Bitter, 1998).

REORIENTATION AND REEDUCATION

Direct interpretations and readjustments may not always be necessary in the group setting (Sonstegard and Bitter, 1998). The unique format of groups—what Yalom (1995) describes as interpersonal learning—may be in and of itself the intervention that offers reorientation for individual group members. Nevertheless, it may be both necessary and appropriate to be more directive in this phase by using the group as an opportunity to practice or integrate new components into the lifestyle of each member. The group offers a safe place to "try on" new behaviors and receive helpful feedback, as well as an opportunity to explore future concerns.

Because this is the phase in which actual change is attempted, encouragement is especially important. School counselors should structure some specific group activities that illuminate individual strengths as well as the benefits of group membership. In addition, school counselors should plan closure activities that emphasize commitment to change, tangible goals and plans, and integration of group learning.

Classroom Guidance Applications

"Adlerian psychology is perhaps the only personality and counseling theory that provides a useful theoretical framework from which to develop classroom guidance programs" (Nicoll, 1994, p. 361). According to the American School Counselor Association (2005), the guidance curriculum component of a counseling program consists of "structured developmental lessons designed to assist students in achieving the competencies and is present systematically through classroom and group activities K-12" (p. 22). Competencies include academic development, career development, and personal/social knowledge and skills.

These competencies are strikingly similar to four of the five life tasks emphasized in Adlerian theory: (a) work/school, (b) friendship/society, (c) love/intimacy, and (d) self (Kottman, 2003b; Watts, 1999). The fifth life task, spirituality, usually is not addressed in a school setting, though in some parochial schools this task, too, may be within the school counselor's purview.

Related to the life task of school/work, ASCA (2005) competencies include the following:

1. Improve academic self-concept
2. Acquire skills for improving learning
3. Achieve school success
4. Improve learning

5. Plan to achieve goals
6. Develop career awareness
7. Develop employment readiness
8. Acquire career information
9. Identify career goals
10. Acquire knowledge to achieve career goals
11. Apply skills to achieve career goals

The Adlerian school counselor designs lessons to help children master each of these competencies in a developmentally appropriate way. The counselor might include information about students' lifestyles and how their personality priorities, Crucial Cs, and goals of behavior can have an impact on their academic and career development.

Guidance lessons in personal/social development across a K–12 spectrum could include activities to increase social interest and help students master the life tasks of friendship/society, love/intimacy, and self. In ASCA's model (2005), the competencies in this area include the following:

1. Acquire self-knowledge
2. Acquire interpersonal skills
3. Apply self-knowledge
4. Acquire personal safety skills

Some lessons that clearly reflect Adlerian sensibility include those on developing understanding of self and others, empathy skills, communication skills, cooperation skills, and responsibility skills (Brigman & Molina, 1999; Nicoll, 1994). Other lessons appropriate for an Adlerian school counselor include

- managing stress,
- resolving conflict,
- preventing bullying and violence,
- assessing and acknowledging personal assets,
- developing and maintaining friendships,
- appreciating differences,
- enhancing social skills,
- exploring family roles and interactional patterns,

- coping with feelings of inferiority,
- developing positive strategies for belonging and gaining significance, and
- clarifying personal values.

These lessons can be carried out using a variety of techniques including bibliotherapy, role-playing, small-group activities, experiential learning, energizer activities, art, paper-and-pencil activities, and discussion.
To build community, a helpful classwide and sometimes even schoolwide
activity may be, "Don't Feed the Monster on Tuesday" (Moser, 1991) day,
in which students keep track of positive self-talk and collectively "shrink
the monster" that day.

Strategies for Working with Teachers and Parents

"The most influential and important people in the social context of children are their parents and teachers" (Kottman, 2003b, p. 65). Whenever
possible, then, the school counselor must consult with parents and teacher
(Kottman, 2003b, 2005a; Kottman & Johnson, 1993)

1. as a vehicle for gaining a better understanding of the child,
2. as a means to help the important adults in his or her life understand the child better, and
3. as a way to teach concepts and intervention strategies that help
   make home and school a more positive environment for the child.

Consultation using the Adlerian approach has been found to be effective for school counselors (Bundy & Poppen, 1986; Dinkmeyer &
Carlson, 2006; Otwell & Mullis, 1997). They are in an excellent position
to work with teachers to help them with specific children, offering insight
into lifestyles, assets, communication patterns, goals of misbehavior, relationship skills, coping strategies, private logic, and so forth.

Also, consulting with parents is helpful, though this might not happen
as regularly as teacher consultation. Through parent-education classes,
periodic phone conversations, and meetings with parents, the school counselor can obtain information about the child's functioning in settings other
than school, about family dynamics that could be affecting the child, and
about the child's assets. These interactions could also be opportunities for

suggesting different ways of handling problems and new ways of relating to the child at home.

Consultation with the significant adults in the child's life follows the same four phases as the counseling process with the child. During the first phase the counselor uses paraphrasing, summarizing, reflecting metacommunicating, and encouragement, to build a relationship with parents and teachers (Kottman, 2005a).

During the second stage the counselor asks questions to learn more about parents' and teachers' perceptions of and attitudes toward the child. The counselor may also explore the lifestyles of the significant adults in the child's life to determine the impact that those adults are having on the child's interpersonal and intrapersonal development. The counselor might ask parents about their family-of-origin, the marital relationship, family values, parenting methods, and so forth. The counselor might ask teachers about their discipline philosophy and procedures, classroom rules, and attitudes toward certain types of children and certain types of classroom behaviors.

In the third phase counselors work with the adults to gain a better understanding of the child and gain clarity about counselors' own lifestyle issues that might be interfering with their ability to interact optimally with the child. As the child and any involved adults gain insight into their own lifestyles, they begin to change their attitudes toward themselves, one another, other people, and the world, in preparation for the fourth phase.

The fourth phase—reorientation/reeducation—entails the use of teaching techniques such as discussion, modeling, and behavior rehearsal with parents and teachers. They learn new skills connected to parenting and classroom management, such as employing logical consequences, encouraging, fostering the Crucial Cs, tailoring discipline to the child's goals of misbehavior, developing communication skills, and determining problem ownership. With many parents (and sometimes teachers) providing information about developmental patterns ("typical" behaviors at different ages) can be extremely helpful.

In the following case studies, two of the authors (Jen Alexander, an elementary school counselor, and Terry Kottman, a former secondary counselor) illustrate the application of Adlerian counseling principles and intervention strategies.

• •

CASE STUDY: MANUEL

After consulting with Manuel's third-grade teacher, parents, and possibly his first- or second-grade teacher, I [Jen Alexander] would begin individual counseling sessions with Manuel, using Adlerian play therapy techniques (Kottman, 2003b). A play therapy approach is appropriate for this student because of his young age, his tendency to be easily distracted, and his preference for high-activity levels. Manuel lacks independence and, as a result, is easily discouraged. Counseling sessions could provide an opportunity for him to take "fun" risks, make decisions, express himself, and gain awareness of his perceptions of self, others, and the world. Ultimately, the school counselor would attempt to help Manuel change his beliefs of inadequacy and teach him healthy ways to assert himself at school, at home, and in his relationships, so he can feel more successful.

I would consult with Manuel's teacher, arranging for sessions of approximately half an hour each, weekly or every other week. Seeing most clients every week in a school setting would be difficult, as the ratio may be one counselor for every 400 students. I would tell Manuel that I plan to see him in the afternoon on some, but not all, Tuesdays. I would not promise to have these sessions every week. This gives children some predictability but also allows flexibility for classroom schedule changes and crises that arise. Depending on Manuel's progress, he most likely would participate in six to 10 sessions with possibly one or two subsequent check-in appointments.

In my first session(s) with Manuel, the goal would be to build an egalitarian relationship. I would start by honestly explaining to him why I have asked to see him. For example, I might say, "Manuel, I'm seeing you today because your parents and teacher came to talk with me. They have some concerns about you and asked me to help. Did you know about that?"

If Manuel acknowledges that he is aware of these adult concerns, I'd ask him about it to gain understanding of his perceptions. If Manuel were surprised, I would explain the concerns honestly by saying, "Your teacher and parents told me that you get frustrated about schoolwork sometimes."

At that point I'd pay attention to Manuel's verbal and nonverbal responses. He might tell me a bit about his frustrations, or show little reaction, or appear uncomfortable and wish to change the subject. Following his lead, I might ultimately say something like, "We don't need to talk much about those things today, but I would like you to know that I'm here to help you. One of the ways I help kids your age is by playing with toys."

Children generally are excited and express interest in working together. While showing Manuel the playroom, I would explain that he will be able to do a lot of things he wants to do here and that we will share "being the boss." Sometimes when he comes, he will get to make decisions about what we do, and sometimes I will choose. I would tell him that he gets to choose what he shares with me and that, although I will not tell others what he tells me, I will be talking with his teacher and parents about ways they might be able to help him. I would explain that if I am concerned about anyone getting hurt, I will talk with other adults about how to keep everyone safe.

In at least the first session, Manuel will be the "boss" in the playroom. I would track his play by acknowledging what I see him doing, reflecting feelings, and encouraging him to make his own decisions. Sometimes children who lack confidence and independence say, "I don't know what to do. You decide."

Instead of making choices for children, I would respond, "Sometimes it's hard to know what to do. I trust you'll find something." Or, "I know you can figure that out." Eventually I would metacommunicate about Manuel's tendency to let others do things for him by saying, "I've noticed that when you don't feel sure about what to do, you often ask me to make choices for you. I wonder if that happens in your classroom and at home." I would look for nonverbal reactions signaling whether my statements are true or not. When Manuel does choose for himself, I would metacommunicate about that, too. "You didn't know where to start, but you figured out what to do. You didn't give up. That takes courage!"

Manuel's distractibility and frustration, I hypothesize, would be evident in the first play sessions. He might give up easily when something doesn't turn out the way he wants it to. He might put away toys quickly and do something else when he feels unsure of himself or frustrated. Manuel would likely be quick to ask for assistance. I would acknowledge his frustration and the underlying worry related to facing difficulties. I would also return responsibility to Manuel for solving these problems.

If he takes out his anger on toys in a manner that may break something or hurt either of us, I would set limits with him by saying, "It's against playroom rules to hurt people or things. If you want to hit, I'll bet you could find something safe to hit." These responses would set the stage for showing Manuel that he is responsible for the choices he makes. Owning his choices would eventually give him a sense of power and accomplishment.

In the second stage of our work together, I would collaborate with Manuel to gain an understanding of his lifestyle. Typically, this requires one or two sessions. I would want to know how he views himself, others, and the world. I would also want to understand the pattern of behavior he has developed in relation to those beliefs. How does his pattern of depending on others help him build and maintain relationships? I would question whether his avoidance behaviors (e.g., highly distractible, off task) and angry outbursts help him gain attention, power, revenge, or prove inadequacy. I would also want to learn more about Manuel's sense of feeling *connected* with others, feeling *capable*, believing that he *counts*, and demonstrating *courage* (the Crucial Cs). I should appreciate Manuel's strengths so we can build on them.

Some children play out metaphors on their own that emphasize lifestyle information. Others do not, so the counselor's direction is required. I could use a variety of techniques with Manuel, depending on his preferences in the playroom. I might ask him to draw a picture of himself doing something at school and then ask him questions about the thoughts and feelings of those illustrated (e.g., Kinetic School Drawing). I could ask Manuel to pretend that he is a talk show host, interviewing several students from his class about what it's like to be a third grader. To learn more about family dynamics, I might ask him to select an animal to represent each member of his family and then make a family collage. Because Manuel likes sports, I could ask him to pretend that everyone in his family is on a baseball team. I'd ask him to draw the players so we could talk about individual roles, thoughts, and feelings.

To further investigate his assets, goals of behavior, Crucial Cs, personality priorities, mistaken beliefs, and patterns of behavior, I might ask Manuel what cartoon, movie, or video game character he would like to be if he could be anyone. I would ask him to tell me a story about that character, pretending that he has been asked to save the day using one "super power." The contents of his story would tell me volumes about his perceptions, beliefs, and patterns of relating in the world.

No matter what activities are used during the second stage of counseling, the goal is to gain insight into the child's lifestyle, not to "change the child." At this point I would check in with his teacher and let her know what I'm seeing in the playroom. If possible, I would do the same with his parents, separate from my meeting with the teacher.

Asking how my interpretations fit with what adults see in the classroom and at home tends to be helpful. I would explain that I notice Manuel giving up easily in the playroom and am sensing that he does not trust himself to face difficulties. The adults typically share examples of times when they have noticed similar patterns with the child. This allows me to further build rapport with them through paraphrasing and reflecting feelings.

From there, we may discuss typical adult reactions to the child in such situations. Depending on the trust established in my relationship with the teacher and parents, I may metacommunicate about what I believe is motivating adult reactions or behavior, to help them gain insight into their own lifestyles. "I wonder if you, as parents, believe that helping Manuel is the way to be a good parent when you notice him feeling frustrated, especially because he is the youngest, and your only son." If parents acknowledge this, we could talk about the difficulty of finding a balance between being there for our children and doing too much for them.

We can use butterflies as a metaphor to illustrate this concept. As a butterfly starts to emerge from its chrysalis, it struggles and appears distressed. A human onlooker, who understands and values the emergence of the new creature, may wish to help, fearing that the butterfly will not emerge without help. Helping the butterfly, however, ultimately disrupts natural chemicals on its wings, inhibiting its ability to fly. The butterfly has to work its way out on its own. This metaphor points out the good intentions of the human (representing the parents) but emphasizes that working through frustration is critical for healthy development.

It would also be important to discuss what is motivating Manuel's behavior patterns. Commenting that all children strive to find unique places of strength in their families and classroom communities may be beneficial. When it comes to schoolwork, I would share my hypothesis that Manuel feels inferior to family members and has developed the erroneous belief that he is less capable than everyone else. He has decided that not trying at schoolwork is better than trying and failing. In his eyes, failure is likely anything less than family members' high level of achievement. To compensate for his feelings of inferiority, Manuel has thrown himself into sports, sometimes so much so that he takes unhealthy risks as he plays. Explaining that my goal is to help Manuel realize his own potential in multiple areas might help the adults express an interest in striving for the same.

And I might offer a suggestion or two for adults to use as an experiment with the child in future encounters. Adults tend to want concrete things to try with children in their care, especially because time for consultation and family counseling is limited in the school setting. I would encourage all adults to communicate with Manuel about his athletic interests. Sports are a source of confidence for him and should be embraced. Acknowledging his hard work and courage will eventually allow for communication about those topics in relation to school and other tasks: "I've noticed that when you play soccer, you keep going after that ball even if it doesn't go in the direction you wanted it to go. I bet you could do the same thing with your schoolwork."

I would explain to Manuel's teacher and parents the importance of encouragement, offering many examples of ways to encourage instead of help or praise in relation to his schoolwork. They would have to be patient with Manuel because he takes longer to do tasks on his own. He might beg, plead, whine, and eventually threaten in an attempt to prove that he is not able to do things on his own. Adults should give Manuel tasks that he is able to complete, but they should not be too easy for him. Manuel needs to experience frustration so adults will have an opportunity to acknowledge his feelings and verbalize their belief in his ability to succeed.

If Manuel pushes his work on the floor in frustration and comments that he is stupid, adults might be inclined to jump in, hoping to rescue him from self-defeating thoughts by saying, "You're not stupid. I'll help you get this done." Taking responsibility for his emotions and behavior, however, would only increase his dependence. Utilizing responses such as the following are more helpful: "It looks like you're frustrated, Manuel. It's okay to be frustrated, but put-downs aren't helpful. Stick with it. I know you can do it. Let me know if you have a question. Otherwise I'll talk to you when you finish the next step."

Choosing not to respond to many of Manuel's negative comments about himself or his outbursts would show that they are not effective ways to get out of uncomfortable tasks. I would encourage Manuel's parents and teacher to expect him to complete his work because they believe in him.

When Manuel demonstrates persistence, his hard work should be acknowledged: "Manuel, you're working hard. You didn't think you could do this, but you're doing it!" To highlight the changes Manuel is making, adults might say, "You're showing more and more courage, Manuel. What have you been saying to yourself to help yourself?"

Teaching adults about logical consequences could also be helpful. At school, recess is a break from work. When Manuel works, breaks should follow. If he chooses not to work, he might be given extra work time instead of a break. I tend to discourage teachers and parents from using tangible rewards for completing work, especially when students' academic skills match the work they are given. External rewards tend to discourage intrinsic motivation for learning.

Unexpected "celebrations" for effort and hard work are a good idea. After several days of courageous effort on schoolwork, his parents might say, "Manuel, your teacher mentioned that you've been working hard at school the past few days. When you're frustrated, you've chosen to keep at it, asking for help when you needed it. We're proud of you! Let's celebrate by watching the game together or going to the park to play catch." Celebrations, it must be noted, should not be based on grades or other outcomes. Effort is most important, especially when children lack confidence, perceive themselves as being inferior to others, and are generally discouraged.

For adults in Manuel's life to understand the goals of his behavior is not enough. Manuel needs to gain insight into his lifestyle, too. That is the focus of the third stage of Adlerian counseling, which usually requires one or two sessions. Although several techniques could help Manuel gain insight into his lifestyle, I would probably create a metaphor for him in the sand tray, highlighting his perceptions of self, others, and the world (Kottman, 2003b; Kottman & Ashby, 2002). I would incorporate aspects of his life story in my story, but the metaphor would not match his situation entirely. If the stories hit too close to home, children often shut down. The power of metaphor is in its ability to promote new understanding without focusing primarily on the client. I would tell my story while illustrating it in the sand tray. It might go something like this.

• • • • • • • • • • • • • • • •

In a land far, far away, there once was a kingdom ruled by a very kind king and queen. The king's name was _____ [child supplies name], and the queen's name was _____ [child supplies name]. They had ruled the land for many, many years. All the people in the kingdom trusted and respected the rulers because the kingdom was a safe, fair, and fun place to be. This was partly because all people in the kingdom had their very own job to do. The job was given to them on their fifth birthdays at a special celebration.

Getting the job was a very big deal, and all little ones in the kingdom looked forward to receiving their responsibilities. It was something that parents talked about with their children over and over again in the years leading up to the party. Some in the land had been given the jobs of builder, scientist, teacher, medic, artist, or historian—to name only a few. There were as many jobs as there were people.

Although many princes and princesses lived in this kingdom, there was only one Frog Prince, and his celebration day had come. Like all the others around him, he had been anxious for his celebration day for a long time. Now that the day was here, he felt excited and also a little nervous. "What if I get a job I don't like? What if I'm not any good at the job I'm given?" he wondered.

Others in the land told him not to worry, but it was hard not to worry. Once the party began, he forgot about his fears because there was so much to do. Music and laughter filled the air as everyone ate candy and rode amusement park rides. Finally it was time for the announcement. Out came the king and queen. They welcomed little Frog Prince and announced that he had been given the job of runner in the kingdom. Every day he ran around the kingdom, taking things from here to there. The king and queen explained that Frog Prince's job was very important. People all over the land would be counting on him to deliver messages and things they needed. He had been chosen for his speed.

Frog Prince felt very excited. He liked to run, and started his responsibilities that very afternoon. Day after day he ran from here to there. Deliveries were on time. People were happy, and Frog Prince felt proud of himself.

That is—until one stormy day. The queen called for little Frog Prince, and when he arrived, she gave him a large envelope. She told the Frog Prince to run as fast as he could to the other side of the kingdom. There wasn't much time. It had been storming all night, and the bridge over the magical stream was damaged and in danger of being washed away. The builders on the other side of the kingdom needed plans from the castle to rebuild the bridge if it was destroyed. If little Frog Prince didn't get to the builders in time, they would not be able to rebuild the bridge.

"Without the bridge, the only way across would be through the water," explained the queen.

"Through the water?" asked the Frog Prince in a trembling voice. "We can't go through the water. That's where the dragon lives."

"That's right," said the queen. "You must hurry. If the bridge is washed away, it has to be rebuilt or someone will have to face the dragon."

Off went little Frog Prince. He ran as fast as he could through the rain. Thunder boomed all around, and lightening lit up the sky. He came to the bridge and found that it was very damaged indeed. Boards had been blown away. He felt a lump in his throat as he took the first step onto the bridge. It was scary to cross. "What if I'm not fast enough?" "What if the wind blows the bridge down, and I fall into the water with the dragon?" he wondered. As soon as he asked those questions, he seemed to have answers, though. "I'll do my best. This is my job."

With that, he took a run for it and made it across to the other side. As he stepped on the land, the bridge gave way. He had made it in time. He gave the plans to the builders and felt so relieved that they would be able to rebuild the bridge for all in the land.

The builders felt relieved, too. They opened the envelope as fast as they could, but their faces dropped when they saw the pages. "We don't know how to read the language of the people on the other side of the Kingdom. You must help us, Frog Prince. Please read the directions to us so we may rebuild the bridge."

Frog Prince's heart sank. "Read?" he asked. "I hate to read. I haven't had much practice because it's not my job. There are others in the kingdom who were given the job of reading. Why don't you ask them?"

"They have no way to get here without a bridge," replied the builders. "We need your help. All we ask is that you do your best. Your reading may not be perfect, and that's okay. Whatever you are able to read will help us build the bridge."

[Pause here in the telling, and ask the child what he or she thinks Frog Prince would do.]

The little Frog Prince thought for some time. "Well, I wasn't sure I would be able to cross the bridge today. That was scary, and I tried my best. I guess I could do the same thing reading these directions."

With that, he read slowly, especially at first. He didn't read all the words correctly, but with his help, the builders understood the directions and the bridge was rebuilt. As soon as it was finished, all the builders and the little Frog Prince ran across it to the other side. The builders told all in the kingdom of the Frog Prince's courage in crossing the bridge in the storm and, most important, doing his best at reading the directions, even though they were hard. Everyone in the kingdom cheered and felt so proud of the little Frog Prince, but most of all, he felt proud of himself!

• • • • • • • • • • • • • • • • • •

In the next session I might ask Manuel to tell me a story about a character who felt like giving up but, instead, showed courage to keep going. If he were to tell the story with an unfavorable ending, I might use the mutual storytelling technique (Gardner, 1986; Kottman, 2003a) to retell the story with a more positive ending.

In the reorientation and reeducation phase I would teach Manuel healthy self-talk strategies to use when he feels frustrated. One option would be to ask him to tell me about a character from a video game, cartoon, or television show that he sees as being down in the dumps. The example I often use with children is Oscar the Grouch from Sesame Street. Oscar always has something negative to say. Manuel could use that character or name another character instead. I would ask him to draw a picture of his character in the middle of a blank piece of paper, and together we would write things around the picture that the character might say to Manuel if he were working on schoolwork and became frustrated. For example, Oscar the Grouch (or another similar character) might say, "You're not any good at this. Why don't you just give up?" Or, "This is stupid. Throw it on the ground!" Manuel and I could then explore how he would feel at hearing these statements. I would ask Manuel if these words help him or hurt him.

From there, I would ask Manuel to pick a character who is the opposite of the one he just chose. This character has to be positive and helpful. I would ask Manuel to draw a picture of this character, and we would write down things the character might say to Manuel when he feels frustrated about schoolwork. We might write things like, "We all get frustrated sometimes. Stick with it." Or, "We all make mistakes. That's the way we learn. Don't give up!"

Again, we would discuss how these statements are more helpful than the others. I would explain that we all feel frustrated in life sometimes, and it's our job to choose whether we're going to say things to ourselves like Oscar the Grouch might say or if we're going to say more helpful things to ourselves. Our last session or two could be devoted to using positive self-talk in specific situations. This could be accomplished through games or a variety of role-playing scenarios.

Before terminating the counseling sessions, it is important to schedule another check-in with Manuel's parents and teacher. This contact allows for consultation in regard to the adults' progress with the strategies we discussed, and it gives the adults an opportunity to share feedback about Manuel's progress at home and school. As Manuel showed progress in terms of demonstrating courage instead of distractibility, discouragement, angry outbursts, or underlying anxiety in relation to schoolwork, Manuel and I would talk about the progress he has made, celebrate his success, and terminate regularly scheduled counseling sessions.

CASE STUDY: AMY

Even before I [Terry Kottman] started working with Amy, I would be thinking about the prereferral information and working to conceptualize her lifestyle. With the information from her English teacher and her mother, I would begin to develop a picture of her as a relatively typical oldest child who has high standards for herself that she is not meeting. This is resulting in moderate discouragement that Amy is experiencing as depression.

With these basic assumptions, I would begin work with Amy, using individual counseling sessions to build the relationship and explore other factors related to her view of herself, others, and the world. In the first session or two I would simply listen to Amy and use paraphrases, summaries, reflection of feelings, and encouragement to establish rapport and trust with her—to communicate to her that I am "on your side." It also might be helpful to ask her to bring in some of her poetry and discuss the feelings and ideas expressed there.

Based on Amy's history of seeking out close connections with teachers, in both junior high and high school, she sounds like a young woman who craves a close connection with a significant adult. In the first phase of counseling, I would be willing to be that adult while still setting appropriate professional boundaries. It also would be essential to revisit her—having said that she might like to die—to make sure that she did not have any intention of following through with any suicidal ideation.

While working to establish the relationship, I would be listening for information related to Amy's lifestyle—her perceptions of herself, others, and the world; her mistaken beliefs; her private logic; her patterns of communication, building relationships, and solving problems; her personality priorities; her goals of misbehavior; and her Crucial Cs. After coming to believe that the relationship is strong enough for me to be more directive (usually after one to three sessions), I would move into the second phase by asking questions related to lifestyle. I would ask Amy to describe

- family members and relationships between herself, her siblings, and her parents;
- situations (both at home and at school) in which she "gets in trouble," what happens as a result of these problem situations, and what she wishes would happen instead;
- any changes she would make in her family, in her classes, and in school;
- what she likes about her family, her classes, her school, and her teachers;
- what she likes about herself in the context of both school and home;
- what she would change about herself if she could;
- how she gets along with others (both adults and peers);
- strategies she uses to solve problems (both at home and school); and
- how she copes with a variety of different feelings (e.g., fear, happiness, anger, pride, sadness, hurt).

Further, I might ask her more generic questions about her preferences in activities, movies, books, and television shows. I would limit the questions each session to five or six so Amy does not feel as though I have turned into a member of the Spanish Inquisition. I always have "fiddling toys" in my office so students can have something to do with their hands while we talk. That way, they don't feel pressured to make eye contact with me but can focus on the "fiddling toy" while we talk.

In addition to asking questions, I would take part in more active, experiential activities with Amy. She has shared poems with her English teacher, so I would bring in my magnetic poetry, requesting that she compose poetry to related to the topics I want to explore. If she would be willing, we could do some adventure therapy exercises (Ashby, Kottman, & DeGraaf, 2008; Kottman, Ashby, & DeGraaf, 2001) or art techniques, such as the Kinetic Family Drawing, the Kinetic School Drawing, animal phototherapy, mask-making, or collages (Knoff & Prout, 1985; Kottman, 2001, 2003b). How long to devote to the second phase of counseling varies from student to student, but I would guess that this phase would take only two or three sessions with Amy. She is already primed to explore her issues; and she is bright, motivated, and thrives on attention.

Amy seems to believe that she is "less than" others, and she does not experience her environment to be supportive or encouraging. She has many mistaken beliefs related to her academic abilities, her appearance, and her social relationships. Her private logic seems to engender discouragement because of her inability to live up to her own high personal standards. She has a pattern of complaining and denigrating herself, which has put a strain on her relationships with family members, peers, and teachers. Amy seems to expect others to solve her problem for her rather than taking action herself. She believes that she is depressed, but my assessment is that she is discouraged rather than depressed.

I would speculate that Amy's personality priorities are superiority and comfort. In her striving for superiority as a way of avoiding her feelings of inferiority, she seems to vacillate between appropriately compensating for her feelings of inferiority with a strong academic performance and verbalizing her desire to give up and not try to accomplish anything. Her other personality priority seems to be comfort, as she constantly referred to the stress she was experiencing as a result of trying to keep up with her work. Her belief that the normal workload at school and home are excessively stressful and her desire to avoid this stress suggests that she experiences even a minor amount of stress as debilitating.

Although Amy does not manifest many misbehaviors, her patterns of interaction with others suggest that the goal of her misbehavior is attention. Her patterns of complaining, excessive neediness, and putting herself down suggest that she is using her behavior in active, potentially destructive ways to get attention. She likely does not believe that she gets enough positive attention in her family, from friends, or at school, and resorts to inappropriate behaviors to garner attention.

As I consider Amy's Crucial Cs, I conceptualize her struggling to a mild to moderate extent with all of them. *Connect* may be her strongest Crucial C, as she does have friends and adults who care about her. Still, she seems to undermine her ability to connect with her neediness and her self-doubts. As for courage, she is unwilling to take many risks or try activities in which she is not guaranteed success, which may indicate a deficit in this Crucial C. Her attitude is pervaded with discouragement—a lack of courage. Although to outside appearances she is capable, her verbalizations suggest that she does not believe that she is capable. Her lack of confidence in her own abilities is undermining her capabilities. The biggest problem area for Amy may be the Crucial C of *count*. She does not seem to believe that she is inherently valuable or valuable enough. Her striving for attention seems to be an attempt to prove to herself that she counts, but her style of getting attention in negative ways is self-defeating.

At the same time I was working with Amy exploring her lifestyle, I would consult with Amy's teachers and her parents. I would solicit information from her English teacher about her concerns regarding Amy and her behavior, monitoring whether Amy continued to seek inappropriate extracurricular contact. It would also be helpful to talk with Amy's other teachers to get a picture of how she acts in class, how she relates to teachers and students, and her usual patterns of problem-solving and coping.

I would probably make several phone calls to Amy's mother, working to establish a relationship with her and to gather information about her relationship with Amy, her perceptions of the dynamics in the family, and her thoughts about Amy's lifestyle. This interaction, I hope, would set the stage for the third and fourth phases of counseling, when I might want to help Amy's mother make some changes in her interactions with Amy. Based on my initial conversation with Amy's mother, I would guess that she is feeling discouraged about her relationship with Amy and disheartened about Amy's attitudes and behavior.

Based on my conceptualization of Amy's lifestyle, I would plan my third-phase interventions. The primary focus would be on encouraging Amy and helping her understand herself better. I would use a variety of active intervention strategies to help her gain insight into the self-defeating patterns of thinking, feeling, and behaving. By combining sand tray techniques, art activities, poetry, journaling, and storytelling/metaphors, I would engage Amy in looking more closely at her attitudes and beliefs about herself, others, and the world.

The techniques of metacommunication; encouragement focused on assets, efforts, and progress; and "spitting in her soup" would deepen her insight. Because Amy is such an intelligent student, I would teach her about personality priorities, goals of misbehavior, and the Crucial Cs, and solicit her opinions about how these factors are influencing her thinking, feeling, and behaving. I would suggest that we find ways to capitalize on the strengths inherent in each of her personality priorities, shift the goal of her behavior toward more positive ways of gaining attention, and enhance all four of her Crucial Cs. When she expresses a willingness to do these things, we would be ready to move into the fourth phase of counseling.

During the third phase of counseling, I would also consult with Amy's teachers and her mother. Without revealing the content of our counseling sessions, I would explain some of my ideas about Amy's lifestyle—both the aspects that I think are working for her and the aspects that are getting in her way. I might also ask them to look at elements of their own lifestyles (e.g., personality priorities, or Crucial Cs) and how they interact with Amy's lifestyle. For example, my guess about Amy's mother is that she might have pleasing and/or comfort as personality priorities, which would contribute to her frustration with Amy's complaining. Understanding how her own lifestyle interacts with Amy's lifestyle might help Amy's mother become more tolerant of Amy's behaviors. It also might be helpful to give the mother more information about adolescent development, given that many aspects of the presenting problem seem to be a function of Amy's being a teenage girl.

During the fourth phase of counseling, Amy and I would discuss attitudes, behaviors, thoughts, and feelings that she would like to change. We would develop a plan for teaching her skills that she wants to learn (e.g., friendship skills, negative thought-stopping techniques, relaxation skills) and discuss strategies for her substituting positive self-talk for private logic and mistaken beliefs. We would work on capitalizing on the strengths of her personality priorities of superiority and comfort. I would suggest that she notice when she is feeling inferior and consider this as a positive challenge rather than a discouragement. She could write a poem or make up a story about the fun aspect of having "comfort" as a personality priority, focusing on spontaneity and stress reduction as a way to enhance peer and family relationships.

We might use role playing or art activities to practice appropriate, constructive ways of gaining attention and feedback that she is capable and that she counts. Using adventure activities and homework assignments, we could practice ways of taking risks and trying things even when there is no guarantee of success. This phase might also involve inviting Amy to participate in a counseling group with other freshman and sophomore girls so she would have a chance to practice new ways of being in the world in a safe environment and receive feedback about her impact on others from her peers. Depending on Amy's commitment to making changes and my time constraints, this phase of the counseling could last from three sessions to an entire semester.

Conclusion

Adlerian theory and therapeutic practices have much to offer school counselors. Adlerian theory is both practical and useful in a school setting in light of its basic principles, the structured method of conceptualizing children and their problems, its emphasis on encouragement and assets, the strategic use of intervention strategies, and the variety of relevant techniques.

References

Adler, A. (1937). Psychiatric aspects regarding individual and social disorganization. *American Journal of Sociology, 42,* 773–780.

Adler, A. (1956). *The Individual Psychology of Alfred Adler.* In H. Ansbacher & R. Ansbacher, (Eds.) New York: Basic Books.

Adler, A. (1958). *What life should mean to you.* New York: Putnam. (Original work published 1931).

American School Counselor Association. (2005). *The ASCA national model: A framework for school counseling programs* (2nd ed.). Alexandria, VA: Author.

Ansbacher, H. (1991). The concept of social interest. *Individual Psychology, 47,* 28–46.

Ansbacher, H., & Ansbacher, R. (Eds.). (1956). *The Individual Psychology of Alfred Adler.* New York: Basic Books.

Ashby, J., Kottman, T., & DeGraaf, D. (2008). *Active interventions for kids and teens: Adding adventure and fun to counseling.* Alexandria, VA: American Counseling Association.

Beames, T.B. (1992). *A student's glossary of Adlerian terminology* (2nd ed.). Chicago: Adler School of Psychology.

Breen, D. (2005). Metaphorical thinking with adolescents. In L. Gallo-Lopez & C. Schaefer (Eds.), *Play therapy with adolescents* (pp. 159–174). Lanham, MD: Jason Aronson.

Brigman, G., & Molina, B. (1999). Developing social interest and enhancing school success skills: A service learning approach. *Journal of Individual Psychology, 55,* 342–354.

Bundy, M., & Poppen, W. (1986). School counselors' effectiveness as consultants: A research review. *Elementary School Guidance and Counseling, 21,* 215–222.

Campbell, C. (2003). Student success skills training: An Adlerian approach to peer coaching. *Journal of Individual Psychology, 59,* 327–333.

Canino, I.A., & Spurlock, J. (2000). *Culturally diverse children and adolescents: Assessment, diagnosis, and treatment* (2nd ed.). New York: Guilford.

Carlson, J., & Slavik, S. (1997). (Eds.), *Techniques in Adlerian psychology.* Washington, DC: Accelerated Development.

Clark, A. (1994). Early recollections: A personality assessment tool for elementary school counselors. *Elementary School Guidance and Counseling, 29,* 92–102.

Corey, G. (2004). *Theory and practice of group counseling.* Belmont, CA: Brooks/Cole-Thomson.

Dinkmeyer, D., & Carlson, J. (2006). *Consultation: Creating school-based interventions* (3rd ed.). New York: Routledge.

Dinkmeyer, D., Dinkmeyer, D., & Sperry, L. (1987). *Adlerian counseling and psychotherapy* (2nd ed.). Columbus, OH: Merrill.

Dreikurs, R., & Soltz, V. (1964). *Children: The challenge.* New York: Hawthorn/Dutton.

Dustin, D., & Ehly, S. (1992). School consultation in the 1990s. *Elementary School Guidance and Counseling, 26,* 165–175.

Edwards, D. (2004). The relationship between social interest and coping resources in children. *Professional School Counseling, 7,* 187–194.

Edwards, D., & Gfroerer, K. (2001). Adlerian school-based interventions for children with attention-deficit/hyperactivity disorder. *Journal of Individual Psychology, 57,* 210–223.

Fallon, M. K. (2004). Adlerian therapeutic techniques for professional school counselors. In B. Erford (Ed.), *Professional school counseling: A handbook of theories, programs, and practices.* Austin, TX: Pro-Ed.

Gardner, R. A. (1986). *The psychotherapeutic techniques of Richard A. Gardner.* New York: Creative Therapeutics.

Gil, E., & Drewes, A. (Eds.). (2005). *Cultural issues in play therapy.* New York: Guilford.

Gilbert, J., & Morawski, C. (2005). Stress coping for elementary school children: A case for including lifestyle. *Journal of Individual Psychology, 61,* 314–328.

Herring, R., & Runion, K. (1994). Counseling ethnic children and youth from an Adlerian perspective. *Journal of Multicultural Counseling and Development, 22,* 215–226.

Holmgren, V.S. (1996). *Elementary school counseling: An expanding role.* Boston: Allyn & Bacon.

Homeyer, L., & Sweeney, D. (1998). *Sandtray: A practical manual.* Canyon Lake, TX: Lindan Press.

Kestley, T. (2005). Adolescent sand tray. In L. Gallo-Lopez & C. Schaefer (Eds.), *Play therapy with adolescents* (pp. 18–29). Lanham, MD: Jason Aronson.

Knoff, H., & Prout, H. (1985). *Kinetic drawing system for family and school: A handbook.* Los Angeles: Western Psychological Services.

Kottman, T. (1999a). Group applications of Adlerian play therapy. In D. Sweeney & L. Homeyer (Eds.), *The handbook of group play therapy: How to do it, how it works, whom it's best for* (pp. 65–85). San Francisco: Jossey-Bass

Kottman, T. (1999b). Play therapy. In R. Watts & J. Carlson (Eds.), *Interventions and strategies in counseling and psychotherapy* (pp. 161–180). Philadelphia: Accelerated Development.

Kottman, T. (2001). *Play therapy: Basics and beyond.* Alexandria, VA: American Counseling Association.

Kottman, T. (2003a). Mutual storytelling: Adlerian style. In H. Kaduson & C. Schaefer (Eds.), *101 play therapy techniques* (Vol. 3). Northvale, NJ: Jason Aronson.

Kottman, T. (2003b). *Partners in play: An Adlerian approach to play therapy* (2nd ed.). Alexandria, VA: American Counseling Association.

Kottman, T. (2005a). Adlerian case consultation with a teacher. In A.M. Dougherty (Ed.), *Psychological consultation and collaboration in school and community settings: A casebook* (4th ed.). Belmont, CA: Thomson.

Kottman, T. (2005b). *Partners in the sand: Adlerian application of sand tray play therapy.* 22nd Annual Association for Play Therapy International Conference Proceedings, Fresno, CA.

Kottman, T., & Ashby, J. (2002). Metaphoric stories. In C. Schaefer & D. Cangelosi (Eds.), *Play therapy techniques* (2nd ed., pp. 233–242). Northvale, NJ: Jason Aronson.

Kottman, T., Ashby, J., & DeGraaf, D. (2001). *Adventures in guidance: How to integrate fun into your guidance program.* Alexandria, VA: American Counseling Association.

Kottman, T., & Johnson, V. (1993). Adlerian play therapy: A tool for school counselors. *Elementary School Guidance and Counseling, 28,* 42–51.

Kottman, T., & Stiles, K. (1990). The mutual storytelling technique: An Adlerian application in child therapy. *Journal of Individual Psychology, 46,* 148–156.

Landgarten, H. (1993). *Magazine photo collage; A multicultural assessment and treatment technique.* New York: Brunner/Mazel.

Lew, A., & Bettner, B.L. (1996). *Responsibility in the classroom.* Newton Center, MA: Connexions.

Lew, A., & Bettner, B.L. (2000). *A parent's guide to motivating children.* Newton Center, MA: Connexions.

Malchiodi, C. (1998). *Understanding children's art.* New York: Guilford.

Manaster, G., & Corsini, R. (1982). *Individual psychology: Theory and practice.* Itasca, IL: F. E. Peacock.

McGoldrick, M. (1998). *Re-visioning family therapy: Race, culture, and gender in clinical practice*. New York: Guilford.

Mosak, H. (1977). *On purpose*. Chicago: Alfred Adler Institute.

Mosak, H. (1995). Adlerian psychotherapy. In R. Corsini & D. Wedding (Eds.), *Current psychotherapies* (5th ed., pp. 51–94). Itasca, IL: Peacock.

Moser, A. (1991). *Don't feed the monster on Tuesday*. Kansas City, MO: Landmark.

Muro, J., & Kottman, T. (1995). *Guidance and counseling in the elementary and middle schools: A practical approach*. Dubuque, IA: Brown & Benchmark.

Myer, R., & James, R. (1991). Using early recollections as an assessment technique with children. *Elementary School Guidance and Counseling, 25*, 228–232.

Nicoll, W. (1994). Developing effective classroom guidance programs: An integrative framework. *School Counselor, 41*, 360–364.

Oberst, U., & Stewart, A. (2003). *Adlerian psychotherapy: An advanced approach to Individual Psychology*. New York: Brunner/Rutledge.

Otwell, P., & Mullis, F. (1997). Counselor-led staff development: An efficient approach to teacher consultation. *Professional School Counseling, 1*, 25–29.

Poorman, P. (2003). *Microskills and theoretical foundations for professional helpers*. Boston: Pearson.

Pryor, D., & Tollerud, T. (1999). Applications of Adlerian principles in school settings. *Professional School Counseling, 2*, 299–304.

Riley, S. (1999). *Contemporary art therapy with adolescents*. Philadelphia: Jessica Kingsley Publishers.

Riviere, S. (2005). Play therapy techniques to engage adolescents. In L. Gallo-Lopez & C. Schaefer (Eds.), *Play therapy with adolescents* (pp. 121–142). Lanham, MD: Jason Aronson.

Schmidt, J. (1999). *Counseling in schools: Essential services and comprehensive programs* (3rd ed.). Needham Heights, MA: Allyn & Bacon.

Sciarra, D. (2004). *School counseling: Foundations and contemporary issues*. Belmont, CA: Brooks/Cole.

Sonstegard, M. (1998). A rationale for group counseling. *Journal of Individual Psychology, 54*(2), 164–175.

Sonstegard, M. & Bitter, J. (1998). Counseling children in groups. *Journal of Individual Psychology, 54*(2), 251–267.

Stiles, K., & Kottman, T. (1990). Mutual storytelling: An alternative intervention for depressed children. *School Counselor, 38,* 36-46.

Thompson, C., & Rudolph, L. (2000). *Counseling children* (5th ed.). Pacific Grove, CA: Brooks/Cole.

Vargas, L., & Koss-Chioino, J. (Eds.) (1992). *Working with culture: Psychotherapeutic interventions with ethnic minority children and adolescents*. San Francisco: Jossey-Bass.

Watts, R. (1999). The vision of Adler: An introduction. In R. Watts & Carlson, J. (Eds.), *Interventions and strategies in counseling and psychotherapy* (pp. 1–14). Philadelphia: Accelerated Development.

Yalom, I. (1995). *The theory and practice of group psychotherapy*. New York: Perseus.

CHAPTER 3

MULTIMODAL CHILD COUNSELING IN SCHOOL SETTINGS

● ●

Matt Englar-Carlson and Alison Englar-Carlson

● ●

Overview

Building upon Lazarus's (1976, 1989, 1997) BASIC I.D. multimodal theory, this chapter presents a holistic counseling approach specifically tailored for children. Multimodal counseling is holistic because it systematically considers seven areas of a child's life in planning treatment interventions. Though a child may present with one initial concern, the multimodal approach assumes that clients are often troubled by a variety of specific problems that can be addressed using a wide range of techniques (Lazarus, 2005).

Keat (1990) developed the HELPING model as an adaptation of Lazarus' multimodal approach to tailor the model specifically to the needs of children. Using the acronym HELPING (rather than Lazarus' acronym BASIC I.D.), the HELPING model presumes that children may need help in the modes of: Health, Emotions, Learning, Personal Relationships, Imagery-Interests, Need-to-know (Notions), and Guidance of actions, behaviors, and consequences (see Table 3.1). In a comprehensive and systematic manner, multimodal counseling assesses each aspect of a person across all seven modes to develop a tailored treatment plan.

The seven HELPING modes are analogous to the seven notes of a musical scale (Keat & Englar-Carlson, 2006). The counselor and the client together assess and choose which notes to play to orchestrate an appropriate multimodal musical menu (Ortiz, 1997). Thus, the goal of multimodal counseling is to make menu choices so dissonance can be decreased and consonance increased in their lives. By selecting the most appropriate notes (concerns), the school counselor can be instrumental in helping the child compose a more harmonious life. This balanced approach represents effective counseling in that it first identifies problems and then utilizes intervention strategies to ameliorate the client's problems.

One facet of this approach that school counselors will find helpful is to utilize whatever technique/procedure is deemed to be potentially most effective in helping the child. Referred to as *technical eclecticism* (Keat, 1990; Lazarus, 1997; Lazarus & Beutler, 1993), this approach addresses how intervention strategies are tailored to fit children's concerns. From the multimodal perspective, specific techniques and procedures are selected based on a careful assessment of their potential effectiveness in the individual counseling situation to help in any or all of the modes. In this manner, conceptualization and intervention are not necessarily theoretical but, rather, aimed at selecting and applying practical, effective approaches. Thus, the multimodal approach can be considered a brief, time-limited model that is both flexible and versatile, matching techniques with the specific needs of each child. The approach seems ideal for school counselors.

This chapter is aimed at counselors and therapists who work with children, parents and families in a school setting. The school setting comprises such an important part of a child's life (a child will spend more that half of his or her daylight hours in school each week) that any effective therapeutic intervention with a child must inherently involve intervention and collaboration within the school setting. The multimodal approach can work well in school settings because of its practical focus. Yet, practicality in counseling is not just a function of intervention or technique but, rather, is often the product of an effective theoretical strategy that guides and grounds practice. Therefore, in our attempt to outline pragmatic procedures, we begin with a simple, straightforward, child-focused theoretical model. Before examining the HELPING model in detail, we will review Lazarus's multimodal theory and BASIC I.D. model, and then look at the transition into the HELPING model for work with children.

Major Constructs of the Multimodal Approach

Arnold Lazarus developed multimodal therapy in the 1960s. Originally trained as a behaviorist, Lazarus recognized that behavioral methods alone usually were not sufficient to bring about lasting change (Lazarus, 2005). He noticed that "narrow band" interventions tended to be less effective than "broad spectrum" interventions (Lazarus, 2000b). Thus, he began to look at a therapy approach grounded in therapeutic breadth. At the same time, he wanted to be able to tailor counseling to determine which counseling techniques would work best with which types of people and which types of problems.

As he investigated these questions, he began to develop his own therapeutic approach and way of understanding clients and the process of counseling. His approach, which he termed multimodal therapy, emphasizes tailoring treatments to individual clients. The approach provides a structured, organized way to answer the questions: What works? For whom? Under which conditions? (Lazarus, 2005).

The multimodal approach is viewed as one of the more comprehensive and established integrative models for counseling. Theoretically, the multimodal approach is grounded primarily in broad social and cognitive learning theory (Bandura, 1986), which emphasizes observing and modeling the behaviors, attitudes, and emotional reactions of others. In regard to the interactive and influential nature of the various facets of personality, the model also draws upon general systems theory and group and communications theory (Lazarus, 2002a; 2005). Multimodal counseling goes beyond the specific focus on behavior and cognition to draw on effective techniques from a broad range of theoretical perspectives without specifically adhering to the theoretical suppositions (i.e., technical eclecticism).

Multimodal therapy is predicated on the belief that most psychological concerns are multifaceted, multidetermined, and multilayered. Thus, a complete therapeutic approach calls for careful assessment and intervention across seven parameters or modalities (Lazarus, 2000b). Lazarus (1997) posited that people use seven modalities to experience themselves and their world, which he referred to using the acronym BASIC I.D. Each letter represents a specific mode, originally addressing the areas of Behavior, Affect, Sensation, Imagery, Cognition, Interpersonal Relationships, and Drugs/ Biological Process. In contrast to the common biological intervention of using psychotropic drugs, in the BASIC I.D., the "D" modality represents the entire range of medical, biological, and health factors (Lazarus, 2000b). The BASIC I.D. acronym is a tool for assessing and understanding a person, and a vehicle for specifying the content for counseling and for guiding the counselor in selecting specific and effective interventions in each mode.

Lazarus (1997) outlined four basic theoretical principles for the multimodal approach.

1. People act and interact across all seven modes of the BASIC I.D.
2. All of the modalities are interconnected and, therefore, must be treated as an interactive system.
3. An accurate assessment and diagnosis is best accomplished by assessing all seven modes and the interaction between them.
4. A comprehensive approach to treatment ameliorates specific problems across the BASIC I.D.

The BASIC I.D. modal has been modified for work with children by adapting some of the procedures used with adults to make them developmentally appropriate for children. The main component of the multimodal evolution involves adapting the BASIC I.D. multimodal modes into the HELPING modes. Don Keat, trained in multimodal therapy by Lazarus, began to apply the model to his work with children. Keat (1990) reflected:

> When I asked myself what I thought I did, I came up with the idea that as a child therapist, I'm primarily a helper. Therefore, I proceeded to develop another acronym which I feel is more easily remembered by parents and teachers when they are interested in helping a child. The question that I ask, therefore, is "Are you interested in helping your child?" The answer, of course, is usually "yes." Therefore, the multimodal evolution has to do with the shift in my work from the BASIC I.D. acronym to the HELPING acronym which would lead to more basic understanding by the persons to whom I'm trying to convey what the seven modes are. (p. 9)

Table 3.1 provides a descriptor of the multimodal evolution and the change from the BASIC I.D. modes to the seven HELPING modes—Health, Emotions (feelings), Learning (school), People (personal relationships),

TABLE 3.1   *Multimodal Evolution*

Letter	HELPING Modes	BASIC I.D. Modes
H	Health	Drugs Diet (D)
E	Emotions/Feelings	Affect (A)
L	Learning/ School	Sensation (S)
P	People/Personal Relationships	Interpersonal Relations (I)
I	Imagery/Interests	Imagery (I)
N	Need to Know/Think	Cognition (C)
G	Guidance of A, B, C's	Behavior (B)

Imagery (imagination, interests), Need to know (cognitions), and Guidance of actions, behaviors, and consequences (behavior). The first letter of each of these words forms the HELPING acronym, which is particularly useful in communicating these concepts to parents, teachers, and children.

The main difference between the BASIC I.D. and HELPING is in changing the S mode of Sensation in the BASIC I.D. to the L mode of Learning. Because school serves as major event in a child life, the Learning mode addresses all aspects of school and the learning process as well as sensation (which includes all visual, auditory, tactile, olfactory, gustatory sensory complaints and concerns). Thus, the multimodal model and approach are mostly the same, but the modes have different names. A counselor's choice to use either the BASIC I.D. or the HELPING acronym depends on the person to whom the ideas are being communicated (Keat, 1990). Table 3.2 further defines each of the modes and provides some examples.

By thinking in HELPING terms, a counselor is apt to leave fewer avenues unexplored because the child is being assessed across the full range of the personality spectrum. Within each mode, a counselor may be guided by the following questions:

- Health: What are the important facts about the child's health or general medical–biological well-being?

TABLE 3.2   *Multimodal Personality Spectrum*

Letter	Mode	Examples
H	Health	Diet, exercise, sleep patterns, biological state
E	Emotions	Feelings, Moods (mad, sad, glad, scared)
L	Learning	School environment, senses (sound, smell, taste, touch, etc.)
P	People	Personal relationships: family (parents), friends (peers), community, cultural
I	Imagery	Self-image, fantasies, mental pictures, daydreams
N	Need to Know (Cognitions)	Beliefs, values, attitudes, problem solving, cultural identity
G	Guidance of A, B, Cs:	Acts, behaviors, consequences (outcomes), habits, activities

- Emotions: What emotional reactions are proving to be difficult or concerning?
- Learning: What is the child's experience at school, and are there any concerns about the child's learning?
- Personal Relationships: Who are the client's significant others, and what essential processes are involved in the child's interpersonal network?
- Imagery: What negative or intrusive images have to be replaced with positive visualizations?
- Need to Know mode: What dysfunctional beliefs and faulty cognitions require restructuring?
- Guidance of ABCs mode: What behaviors does the child want to increase or decrease?

When counseling a child, besides gaining an understanding of the separate HELPING components, the counselor must appreciate the interactive effects between and among the modes to see the reciprocal influences.

The multimodal tables in this chapter can help counselors organize the practical procedures by mode so they can be integrated into a working program. One of the best ways to understand the multimodal approach is to create a multimodal self-growth profile. A self-help example is provided in Table 3.3 to illustrate how you can apply this model. Keat (1979, 1990) previously presented multimodal growth profiles to help therapists and counselors. Creating a self-growth profile and self-assessing across the HELPING modes is typically the best way to learn about the approach because once you apply it to yourself, you can understand more clearly how to apply it to children. For another idea of how to use the multimodal model, look at Lazarus (2000a) for applying the multimodal model for personal replenishment for counselors. As counselors, we are constantly looking to improve ourselves and engage in self-growth. Therefore, these types of experiences can be part of our lifelong journey in the process of growth toward being our best personal self.

Goals of Counseling

One of the main tasks for school counselors is to help children realize success and overcome areas in life where they remain stuck. A child may have difficulty completing schoolwork, getting along with others, be experiencing anxiety, displaying inappropriate expressions of anger and fighting, and so forth. The multimodal approach provides a comprehensive HELPING map for each child, which evolves through each contact as the school counselor determines the main therapeutic tasks to ameliorate the child's problems, concerns, and troubles (Keat, 1990).

At the core of the multimodal approach is the counselor's formulation of an assessment of the concern or problem across the HELPING modes. This systematic problem-solving approach gives the counselor some idea of where the child is primarily having concerns. Within multimodal counseling the work of the client, much like the work of the counselor, depends on the nature of the problem and on the interventions selected. Multimodal counseling is directive and goal-directed, with the client's goals largely mirroring the counselor's goals. At the onset of counseling, the counselor makes a complete HELPING assessment of the child and

TABLE 3.3	**Multimodal Growth: HELPING Yourself**	
Modality	**Task, Skill, Concern**	**Training**
Health	Weight Smoking Alcohol Physical Conditioning	Diet Count, Saturation Monitor Club (AA) Running/ Cross Training
Emotions Feelings	Joy Anxiety Anger Stresses	Fun Training Relaxation Training, TM Anger Management Stress Inoculation
Learning School	Aural Appreciation Visual Aesthetics Sexual Skills Kinesthetic Abilities	Music Listening Art Appreciation Sex Education Dance, Yoga
Personal Relationships	Getting Along With Others Listening and Responding Time with Children	Friendship Training Communication Training Quality Time Alone
Imagery Interests	Self-Concept Train Imagery	Self-Esteem Training Reward Survey for Children Fire Drills
Need to Know	Irrational Ideas Decision Making How to Study	Rational Thinking Training Problem Solving Practice Study Skills
Guidance of A, B, Cs	Time Use Lack Assertiveness General Behavioral Skills	Scheduling Assertiveness Training Behavior Rehearsal

notes concerns within each mode. This assessment can be a combination of concerns and problems identified by a teacher, a parent, or the child.

To keep counseling brief and time-limited, the counselor chooses three or four concerns to address in more detail, and selects appropriate interventions to target each of these concerns. For example, if the treatment plan calls for work in the Imagery mode, the child will be educated on self-imagery techniques, and the counseling will be a collaborative effort to tailor the imagery exercises to the child's needs.

Role of the Counselor

Because this is an approach with a wide range of techniques, it is most effective when the counselor can be flexible, versatile, well informed on a variety of techniques and procedures, and able to connect with a child. In that sense, the counselor is a veritable jack-of-all-trades and a true integrative counselor. Multimodal counseling is an active and demanding approach that is often more demanding on the counselor than the client (Dryden & Lazarus, 1991). Because multimodal therapy requires counselors to be informed about techniques and able to administer a wide range of interventions, the multimodal counselor has to make a commitment to lifelong learning and keep up-to-date on clinical research and interventions.

Thus, one of the crucial roles for multimodal counselors is to be consumers of a wide range of information (clinical, developmental, self-help, etc.) and material that may come to bear on the school counseling setting. This knowledge base allows counselors to select the most relevant and effective interventions. Advanced counselors learn to pace multiple treatment strategies according to the client's resources and needs.

The Nature of Counseling Relationship.

Although multimodal counseling emphasizes assessment, intervention, and technique, the counseling relationship is no less important. Lazarus (1997) noted that

> effective therapy calls for appropriate techniques, correctly administered, within the context of a trusting and caring relationship. The relationship serves to educate, motivate, generate, formulate, and separate problems and solutions. (p. 12)

In a sense, the relationship is "the soil that enables the techniques to take root" (Lazarus, 2002a, p. 243). Thus, the nature of and importance placed on the counseling relationship seem to be driven more by client need than a set of dictates and directives about the need for a specific type of counseling relationship. School counselors often have to connect with children to develop trust and understanding that will increase compliance and motivation to change.

A flexible repertoire of relationships styles, paired with a wide range of pertinent techniques, enhances treatment outcome. Thus, to vary relational stances with clients, the school counselor has to be "an authentic chameleon" (Lazarus, 1997; 2005). Tailoring treatment to clients includes shifting the therapeutic style to match the child's needs, preferences, and developmental level. For example, with a shy or withdrawn child, the school counselor may be more directive and animated to draw out the child; with a socially engaging child, the school counselor may follow the child's lead and be more active within the session.

Multimodal counseling in schools assumes that counseling relationships will be formed best in settings and environments suited to children according to their developmental and cultural needs. School counselors, therefore, should be flexible enough to vary their therapeutic approach and style to match the child's needs. For example, I (Matt Englar-Carlson) recall fostering many of my counseling relationships with elementary school boys while playing games in the gym or by walking around the school grounds rather than sitting in my office. Although I might have been more comfortable remaining in my office talking or playing board games with the boys, I sensed that many of them would prefer to build our relationship through more active means.

Change/Stages of the Counseling Process

One of the greatest contributions of multimodal counseling is its precise and structured framework for comprehensive counseling. Further, the model is conducive to brief counseling— which comprises the majority of school counseling. Lazarus (1997) highlighted four stages of multimodal therapy, adapted to fit both the HELPING model and work within school settings.

1. Evaluate the child across all seven HELPING modes, and determine the concerns in each mode. This stage concentrates on information gathering from referral sources and other assessments.
2. Select three or four main concerns that require attention and intervention. For children in schools, selection of these concerns can be guided by the child's desires ("What would you like to be different?") and also the needs of the school and the child's parents.

3. Determine if further specific evaluation or testing, including a physical evaluation, is needed to gather more information about the child's concerns.
4. Apply empirically or clinically validated interventions to the specific concerns in each mode. The bulk of direct counseling occurs at this fourth and final stage.

The HELPING process begins with a precise and systematic assessment of each child's HELPING modes. Referrals represent the mechanism by which the counselor becomes aware of the child's difficulties and as an invitation to begin providing service. As such, referrals maintain a unique and important position in the help-seeking process. At home, parents are often the primary referral source. At school, teachers are often the primary referral sources.

Various multimodal referral forms are available for use in school settings. Although Keat's (1990) multimodal referral form was developed primarily for referrals from the home and for professionals in private practice, it has been adapted for use in schools. This form is presented in Figure 3.1. Some innovative school counselors have adapted the form for use in both school and agency settings (Keat & Englar-Carlson, 2006). It can help the school counselor gain a comprehensive picture of a referred client across the seven HELPING modes. The revised multimodal referral form for children utilizes a 5-point rating scale for each item (1 = Deficient and 5 = Adept). The total score for each mode can be added, then converted into a percentage to enable charting a profile. In addition, the rating system allows numerical comparisons to be charted throughout the counseling process to see how a child is progressing in the different modes.

Usually the multimodal referral form is completed by a child's parent(s), or it can be administered orally during a parent interview. An in-person parent interview is often preferred to gain a more accurate assessment of the child. In the first interview the counselor typically meets with the parent(s) alone and goes over the major concerns at the moment. The aim is to get some idea about the family structure—the children involved, their ages, their grades, how they are doing in school, and so forth. After the parents have provided a broad description about the family and the presenting concerns, the counselor can move to more specific questions.

Child's Name: DOB: Grade:

Parent's Name: Phone Number:

Reasons for Referral:

General Description of the Problem:

Please circle the number which best describes this child's behavior at this time. Please comment on items that are outstanding strengths or weaknesses (difficulties).

Deficient	1	2	3	4	5	Adept
HEALTH						**COMMENTS**
Is generally healthy			1 2 3 4 5			
Gets enough exercise during day (e.g., recess)			1 2 3 4 5			
Is energetic			1 2 3 4 5			
Is physically fit			1 2 3 4 5			
Seems to be well rested when in school			1 2 3 4 5			
Consistent attendance			1 2 3 4 5			
Appropriate hygiene			1 2 3 4 5			
Any vision or hearing concerns?			Y N			

Medication

Other

                                           Total _____ /35 = _____ %

EMOTIONS						**COMMENTS**
Seems generally happy and has fun			1 2 3 4 5			
Accepts criticism			1 2 3 4 5			
Accepts praise			1 2 3 4 5			
Appears relaxed and comfortable			1 2 3 4 5			
Handles ups and downs easily (seems emotionally well-adjusted)			1 2 3 4 5			
Expresses feelings			1 2 3 4 5			
Expresses anger appropriately			1 2 3 4 5			
Identifies feelings			1 2 3 4 5			
Communicates feelings			1 2 3 4 5			
Is pleased with accomplishments			1 2 3 4 5			

Other

                                           Total _____ /50 = _____ %

Deficient	1	2	3	4	5	Adept
LEARNING						**COMMENTS**
Adequate gross motor (coordinated physically)			1 2 3 4 5			
Adequately developed fine motor tasks			1 2 3 4 5			
Average language development			1 2 3 4 5			
Is generally performing to expectancy/ works to potential			1 2 3 4 5			

(continued)

FIGURE 3.1
Multimodal Referral Form

Current grades and present levels

Reading	_____	Social Studies	_____
Math	_____	Science	_____
Language	_____	Handwriting	_____
Spelling	_____	Other	_____

Is well organized	1 2 3 4 5	
Works neatly	1 2 3 4 5	
Applies learning	1 2 3 4 5	

Favorite subjects are _____

Other _____

Total _____ /65 = _____ %

PEOPLE PERSONAL RELATIONS   COMMENTS

Gets along well with other children in a group	1 2 3 4 5	
Relates well to children one on one	1 2 3 4 5	
Handles conflict appropriately	1 2 3 4 5	
Is well liked by peers	1 2 3 4 5	
Has friends	1 2 3 4 5	
Can share things easily	1 2 3 4 5	
Enjoys helping others	1 2 3 4 5	
Relates well to adults	1 2 3 4 5	

Life stressors of which you are aware _____

Other _____

Total _____ /40 = _____ %

IMAGERY/INTERESTS   COMMENTS

Is generally confident/knows strengths and weaknesses	1 2 3 4 5	
Expresses feelings of adequacy and security	1 2 3 4 5	
Is creative	1 2 3 4 5	
Has good sense of humor	1 2 3 4 5	
Shows good curiosity	1 2 3 4 5	
Shows interest and imagination	1 2 3 4 5	
Feels good about self	1 2 3 4 5	
Seems to like school	1 2 3 4 5	

His/her primary likes are _____

Child seems to dislike _____

Other _____

Total _____ /40 = _____ %

NEED TO KNOW   COMMENTS

Distinguishes between right and wrong	1 2 3 4 5	
Good decision-making skills	1 2 3 4 5	
Can set realistic goals for self	1 2 3 4 5	

(continued)

FIGURE 3.1
Multimodal Referral Form *(continued)*

Displays positive/rational outlook	1 2 3 4 5	
Demonstrates accurate perceptions of situations	1 2 3 4 5	
Knows when to ask for help	1 2 3 4 5	
Other		

Total _____ /30 = _____ %

GUIDANCE OF ACTIONS, BEHAVIORS, CONSEQUENCES		COMMENTS
Attends to task	1 2 3 4 5	
Appropriate attention span	1 2 3 4 5	
Is satisfied with appropriate amounts of attention	1 2 3 4 5	
Accomplishes tasks successfully within a given timeframe	1 2 3 4 5	
Respects property	1 2 3 4 5	
Respects rights of others	1 2 3 4 5	
Follows rules	1 2 3 4 5	
Follows directions	1 2 3 4 5	
Works well independently	1 2 3 4 5	
Completes work	1 2 3 4 5	
Is generally cooperative	1 2 3 4 5	
Exhibits self-control	1 2 3 4 5	
Can be motivated by		
Other		

Total _____ /60 = _____ %

Involved in special programs?   Yes _____   No _____

Check appropriate ___Speech ___Learning Support ___Chapter Math ___Chapter Reading

Attendance to date: Days Absent _____   Days Tardy _____

Parental contact?   Conference   Phone Call   Letter/Note

Results of contact _____

FIGURE 3.1

Multimodal Referral Form (continued)

In that way, the counselor fills in specific information that can be useful to assess the overall family situation and the child in particular. The goal is to determine the major concerns so counseling can begin to concentrate on these concerns and solutions can begin to emerge.

The second major area of inquiry prior to seeing a child consists of contact with the child's teacher. Because the school environment is one of the two major life areas of concern for the child (home is the other one), the counselor's formal contact with the teacher can provide information relevant to HELPING the child. The interview with the teacher should be conducted in a manner similar to that of the interview with the parent, beginning with open projective questions (e.g., "Describe Jan to me") and moving to more specific questions that assess each mode. These questions can be guides in gaining a comprehensive picture of the whole child.

Once concerns have been determined in each mode, they are ranked-ordered from 1 to 7. For school counselors, the rank order is often guided initially by the presenting problem or the referral from the classroom teacher or the parent. In some circumstances, particularly self-referrals, students can choose the mode of intervention based on their concerns and goals. After beginning to work within the initial mode, counseling turns to other areas that the school counselor deems important. The counselor often seeks to link a preferred mode (for example, a child referred for difficulties with homework or school performance might have the Learning mode ranked as #1), and a lesser preferred mode (for example, the Personal Relationships mode and how inadequate performance in school influences friendships). This process is called *bridging*, because it connects a preferred modality to a less familiar one.

After the modes have been rank-ordered, the counselor selects appropriate interventions for the modes requiring immediate attention, with other concerns in other modes addressed as needed. The main criterion for selecting an intervention is the effectiveness of the procedure for helping the child. By organizing a person and his or her experience of the world within the seven modes, Lazarus was interested in understanding how an individual uses all of the modes, as well as which modes seemed to be most important to a person at any given time. Lazarus (1997) used the term *firing order* to describe the sequence of modalities a person uses when confronted by an event. The process of understanding a client's firing order is called *tracking*. Lazarus (2005) provides an example of tracking the firing order using the BASIC I.D.

> Some clients tend to generate negative emotions by dwelling first on sensations (S; a slight dizziness accompanied by heart palpitations), to which they attach negative cognitions (C; ideas of illness and death), immediately followed by adverse images (I; pictures of hospitals and catastrophic disease), culminating in maladaptive behavior (B; unnecessary avoidance or withdrawal). (p. 340)

In this example, the client has an SCIB firing order outlining his or her experience of a specific problem and how he or she responds to it. Clearly, tracking order is not a fixed tendency and can be adapted and changed through intervention. By tracking the firing order and sequence of events that leads to disturbance, the counselor gains insight into the antecedent events and learns how the client reacts to events. Further, tracking enables the counselor to determine where appropriate intervention should take place. From here, specific interventions can be tailored accordingly.

Multicultural Applications

Although multimodal therapists acknowledge multicultural issues, these are not listed specifically as one of the seven modes. Yet, at its core, multimodal counseling emphasizes individual differences. Corey (2008) noted that multimodal counselors work hard not to force clients into a predetermined treatment but, instead, to remain open to the client's needs. Because of its emphasis on evaluation and assessment, each client can stand out as a unique person rather than a diagnosis (Day, 2004). Multimodal assessment also takes a holistic approach that integrates social, cultural, and interpersonal aspects. For example, three boys who show anger and behavior management problems are unique and will receive different interventions based on their multimodal profile.

Because multimodal therapy is not tied to a set pattern of interventions, counselors can assess a client's cultural background and identity adequately and not be tied to culturally incongruent interventions. The counselor can freely choose directive or nondirective methods, or decide to intervene at the individual, family, or community level (Palmer, 2000). Thus, a multimodal counselor can truly create an individual therapy for each client. If the multimodal assessment reveals that a child is dealing with discrimination, prejudice, or identity issues within one of the modes, an appropriate intervention can be developed to address these concerns. Culturally aware multimodal counseling has much more to do with the counselor's multicultural competence than the cultural sensitivity of the multimodal model.

Interventions

A key concept in multimodal counseling is the use of *technical eclecticism*, in which multimodal counselors consider applying any relationship strategy, intervention, or therapeutic technique. Because clients have a multitude of problems, the multimodal counselor must respond with a variety of effective interventions to bring about change. Though intervention strategies are introduced and refined constantly, the counselor carefully times when to apply the intervention (Corey, 2008).

Another major premise of multimodal interventions is its emphasis on breadth rather than depth (Lazarus, 1997). In that sense, the more coping responses a child learns, the better equipped he or she will be to face future stressors. The school counselor, then, can be viewed as a "coping teacher" (Keat, 1990). When the school counselor identifies an area of intervention (for example, anxiety or drug and alcohol use), the student is taught multiple intervention strategies across the HELPING modes (thought-stopping, behavioral rehearsal, basic breathing and relaxation exercises, imagery techniques, etc.). For example, for a teenager with an alcohol and drug problem, a behavioral management plan might work for drinking alcohol but relaxation training is more effective for pot smoking.

Individual Counseling Applications and Interventions.

As noted previously, the emphasis within individual counseling is on technical eclecticism, applying whatever technique best fits a presenting concern. Thus, the multimodal school counselor borrows and uses techniques from many therapy systems. Whenever possible, the guiding criterion for selecting interventions is based on empirical research and what is known to work. Flexibility, however, does allow other means of applying interventions. Because fewer empirically indicated techniques may be suitable for working with children within schools, a logical or practical rationale can also be used to select interventions.

Counselors should also use their intuition to determine which interventions to apply (Lazarus, 1997). At this point, a key distinction can be made between multimodal counseling and other approaches. Whereas some approaches prescribe specific interventions, multimodal counseling is flexible and integrative enough to allow counselors to carefully select the most appropriate strategies to tailor effective treatment. This ability to tailor interventions is extended to enable culturally appropriate and consistent interventions for children and parents.

When outlining the techniques used in multimodal school counseling, the range truly has no boundaries. Among these techniques are stress-inoculation or anxiety-reduction training, behavioral rehearsal, thought-stopping, bibliotherapy, friendship and social skills training, study skills training, self-esteem and imagery exercises, anger management, self-hypnosis, physical exercise interventions, and time management. Many of these interventions are standard behavioral interventions that work well with children. School counselors can research empirically supported strategies for working with children (additional resources for empirically supported interventions with children and adolescents include Christophersen & Mortweet, 2001; Evans et al., 2005; Lonigan & Elbert, 1998; Shapiro, Friedberg, & Bardenstein, 2006).

Lazarus (1989) outlined 39 common techniques used in multimodal counseling. Beyond standard interventions, Keat and Englar-Carlson (2006) suggested the use of poetry therapy, audiotherapy, music therapy, videotherapy, cybertherapy, cinema/reel therapy, art therapy, magic, and laughter self-therapy. Again, the counselor uses only the techniques, not the conceptualization or theoretical foundation for the technique. Thus, the counselor can apply Adlerian techniques, including acting as-if, the push-button technique, and task setting (Carlson & Englar-Carlson, 2008) without endorsing the Adlerian theory of personality.

The multimodal school counselor does not select interventions randomly. Instead, all interventions are situated within the HELPING theoretical model that guides the counselor in treatment planning and where to proceed. The simple HELPING approach follows the same format: Referral leads to assessment; assessment leads to treatment planning and intervention; and then the child is continually assessed to determine the next step in tailoring the counseling. The format is the same for children or adolescents. The difference is more in tailoring intervention strategies by developmental level.

Group Counseling Applications and Interventions

Group counseling is an essential component of any school counseling program. Within the school context of increasing demands for counseling services paired with fewer school counselors, group counseling interventions comprise one of the more cost- and time-effective strategies for the school counselor. Beyond the clear advantage of using group counseling to assist more students, group counseling interventions are increasingly viewed as the *preferred* school counselor intervention (Gladding, 2007). Groups reach a wide audience of students who share problems and concerns. Further, the group setting reflects the children's social world in the school and community.

Because the multimodal approach works so well in helping children to change their behaviors, it becomes an excellent vehicle to work with children in a group setting. For the most part, multimodal group counseling consists of problem-centered groups that address one specific concern, such as stress or anger. Interventions to address the concern are implemented in each of the seven HELPING modes. In the HELPING modes, group procedures can be used in the following manner:

- *Health:* The group counselor is in an advantageous situation to observe the student's physical health. The counselor can observe energy levels, weight, pallor, cleanliness, and so forth. Sensing a need for change in some of the children, group sessions can be tailored to a discussion of exercise, proper eating habits, care of one's personal self, and the like. Then the group can actively practice some of the activities.
- *Emotions:* Anxiety, stress, fear, and other emotions can be observed readily in a group setting. These emotions can be addressed as part of the group session in which the school counselor asks the children to complete the sentence: "I feel angry (fearful, anxious...) when ...." Interventions for coping can be introduced in the group, and children in the group can talk about how they cope with their emotions.
- *Learning:* School counselors of groups usually make it a point to talk with the classroom teacher regarding students' school progress. If a specific learning need is identified, the group session can be particularly helpful in helping children develop study skills, life skills, listening skills, or thinking skills.
- *Personal Relationships:* Groups provide an arena for helping children make connections with others and build friendships. Often, the focus of the entire group is on ways to make and keep friends.
- *Imagery:* Many students referred for group counseling have a low self-concept. In a group session students can learn and practice

coping skills to deal with put-downs and get feedback to refute negative self-talk. Some techniques that work particularly well with children are to use positive self-imagery, to identify strengths, and to role play things to say when someone puts them down.

- *Need to Know:* Students often lack the information necessary to deal with the complex concerns in their life. A group session lends itself to bibliotherapy approaches that help children gain the necessary knowledge and insight to deal with their concerns more successfully. Some students in the group can provide insight and ideas on how they were able to overcome similar concerns.

- *Guidance of Actions, Behaviors and Consequences:* Children who lack the skills necessary to behave appropriately can be helped through group intervention. Often, techniques such as behavioral contracts, or bar or line graphs can be used to show success (or lack of it) in developing a behavior or giving direct feedback for the child to complete as part of a group process.

Classroom Guidance Applications and Interventions

For the most part, multimodal counseling has been applied in only a limited way in classroom guidance applications and interventions. The main contribution is the HELPING model itself and the structured method of evaluation and intervention. For any classroom guidance lesson or directed intervention, a school counselor can take a HELPING view for planning and implementation. A first step would be to assess the need following an interview with the classroom teacher, and then develop a HELPING chart for the entire classroom.

Appropriate interventions could then be selected for the class. These could involve classroom guidance lessons, small-group experiential exercises, use of films or movies, or more active interventions that get the class out of the classroom. For example, Keat and Englar-Carlson (2006) outlined large-group and classroom HELPING strategies to address cooperation, violence prevention, and health and wellness. Throughout this process, the HELPING model can serve as a schedule or map that consistently asks the school counselor: What are the needs? What works with this concern? What works for this specific class?

Strategies for Working With Teachers and Parents

The two major life environments and influences for children are the school and the home/family. Consultation is one of the treatments of choice for many school counselors to effect change in the classroom and at home. A fundamental belief of consultation is that children tend to fail or have problems because of the context that their parents and teachers create for them. Rather than identifying the child as unhealthy or disturbed and isolating him or her for treatment, consultation works directly with the system. The context and system in which the individual lives and the interpersonal domain become the focus of treatment (Dinkmeyer & Carlson, 2006). Children with problems, therefore, can be viewed as living within unhealthy families, classrooms, or other dysfunctional systems. When interventions are directed to changing the system through work with parents, teachers, administration, and curriculum, students prosper and dysfunctional behavior is reduced.

The multimodal approach can be applied in the realm of consultation with parents and teachers. School counselors can offer the HELPING model as a useful way to understand children and their environment and as a tool to guide parents and teachers toward working with their children effectively. As a consultant, the school counselor educates parents and teachers about ways to intervene in a purposeful, effective, and comprehensive manner. In this capacity the counselor can guide parents to create changes at home in areas where intervention is needed.

For example, when working with parents, a school counselor can use the HELPING model to organize areas of family-wide intervention such as making dietary changes involving consistently healthy breakfasts and lunches in the Health mode; adopting anger management strategies in the Emotions mode; having older siblings tutor younger ones in the Learning mode; installing family council meetings to address family concerns (e.g., family chores, curfews) in the Personal Relationships mode; parents' learning how to aid their children in developing positive self-images in the Imagery mode; exploring rational expectations for parents and children in the Need to Know mode; and establishing behavioral contracts about piano practice or reading time in the Guidance of ABCs mode.

As an illustration of how the HELPING model applies to children, the following two case examples illustrate multimodal mapping. For each of these case examples, the modes are presented in their rank-order of importance for the case.

● ●

CASE STUDY: MANUEL

Manuel is the youngest child, and the only boy, in a Latino family. In a family that values education, he has four high-achieving older sisters. Though the presenting concern from the teacher referral centered on school performance (Manuel "is having difficulty keeping up with his classwork"), he has other concerns that undermine and contribute to his difficulties in the classroom.

Prior to the first session the school counselor spoke with the classroom teacher about the referral concerns and had Manuel's parents complete the multimodal referral form. From these interactions the school counselor was able to create a multimodal profile of Manuel and rank-order the HELPING modes in order of importance as a way to organize counseling and create the treatment plan.

This case is a good illustration of the systemic effect of multimodal counseling. Though the presenting concern fits within the Learning mode, the best way to help Manuel with his classwork may be indirect interventions in other modes to address his behavior, cognition, and imagery. The primary goals in counseling Manuel are to gain more information about his distractibility, develop the ability to remain on-task and complete his homework, help him refute his negative self-talk, and build his self-esteem. The multimodal profile of Manuel in Table 3.4 presents an overview of the HELPING profile, as well as the ranking of his problems in terms of concerns and intervention plans. Under each area of concern, the problem is listed and numbered, along with related treatment options that could be implemented.

The case is presented following the modes as they were determined in rank order of importance. For each mode we go into the details of some of the treatment interventions. In this case Manuel would typically be seen primarily in individual counseling, but the parents might be included at times. Additional contacts would be with the classroom teacher, school psychologist, and family doctor, to coordinate contracts and information and keep Manuel motivated. Therefore, this case shows how a school

TABLE 3.4   *HELPING Manuel*

Mode	Rank	Concern	Intervention Strategy
Health	2	H1 Hyperactivity/ Distractibility	H1 ADHD screening
Emotions	5	E1 Anger	E1 Anger Management/ Bibliotherapy
		E2 Anxiety (grades & report card)	E2 Relaxation Training/ Breathing Exercises
Learning	7	L1 Independent learning in classroom	L1 Classroom desk in carrel; place model learners next to Manuel; chunk work; provide breaks & extra time to complete work.
Personal Relationships	6	P1 Teacher concerns within classroom	P1 Pair with on-task buddy
		P2 Parental Concerns	P2 Role play/ Consultation with parents
		P3 Role of Manuel in family	P3 Consultation with parents/Bibliotherapy
Imagery	4	I1 Low Self-Image: Failure	I1 Self-Esteem Building
		I2 Negative thoughts about school failure	I2 Miracle Question
Need-to-Know	3	N1 Negative Self-talk & self-downing tendency	N1 Cognitive restructuring, bibliotherapy, therapeutic games
		N2 How to Study	N2 Study Skills
Guidance of A, B, Cs	1	G1 Staying on task	G1 Reward Survey for Children, Behavioral Contracting
		G2 Complete homework	G2 Behavioral chart to track homework. Make sure homework time and area are consistent and free of distractions.
		G3 Time Management	G3 Scheduling

counselor uses the broad range of interventions from individual to family to school collaborations.

Guidance of Actions, Behaviors, and Consequences

The younger the child, the more likely will behavioral issues be ranked fairly high in various areas of concern. As a child moves along the developmental spectrum, however, this zone often moves down to somewhere in the middle of the modes (Keat & Englar-Carlson, 2006). Manuel has difficulty staying on-task during independent work times in the classroom, and this is impacting his academic achievement negatively.

A comprehensive behavior plan should be implemented in school, with associated cooperation and follow-through at home. Manuel has to be an integral part of designing this behavior plan. One or two behaviors should be targeted for intervention—for example, time on-task behavior during independent seatwork. Behavioral contracting to address this issue would be implemented. A reward plan for on-task behaviors consistent within home and school settings could be useful. Through these measures Manuel would earn tangible daily rewards for on-task behavior.

The Reward Survey for Children (Keat, 1990) is a good tool for assessing rewards that interest a child. This measure is typically administered to a child during the first session and then completed at home or during ensuing contacts, as the basis for behavioral contracting. Also, because Manuel has difficulty managing his time and completing homework, he will learn time management skills using a homework planner. Manuel could be trained to track and chart completed homework daily at home to help him take more independent responsibility for his work. Homework time should be consistent daily, and he should have a quiet place to work, free from distractions.

Health

The health and wellness of a child is always an important concern. Manuel seems to be a healthy child, active in sports. A lingering question remains, however, as to whether he fits the diagnostic criteria for attention-deficit hyperactivity disorder (ADHD). Therefore, the school psychologist could conduct an ADHD screening, consisting of several time on-task/off-task observations and ADHD checklists (i.e., *Conners' Rating Scales-Revised*,

Conners, 1997; *Attention-Deficit Hyperactivity Disorder Test*, Gilliam, 1995) to be completed by the classroom teacher and parents.

An academic screening can be conducted to rule out any possible learning disabilities. This information would be written up and shared with the family's psychiatrist/family doctor, to conduct any further assessments deemed necessary and make a formal diagnosis, if appropriate. With a formal diagnosis of ADHD, the psychiatrist/family doctor may recommend and monitor a trial of medication.

Need to Know

The need-to-know (notions) mode could become more important as Manuel grows older and learns how to control things he perceives in his head. Cognitive restructuring is helpful in changing a child's perspective. The cognitive awareness (i.e., the audiotapes we play in our head) of Manuel suggested negative self-talk about his abilities in school ("I'm just not as smart as my sisters"; "I'm really good at sports but nothing else") and some distortion regarding his responsibility for his schoolwork. Some of these ideas could be viewed as emanating from his core beliefs associated with his privileged and protected role in the family and how he has learned to gain attention.

Ellis's original ABC model provides a simple, practical tool to help children think about the effects of their thoughts on their feelings and their worldview. Because this model is visual, the school counselor would draw it out for Manuel and help him organize his school experiences in terms of the model. To learn more about cognitive restructuring, he could utilize some developmentally appropriate workbooks such as *Thinking, Feeling, Behaving* (Vernon, 2006) or the *Passport Program* (Vernon, 1998) or games (*Let's Get Rational,* Wilde, 2001). As Manuel gains more understanding about the ABC model, he could begin to test his assumptions against the existing evidence and use some self-instructions ("I can do it, and I'm smart"; "I know this is hard, but I can do it"). To work on Manuel accepting responsibility, the school counselor would consult with the parents about giving him more responsibility at home and reducing the expectation that other family members will dote on him.

Another intervention would be to teach Manuel effective study skills for the classroom and at home. A resource room specialist could possibly offer some ideas for Manuel and his parents. Further, he could be referred to the school's Student Study Team for assistance in learning study skills.

Imagery

In the imagery mode (i.e., the videos we play in our head), enhancing self-esteem is an ongoing task in child counseling. For Manuel, the school counselor would focus on his self-efficacy as a student and use his success as an athlete as a bridge to his strengths. Emphasis might be placed on his fear of failing as a student.

A second concern in this area addresses Manuel's future orientation toward his success in school. He seems to have little hope that his school-work will improve and, thus, lacks the image of a successful future. The school counselor might employ the Miracle Question from solution-focused therapy (de Shazer, 1988) to paint a rich description of Manuel's world if he were a more successful student. Sklare (2004) suggested stating the Miracle Question in magic terms: "If I were to wave a magic wand and wish all your school problems were fixed, what would you be doing if we could video-tape you for one day?" The Miracle Question can be stated in many differ-ent ways, but the bottom line is that the school counselor's goal is to keep the focus on what the child will be doing when the problem is solved.

To expand the Miracle Question, we like to add aspects pertaining to the social environment. For example: "If the miracle were to occur and you have friends, how will your parents/ teachers/ peers know that you are different?"

Emotions

As can be gleaned from the initial presenting problem statement, as well as from the profile, Manuel struggles with anger management at times when he feels frustrated and overwhelmed. Anger management through bibliotherapy (e.g, *The Angry Monster Workbook,* Shore, 1995; *The Very Angry Day That Amy Didn't Have,* Shapiro, 1994) will help him better understand his emotions and reactions and control his outbursts. As Manuel also shows anxiety about his grades and school performance, relaxation training could be introduced. He could apply the ability to relax to anxiety and stress and also to managing his anger.

Relaxation training typically involves a multidimensional approach of first teaching children to breathe appropriately, then to tense and relax muscles, and then to learn self-sentences to say to relax themselves, as well as eliciting appropriate relaxing images from their lives. A good resource for relaxation training is *The Relaxation and Stress Reduction Workbook* (Davis, Eshelman, & McKay, 2000).

Personal Relationships

Manuel often asks for help from the teacher on tasks that he is capable of completing independently. The teacher also observed that he becomes distracted and is discouraged with work that he thinks is "too difficult." Pairing Manuel with a classmate or buddy as a good role model may help him stay on-task. Implementing a classroom rule of "ask three and then me" also could help Manuel attempt work before he gives up and/or asks the teacher for help. This fosters independence and bolsters self-esteem as Manuel finds that he is more capable than he thought.

Based on the referral information, Manuel's parents evidently believe that he is capable of performing better in school and that he is anxious about his grades and burdened with their high expectations. Learning to develop better ways of getting along with the adults and talking about these concerns can help Manuel feel closer to his parents. One possibility is to brainstorm and role-play with Manuel about ways to communicate with his parent about his fears.

Finally, counseling will include consultation with Manuel's parents to address his role in the family system and ways to build responsibility. Manuel could be given daily chores at home to promote a sense of accomplishment, responsibility, and independence. This could teach responsibility and build self-esteem ("I did it by myself").

Learning

The learning zone seems to be the area of presenting concern for Manuel, yet interventions in the other modes all involve his learning indirectly. The school counselor can implement some interventions directly with the classroom teacher—those that involve his learning environment in the classroom. Each of these interventions requires consultation with the classroom teacher, and consistent follow-through. One idea is to pair Manuel with an appropriate on-task classmate as a buddy. This buddy could be changed every week or every second week to build a support system for Manuel.

He also may benefit from a place to work that is relatively quiet (e.g., a study carrel, a seat at the front of the room in proximity to the teacher, a seat away from the window or door). Further, because Manuel seems to become distracted and frustrated easily, his schoolwork could be chunked into tangible segments, with breaks, so he does not become overwhelmed and he stays on-task. Further, he could be given extra time to complete work if needed.

If successful, these interventions could provide evidence that Manuel is truly capable of success in the classroom. At the same time, he would be garnering positive attention from peers, teachers, and parents for his achievements in the classroom.

Multimodal counseling with Manuel would clearly be a collaborative effort between school and home with the school counselor acting as the director. The expected outcome would be a boy with a greater sense of accomplishment as a student and a more positive self-image. Along the way, Manuel would have tangible evidence of success (better grades) and develop lifelong skills (cognitive restructuring, relaxation training) that he could use in other situations.

• •

CASE STUDY: AMY

Amy is 15 years old and the oldest of three children in an intact family. She presents with possible mild/moderate depression and anxiety with some concerns about her peer interactions. She appears to be disconnected from her friends and her mother and has sought closer relationships with her teachers as a forum to talk about her difficulties. She does seem to be experiencing many of the significant transitions of becoming an adolescent (entering high school, beginning to menstruate, having greater expectations for academics and personal responsibility). Further, she is struggling with some body image concerns.

Despite receiving good grades, Amy's elevated and absolute expectations are contributing to her feelings of being overwhelmed and her self-image of not being good enough. Amy believes that she is misunderstood, alone, and not in control of her life. Though she seems to be in good health, she has frequent headaches.

Amy was open to counseling, and the sessions began with a multimodal assessment in all of the HELPING modes. The multimodal profile of Amy is presented in Table 3.5. From the information gathered during the assessment phase, it was evident that the modes that required the most immediate attention were Imagery/Interest, Emotions/Feelings, Need to Know, and Personal Relationships. The following is an expanded description of the modes and interventions, rank-ordered, starting with the immediate mode of intervention.

Emotions/Feelings

As can be gleaned from the initial presenting problem statement, as well as from the profile, the major concerns were in the emotional zone. By her own account, Amy has been in an extended depressed mood. She recounted numerous symptoms common to depressive disorders—somatic complaints (headaches), sadness, argumentativeness, low self-esteem, increased stress, suicidal thoughts, and some isolation from peers (Evens et al., 2005). The school counselor could begin to assess Amy's level of mood using the *Children's Depression Inventory* (Kovacs, 1992) for an ongoing assessment of her mood fluctuations. The counselor would make a referral for a more extensive medical and/or psychiatric evaluation to assess Amy's depressive symptoms, suicidal thoughts, and stress or anxiety. An outcome of this evaluation might include a recommendation for medication (e.g., antidepressants) to address these issues.

Amy said she felt increased stress to perceived higher demands associated with schoolwork. She may benefit from relaxation or mindfulness training to help her feel some control over her stress and anxiety. Some simple relaxation training interventions could be taken from *The Relaxation and Stress Reduction Workbook* (Davis et al., 2000). A more intensive intervention would consist of mindfulness training following the mindfulness-based stress reduction program (Kabat-Zinn, 1990). Mindfulness training could help Amy develop some coping skills in response to stress and anxiety, and in addition serve as an effective intervention against depression (Miller, Fletcher, & Kabat-Zinn, 1995).

Imagery/Interests

The Imagery mode represents a significant area of intervention to address Amy's self-image, body image, and views of the future. Many of the interventions in this mode could come from a feminist theoretical model, to

TABLE 3.5   *HELPING Amy*

Mode	Rank	Concern	Intervention Strategy
Health	5	H1 Headaches	H1 Medical evaluation (incl. vision testing) H1 Teach relaxation and/or massage.
		H2 Exercise	H2 Begin exercise program
Emotions	1	E1 Depression	E1 Medical evaluation including E1 Reduce cognitive distortions and assumptions.
		E2 Stress/Anxiety	E2 Relaxation training/ Mindfulness training
Learning	6	L1 Hard time keeping up with schoolwork	L1 Learn Study Skills & Time Management
Personal Relationships	4	P1 Conflict with parents	P1 Communication skills P1 Planning girl-focused time together P1 Mother daughter group
		P2 Conflicts with peers	P2 Social skills training P2 Social skills group
Imagery	2	I1 Self-Image	I1 Self-Esteem Building
		I2 Body Image (fat & ugly)	I2 Bibliotherapy
		I3 Hopelessness	I3 Skeleton Key/ Miracle Question
Need-to-Know	3	N1 Negative Self-talk & self-downing tendency	N1 Refuting Irrational Ideas & automatic thoughts. Constructive/positive self-talk.
		N2 Absolute Thinking (I must do everything 100% well)	N2 Dispute self-defeating thoughts
		E3 Suicidal Ideation	E3 Suicide prevention contract
Guidance of A, B, Cs	7	G1 Lack of Enjoyable Events	G1 Pleasant Events Scheduling
		G2 Time Management	G2 Scheduling and Using a Planner

empower and strengthen the core of Amy as a girl. To build her self-esteem, she might find images of herself in which she can take pride, and construct a self-concept based on her strengths. Amy would be instructed in constructive and positive self-talk and cognitive restructuring to address her low self-esteem, supplemented by work in the Need-To-Know mode. Ideas for practical interventions in sessions and as homework could be taken from *Things Will Be Different for My Daughter: A Practical Guide to Building Her Self-Esteem and Self-Reliance* (Bingham, Stryker, & Neufeldt, 1995).

Amy's body image concerns seem to be grounded in the developmental context of girls' puberty and the often painful "conventional story of female becoming" (Brown, 1991, p. 72). She is in the midst of the physiological and psychological process of developing a woman's body, which often ushers in the objectification of one's own body by boys, other girls, and oneself (Tolman & Brown, 2001). Amy commented about being "fat and ugly," which speaks to her self-image about her appearance, yet it may indicate a normative discontent of many females in regard to their bodies (Choate, 2005). Choate outlined five protective factors as model of therapeutic intervention for body image concerns:

1. Family of origin support
2. Gender role satisfaction
3. Positive physical self-concept
4. Effective coping strategies
5. A sense of holistic balance and wellness

Thus, interventions could closely align within these areas. In particular, the conflictual relationship with Amy's mother may be making matters worse, as Amy doesn't want to talk with her mother about the physiological changes. Intervention in the Personal Relationship mode to address the relationship between mother and daughter could provide some support. Another source of psychoeducation for Amy could be *Our Bodies, Ourselves: A New Edition for a New Era* (Boston Women's Health Collective, 2005). Other interventions might include examining her beliefs about beauty and attractiveness and modifying her negative core beliefs.

Amy is displaying hopelessness, which is strongly indicated in both depression and suicidal behavior (Shapiro et al., 2006). Therefore, efforts can address the possibilities for future change in her life. The school counselor can use two questioning tools (Skeleton Key and Miracle Question), from solution-focused brief therapy, to shift Amy toward a more positive future orientation and direct her thinking to the good things rather than the bad things happening in her life. The Skeleton Key question (de Shazer, 1985) is simply:

> Between now and the next time we see each other, I would like you to notice the things that happen to you at home and school that you like and would to like to keep happening. By telling me the things you want to have happen in your life, I can learn more about you and what you're up to.

Amy's thoughts about this question will help determine positive areas in her life and goals for counseling. The Miracle Question (de Shazer, 1988) could help Amy imagine a future when she is happier and plant a vision of the future when the problem is not present. Originally stated, the Miracle Question asks: "Should a miracle occur this evening while you were sleeping and when you woke up you suddenly realized that your problems were solved, what would you be doing that would show that the miracle had taken place? What will be a first sign that things are better?" The miracle that Amy envisions is more than just a hopeful wish; it is also the common ground upon which Amy and the school counselor agree to build new foundations in counseling (Nau & Shilts, 2000).

Need to Know

Amy may well benefit from learning skills refuting her irrational ideas, using cognitive restructuring, and incorporating positive self-talk. As an adolescent, Amy would have a greater ability to understand the role of cognition in changing her perceptions and emotions. She might benefit from guided direction and developmental interpretation of some of the lessons drawn from *Feeling Good* (Burns, 1999) about learning the ABC model and then using homework, such as a thought diary, to catch automatic thoughts.

She has shown the ability to use writing as an outlet. Therefore, journal and diary homework may be particularly effective. She could also play some therapeutic games (*Let's Get Rational Game*, Wilde, 2000) and engage in personal experiments to test some of her assumptions about her experience of the world. After gaining more insight into the role of her cognitions, Amy could begin to explore her expectations about being the oldest child, her family dynamics and relationships, and some of her thoughts about friendships. Particular emphasis would be placed on Amy's pressure to be a high achiever and her desire to have things "her way." A goal from this work would be for Amy to develop some coping strategies to create rational cognitions.

The final consideration in this mode concerns Amy's suicidal ideation. Though she denies having a plan to harm herself and confirms that she would not make an attempt, any suicidal ideation calls for an immediate therapeutic response that is strong, decisive, and clear. Further assessment should address the reasons for these suicidal impulses and whether any self-harming behaviors are present or have happened in the past (Shapiro et al., 2006). Though the school counselor can normalize fleeting thoughts about wishing to be dead, an appropriate risk management response would be for the school counselor to make a suicide safety contract with Amy. This contract could be revised over the period of counseling with Amy.

Personal Relationships

Amy seems to be struggling with her personal relationships with her family-of-origin and peers. Her response to these difficulties has been to seek relationships with extended family members who are removed from her immediate surroundings, as well as supportive adults in the school setting. Amy is cognizant of her interpersonal difficulties and wants to make some changes.

The difficulties with her parents seem to center primarily on her mother. The pre-counseling phone interview confirmed the mother's frustration with Amy. Clearly, an intervention to strengthen their relationship is crucial. One suggested intervention is to teach Amy effective communication skills (e.g., "I" statements, active listening) to give her more tools in her relationship with her mother. After gaining some of these skills, the school counselor might encourage a joint session with Amy and her mother to develop a structured plan for their relationship to improve. Prior to that meeting, the school counselor would consult with the mother about her willingness to spend time with Amy and ensure her commitment.

Relationship-building interventions with Amy and her mother would emphasize girl-focused activities, allowing Amy to introduce her mother to things that she knows best and that interest her. These activities could help Amy's mother bridge the generation gap between them and create a common language built on mutually shared experiences. Periodic meetings with Amy, her mother, and the school counselor could be a vehicle for monitoring progress. Referral to a mother–daughter group would be another outlet to strengthen their relationship.

Amy's peer relationships are suffering. Referral to a girls' group or a social skills group can be an effective way to build friendship skills. If a group is not available, the counselor might work with Amy on social skills training. Using behavioral interventions such as covert modeling and role playing, Amy could develop new skills and comfort with her peers (Shapiro et al., 2006). Further, the school counselor can make process comments on Amy's interpersonal style and offer feedback about her presentation in counseling.

Health

Amy has frequent headaches, which may have a medical and/or emotional etiology. When she goes for the medical check-up to have an evaluation for depression, she would speak to her doctor about her headaches and have her vision tested, as there has been some association between adolescent depression and headaches (Pine, Cohen, & Brook, 1996). This evaluation is important in determining the course of treatment. Amy's physician may recommend medication to address the headaches. Amy would also be taught simple relaxation and self-hypnosis to promote self-efficacy in reducing her pain (Sperry, Lewis, Carlson, & Englar-Carlson, 2005). Amy could be guided through relaxation training interventions taken from *The Relaxation and Stress Reduction Workbook* (Davis et al., 2000) to lessen possible somatic tension.

As a second area of intervention in the Health mode, an exercise program could be established for Amy. Physical activity and exercise seem to alleviate some of the symptoms of depression, particularly for people whose level of depression is higher than normal before the start of the exercise program. Further, exercise seems to be useful in managing anxiety, depression, anger, tension, reaction to stress, self-efficacy, and self-esteem (Hansen, Stevens, & Coast, 2001; Tkachuk & Martin, 1999). If possible, Amy would be referred to a female-oriented exercise program such as Curves or programs at the local YWCA.

Learning/School

Amy is having a difficult time keeping up with the schoolwork required in the gifted program. She could be educated about appropriate study skills and encouraged to study with a friend or study group. If she can pair social interaction with effective studying, she might realize progress in her academic work and friendships. Amy could be taught how to use a homework and assignment planner effectively, as well as a calendar to schedule time to study for tests and complete homework and assignments. She could meet with the school counselor to discuss her current classload, and her schedule could be changed as needed and appropriate.

Guidance of A, B, Cs

Amy lacks pleasant and enjoyable events in her daily and weekly life. To address this concern, the school counselor would work with Amy to determine what she considers pleasant and how to make it happen in her life. A first step is to explore what she likes to do for fun. It might be riding her bike, seeing movies, listening to or playing music, or just hanging out. From this list, Amy would list her activities on a 3 x 5 card to document her desires.

The second consideration is: Is she going to do this alone, or with a friend, or a parent or relative? The third concern is how to get started on this type of activity. For example, her father might take her to the movie theater, or she might need a ride to a local park Each activity involves a series of steps and planning. The fourth consideration is to how to get Amy going. We would work to program pleasurable events into her life to give her something to look forward to and keep a positive outlook on life.

Amy seems to be motivated to make changes in her life, and thus would enter multimodal counseling in an action stage. Though her HELP-ING profile presents numerous interventions, success in an individual mode would result in progress across the whole spectrum. If Amy is able to gain some early success and exhibit control in her life, she could develop better coping strategies and skills to improve her relationships and mood.

Conclusion

This chapter presents a comprehensive model of school counseling for successful intervention and outcomes. Above all, multimodal counseling is an organized, systematic model of counseling that applies theory toward practice. Multimodal counseling is widely accepted as an effective therapeutic approach. With the current trend in psychotherapy and counseling toward multidimensional, multidisciplinary, and multifaceted interventions, multimodal counseling has enjoyed a renaissance. It is recognized as one of the few organized and systematic integrative therapies.

The multimodal framework allows counselors to identify cultural and idiosyncratic variables and, thus, avoid placing clients in preconceived treatments. Multimodal counseling has been effective with a wide variety of clients and presenting concerns, including adults, couples, and children. In the school setting, multimodal counseling provides school counselors with a wealth of individual, group, and classroom interventions that all reside within a structured framework.

References

Bandura, A. (1986). *Social foundations of thought and action: A social cognitive theory.* Englewood Cliffs, NJ: Prentice Hall.

Bingham, M., Stryker, S., & Neufeldt, S. (1995). *Things will be different for my daughter: A practical guide to building her self-esteem and self-reliance.* New York: Penguin Classics.

Boston Women's Health Collective. (2005). *Our bodies, ourselves: A new edition for a new era.* New York: Touchstone.

Brown, L.S. (1991). Telling a girl's life: Self-authorization as a form of resistance. In C.Gilligan, A.G. Rogers, & D.L. Tolman (Eds.), *Women, girls, and psychotherapy: Reframing resistance* (pp 71–86). Binghamton, NY: Haworth Press.

Burns, D. (1999). *Feeling good: The new mood therapy.* Avon Books.

Carlson, J.D., & Englar-Carlson, M. (2008). Adlerian therapy. In J. Frew & M. Spiegler (Eds.), *Contemporary psychotherapies for a diverse world* (pp. 93-140). Boston: Lahaska Press.

Choate, L.H. (2005). Toward a theoretical model of women's body image resistance. *Journal of Counseling and Development, 83,* 320–330.

Christophersen, E.R., & Mortweet, S.L. (2001). *Treatments that work: Empirically supported strategies for managing childhood problems.* Washington, DC: American Psychological Association.

Conners, C. K. (1997). *Manual for the Conners' Rating Scales–Revised.* North Tonawanda, New York: Multi- Health Systems.

Corey, G. (2008). *Theory and practice of counseling and psychotherapy* (8th ed.). Belmont, CA: Brooks-Cole.

Davis, M., Eshelman, E.R., & McKay, M. (2000). *The relaxation and stress reduction workbook* (5th ed.). Oakland, CA: New Harbinger Publications.

Day, S.X. (2004). *Theory and design in counseling and psychotherapy*. Boston: Lahaska Press.

de Shazer, J. S. (1985). *Keys to solution in brief therapy*. New York: Norton.

de Shazer, J. S. (1988). *Clues: Investigating solutions in brief therapy*. New York: Norton.

Dinkmeyer, D., Jr., & Carlson, J.D. (2006). *Consultation process and skills: Creating school-based interventions* (3rd ed.). New York: Brunner-Routledge.

Dryden, W., & Lazarus, A.A. (1991). *A dialogue with Arnold Lazarus: "It depends."* London: Open University Press.

Evans, D.L., Foa, E.B., Gur, R.E., Hendin, H., O'Brien, C.P., Seligman, M.E., & Walsh, B.T. (Eds.). (2005). *Treating and preventing adolescent mental health disorders: What we know and what we don't know*. New York: Oxford.

Gilliam, J. E. (1995). *Examiners manual for the Attention-Deficit/Hyperactivity Disorder Test: A method for identifying individuals with ADHD*. Austin, TX: Pro-Ed.

Gladding, S.T. (2007). *Group work: A counseling specialty (5th ed.)*. Upper Saddle River, NJ: Merrill-Prentice Hall.

Hansen, C. J., Stevens, L.C., & Coast, J.R. (2001). Exercise duration and mood state: How much is enough to feel better? *Health Psychology, 20*, 267–275.

Kabat-Zinn, J. (1990). *Full catastrophe living: Using the wisdom of your body and mind to face stress, pain and illness*. New York: Dell Publishing.

Keat, D. B. (1979). *Multimodal therapy with children*. New York: Pergamon.

Keat, D. B. (1990). *Child multimodal therapy*. Norwood, NJ: Ablex.

Keat, D.B., & Englar-Carlson, M. (2006). *Comprehensive child counseling*. Manuscript in preparation.

Kovacs, M. (1992). *Children's Depression Inventory*. North Tonawanda, NY: Multi-Health Systems.

Lazarus, A. A. (Ed.). (1976). *Multimodal behavior therapy*. New York: Springer.

Lazarus, A. A. (1989). *The practice of multimodal therapy*. Baltimore: Johns Hopkins University Press (updated paperback edition).

Lazarus, A. A. (1997). *Brief but comprehensive psychotherapy: The multimodal way*. New York: Springer.

Lazarus, A.A. (2000a). Multimodal replenishment. *Professional Psychology: Research and Practice, 31*, 93–94.

Lazarus, A.A. (2000b). Multimodal strategies with adults. In J. Carlson & L. Sperry (Eds.), *Brief therapy with individuals and couples* (pp. 106–124). Phoenix, AZ: Zeig, Tucker, & Theisen.

Lazarus, A.A. (2002a). Client readiness for change, cultural concerns, and risk taking: A multimodal case presentation. *Clinical Case Studies, 1*, 39–48.

Lazarus, A.A. (2002b).The multimodal assessment therapy approach. In F.W. Kaslow & J.L. Lebow (Eds.), *Comprehensive handbook of psychotherapy: Integrative/eclectic* (pp. 241–254). New York: Wiley.

Lazarus, A.A. (2005). Multimodal therapy. In R. Corsini & D. Wedding (Eds), *Current psychotherapies* (7th ed., pp. 337–371). Itasca, IL: Peacock.

Lazarus, A.A., & Beutler, L.E. (1993). On technical eclecticism. *Journal of Counseling and Development, 71*, 381–385.

Lonigan, C.J., & Elbert, J.C. (Eds.). (1998). Empirically supported psychosocial interventions for children [Special issue]. *Journal of Clinical Child Psychology, 27,* 138–236.

Miller, J. J., Fletcher, K., & Kabat-Zinn, J. (1995). Three-year follow-up and clinical implications of a mindfulness-based stress reduction intervention in the treatment of anxiety disorders. *General Hospital Psychiatry, 17,* 192–200.

Nau, D. S., & Shilts, L. (2000). When to use the miracle questions: Clues from a qualitative study of four SFBT practitioners. *Journal of Systemic Therapies, 19,* 129–135.

Ortiz, J. M. (1997). *The Tao of music: Sound psychology.* York Beach, ME: Samuel Weiser.

Palmer, S. (2000). Developing an individual therapeutic programme suitable for use by counseling psychologists in a multicultural society. *Counselling Psychology Review, 15,* 32–50.

Pine, D.S., Cohen, P., & Brook, J. (1996). The association between major depression and headache: Results of a longitudinal epidemiologic study in youth. *Journal of Child and Adolescent Psychopharmacology, 6,* 153–164.

Shapiro, J.O., Friedberg, R.D., & Bardenstein, K.K. (2006). *Child and adolescent therapy: Science and art.* New York: Wiley.

Shapiro, L. (1994). *The very angry day that Amy didn't have.* Plainview, NY: Childswork/Childplay.

Shore, H. (1995). *The angry monster workbook.* Plainview, New York: Childswork/Childplay.

Sklare, G. (2004). *Brief counseling works: A solution-focused approach for school counselors and administrators* (2nd ed.). Thousand Oaks, CA: Corwin Press.

Sperry, L., Lewis, J., Carlson, J.D., & Englar-Carlson, M. (2005). *Health promotion and health counseling: Effective counseling and psychotherapeutic strategies* (2nd ed.). Boston: Allyn & Bacon.

Tkachuk, G.A., & Martin, G.L. (1999). Exercise therapy for patients with psychiatric disorders: Research and clinical implications. *Professional Psychology: Research and Practice, 30,* 275–282.

Tolman, D.L., & Brown, L.M. (2001). Adolescent girls' voices: Resonating in body and soul. In R.K. Unger (Ed.), *Handbook of the psychology of woman and gender* (pp. 133–155). New York: Wiley.

Vernon, A. (1998). *The PASSPORT program: A journey through emotional, social, cognitive, and self-development (Grades 1?5).* Champaign, IL: Research Press.

Vernon, A. (2006). *Thinking, feeling, behaving: An emotional education curriculum for children (Grades 1-6).* Champaign, IL: Research Press.

Wilde, J. (2000). *Let's get rational.* Centerville, IN: LGR Productions.

CHAPTER 4

BRIEF COUNSELING: PROBLEM SOLVING AND SOLUTION FOCUSED

• • • • • • • • • • •

John M. Littrell

• • • • • • • • • • •

Overview

The practice of brief counseling reaffirms a perspective long held by career counselors to (a) help people identify their strengths, (b) assist them in setting goals, and (c) increase their flexibility to achieve those goals. In working with clients, career counselors spend considerable time exploring clients' talents and interests and direct minimal attention to what does *not* work. So what accounts for the current excitement about brief counseling when career counseling has operated for years with the same assumptions? The answer is that career counseling was perceived for many years as something quite different from personal or social counseling. In the mind of some, helping people with career concerns was not "real" counseling because these counselors did not delve deeply into their clients' past, failed to focus on problems, and believed that change takes a long time.

With the discovery of brief solution-focused counseling in the 1980s by people such as Steve de Shazer (1985, 1988) and others, a movement grew among practitioners who wanted alternatives to counseling models that assumed that unlimited time was available to assist people. Counselors across a variety of settings began to realize that counseling time was indeed limited. With brief counseling, single sessions were

frequent and seeing clients for more than six sessions was a luxury. A real-
ization began to dawn that brief counseling is a viable answer for school
counselors who want to help students in the shortest time while still
engaging in high-quality counseling. In other words, brief does not have
to mean second-rate.

The following two scenarios illustrate the difference between a deficit
and diagnostic counseling approach and a strengths and exceptions
approach. The scenarios differ in their emphasis on delving into the past
versus a more now-and-future orientation, the former addressing problems
versus strengths and believing that change will take a long time versus
assuming that change can occur quickly.

Deficit and Diagnostic Scenario

Pat is a seventh grader who has been diagnosed with a conduct disorder.
She treats classmates with contempt and has bullying tendencies. Pat has
no friends. Academically, she is two grades behind in school, possibly
because of daydreaming a lot in class. Pat does not accept responsibility.
In terms of socioeconomic status, she is in the lower-middle class. Her
parents divorced three years ago, and Pat is reared by a single-parent
mother. Her older brother dropped out of school in the 10th grade.

Strengths and Exceptions Scenario

Pat is a seventh grader who has been diagnosed with a conduct disorder.
She treats classmates with contempt and has bullying tendencies.
Currently Pat has no friends but seems to make an effort to acquire
friends. Academically, when Pat was in third grade, she was two grade
levels behind peers, but in the past four years she has not fallen any further behind. Pat pays attention when the teacher speaks but daydreams a
lot in class. Accepting responsibility seems difficult much of the time, but
Pat definitely accepted responsibility in running the concession stand after
school, diligently making sure that all the money was accounted for (indi-
cating math skills on display). In terms of socioeconomic status, she is in
the lower-middle class. Pat's parents divorced three years ago, and she is
being reared by a single-parent mother. Her father provides regular finan-
cial support and sees her every weekend. An older brother dropped out of
school in the 10th grade.

Question for the Counselor

Which scenario is more hopeful? Both scenarios contain information that may be useful in working with her, but the second holds out more hope. One reason is that the second scenario is not simply a recitation of aspects of Pat's life that are not working. Although it does contain information about what does not work in Pat's life, it also contains information about what *does* work. This chapter will show how brief counselors would be inclined to view Pat from the second perspective: They would actively seek information about her to clarify and amplify her strengths and resources.

History of Brief Counseling

Over the past 25 years, counseling has begun moving away from away from a deficit and pathology model of human beings and toward an emphasis on what works in people's lives. For a long time psychological theories emphasized what can go wrong with people. Even today we see this reflected in the diagnosis of human pathology in the *Diagnostic and Statistical Manual of Mental Disorders* (DSM-IV-TR; American Psychiatric Association, 2000). While abnormal psychology emphasizes human deficits, the trend has been to move away from deficit models. Despite the tenacity of the DSM-IV-TR as a major force in the field of mental health, the school counseling profession has remained adamant that school counselors look at the whole child/adolescent who is in the process of development.

Further, counseling theories formerly tended to be all-encompassing theories of personality as advocated by therapists including Sigmund Freud, Carl Rogers, and Fritz Perls. Brief counseling reflects a movement beginning in the late 20th century to be less grandiose in theorizing. Instead of defining and trying to understand who humans are, as earlier theories did, brief counseling is more interested in how the process of change occurs. Brief counseling places considerably less emphasis on understanding humans and more on how to help people change.

Brief counseling was not developed in isolation. Echoes of brief counseling are found in other theories. Adlerians focused on the world surrounding the client, not just the client's inner world. In 1965, William Glasser first published *Reality Therapy*, in which he abandoned much of the emphasis on the past and placed it on where clients were and where they wanted to go. In the late 1960s, the Mental Research Institute (MRI) group in Palo Alto, California, committed heresy by limiting counseling to 10 sessions. In addition, MRI began to emphasize the interactional nature of problems (Fisch, Weakland, & Segal, 1982; Watzlawick, Weakland, & Fisch, 1974). Rather than looking at problems within people, adherents viewed problems as arising from interactions with others and that this view would better facilitate change. Today, when brief counselors think about problems, they are inclined to think of them as problems in living. Problems are not found within people but, rather, as interactional difficulties within a social context.

A key figure in the brief counseling movement, Steve de Shazer, studied at MRI. Along with Insoo Kim Berg, he founded the Milwaukee Brief Family Therapy Center in 1978. He reversed the MRI's emphasis on starting with problems and wrestled with his associates on answering the question: Why concentrate on problems rather than solutions? They embarked on a systematic program of highlighting when clients did not have problems, called *exceptions*, and the clients' strengths that might be useful in finding solutions.

Characteristics of Brief Counseling

Brief counseling has nine defining characteristics (Littrell & Zinck, 2004). These characteristics are not mutually exclusive from other counseling approaches, but taken together, they confer on brief counseling its uniqueness. Brief counseling is

1. relationship based,
2. humor eliciting,
3. time limited,
4. solution focused,
5. action based,
6. socially interactive,
7. detail oriented,
8. developmentally attentive, and
9. culturally responsive.

Each of these characteristics is discussed in detail in the remainder of the chapter.

Major Constructs of Brief Counseling

All counseling theories address the following constructs: (a) the goals of counseling, (b) the nature of the counseling relationship, (c) the role of the counselor, (d) the process of change and stages of the counseling process, and (e) multicultural applications.

Goals of Counseling

What is the nature of goals in brief counseling? To clarity this question, we must answer four questions.

Question 1: What do goals look like? Brief counselors find that helping clients set goals is a valued process that enhances client movement from where they are currently to a desired state in the future. Goals that meet six criteria have been shown to be valuable in the change process. Goals should be (a) stated in the positive, (b) meaningful to the client, (c) under the client's control, (d) specific and concrete, (e) short-term versus long-term, and (f) small. Examples of goals that meet these criteria are as follows:

- *(6th grader)* During the next 3 weeks, I will have asked five kids in my class to work on projects together.
- *(12th grader)* In 2 weeks, I will have completed submitting applications to my top six colleges.

Question 2: Who sets the goals? The counselor and the client mutually negotiate the goals of counseling. The client has the final say about what the goals will be. This is not to say that counselors do not assist with the process. On the one hand, counselors are skilled in helping clients set goals that meet certain criteria, as explained in the previous question. On the other hand, goals are not imposed on students.

To be motivated to work toward a goal, the goal should be meaningful. Too often in their attempts to be well meaning, counselors—and especially teachers—think they know best what the student should be doing. One way to "unmotivate" students is to give them goals rather than take the time to find out what goals they find meaningful and are willing to exert some effort to achieve.

What if students do not want to work toward what others think are in their best interest? The brief counseling answer is to begin with goals that the student finds meaningful. When the counselor helps students achieve goals that are meaningful to them, they will be much more inclined to trust the counselor with other concerns. Counselors often find that then the students begin to change the behaviors that other people thought they should change.

Say, for example, that a ninth grader is referred to you for skipping school. Many of us might think that the goal is to have the student attend classes regularly. If we were to ask the student what she really found meaningful and might be willing to work on, however, she might answer, "I'd like to have more friends." The irony is that if you help her have more friends, she would probably be more inclined to attend school. Brief counseling starts where the student is motivated, not with our agenda of what we believe is best for the student.

Question 3: How do we know when goals are reached? The student says or indicates one of the following: (a) "I no longer have a problem," or (b) "This is something I can live with." Counselors and students can use the six criteria specified in question 1 to assess whether they have reached their goals. Four possibilities exist: The goal (1) is exceeded, (2) is met, (3) is partially met, or (4) is not met. If (1) or (2)—congratulations for helping another person successfully. If (3) or (4)—brief counselors should reassess whether the goal was meaningful to the student, completely under the student's control, clear, not too big and overwhelming, and based on a realistic timeline. Students' initial goals are often too big. Halving or even quartering their goals frequently brings sighs of relief and reenergizes students.

Question 4: Is all counseling goal oriented? Yes, because a problem, by definition, is a discrepancy between where one is now and where one would like to be. Over the course of counseling—whether 10 minutes or 5 sessions—hopefully, the student moves from a present state, one that is less than desired, to a desired future state. Even students who are dealing with the breakup of relationships will be attempting to avoid having the intensity of feelings and repetitious behaviors that they currently are experiencing.

The Nature of the Counseling Relationship

The nature of the counseling relationship is the defining aspect of all forms of counseling. Two of the nine brief counseling characteristics that shed light on the counseling relationship are the relationship-based and humor-eliciting characteristics.

CHARACTERISTIC #1: RELATIONSHIP BASED

What kind of relationship characterizes brief counseling? The novelist Andre Gide summed up one aspect of relationships:

> The young people who come to me in the hope of hearing me utter a few memorable maxims are quite disappointed. Aphorisms are not my forte; I say nothing but banalities, but I listen to them and they go away delighted.

In brief counseling we agree with Gide that listening is an essential quality. Brief counselors do listen—and listen intently. Brief counselors believe that the research on the counseling process holds some basic truths: The facilitative conditions of warmth, genuineness, and empathy do matter, and they matter greatly. One does not have to be Carl Rogers to care about students, be genuine in one's own nature, and convey empathy as one listens.

Unfortunately, some advocates of solution-focused counseling, even the late Steve de Shazer, advocate a technique-oriented form of brief counseling. Although counselors must be skilled technically, their humanness is more important. To ignore the power and hope-inducing aspects of the counseling relationship is like pressing on the gas petal of the car to go forward while keeping the other foot on the brake. It may work for a while, but the damage is inevitable.

When learning about brief counseling, the tendency is to become technique oriented. The wheels start clicking and the counselor thinks, "This would be a great time to ask the Miracle Question." Although techniques such as the Miracle Question can be highly effective, of greater importance than techniques is the counselor's ability to be present in the counseling relationship. Years ago, behaviorists believed in the "curative" powers of their techniques; however, researchers discovered that the clients of behaviorists who were warm, caring, and empathic did better than did the clients of behaviorists who lacked these qualities.

John Dillinger robbed banks across the Midwest in the 1930s. He was quoted as saying, "You can get so much more out of people with a kind word and a gun than just a gun." I prefer to make this a more positive statement by recasting it as, "You can get so much more out of clients with warmth, genuineness, empathy, *and* techniques than just techniques." If the facilitative conditions are present, we increase our chances of being the helpers we want to be, even as we use some powerful brief counseling techniques.

CHARACTERISTIC #2: HUMOR ELICITING

An underrated aspect of most forms of counseling is the use of humor. The counselor who elicits humor and laughter from people has an advantage over the solemn counselor who dwells on the heaviness of problems. The use of humor and laughter is not intended to minimize suffering but, instead, to place suffering within a larger perspective that includes life's resources and opportunities.

A second benefit of eliciting a student's sense of humor is that it allows students to have more choice in their worlds. Jean Houston understood this with her succinct phrase, "At the height of laughter, the universe is flung into a kaleidoscope of new possibilities." New perspectives and new possibilities emerge as students take themselves and their problems less seriously.

Like Adlerians and reality/choice therapists, brief counselors celebrate the appropriate use of humor within counseling. Students are perceived as having a sense of humor that can be tapped to facilitate change. Laugher is viewed as a lubricant to aid in taking steps in new directions. Fun (including pleasure and enjoyment) is recognized in reality/control therapy as a major human need, along with some heavy-duty needs such as power, love and belonging, freedom, and survival. The process of making changes can be fun. Counselors who elicit a client's sense of humor add another dimension to their work. Brief counselors would agree with Woody Allen's statement, "I am thankful for laughter, except when milk comes out of my nose."

Role of the Counselor

Brief counselors often are defined by the roles they assume. A study of an exemplary elementary school counselor, Claudia Vangstad, found that the school counselor expressed her overall role as a counselor by exhibiting 12 capabilities (Littrell & Peterson, 2005), outlined in Figure 4.1. When these capabilities are developed and employed, the synergistic effect in

I.   Grounding the Self
    A.   Understanding Self (Capability 1)
        1.   Vision
        2.   Identity
        3.   Core Beliefs
        4.   Basic Values
    B.   Understanding Change (Capability 2)
II. Realizing a Vision
    A.   Reading a School Culture (Capability 3)
    B.   Acting Contextually (Capability 4)
    C.   Designing a Developmental Curriculum (Capability 5)
    D.   Guiding Students in Classrooms (Capability 6)
    E.   Facilitating Groups (Capability 7)
    F.   Counseling Individuals (Capability 8)
    G.   Building Partnerships (Capability 9)
    H.   Advocating for Children (Capability 10)
III. Staying the Course
    A.   Planning, Organizing, and Persevering (Capability 11)
    B.   Ensuring Comprehensive Renewal (Capability 12)

Based on an exemplary school counselor who transformed the culture of a school. See *Portrait and Model of a School Counselor,* by J. M. Littrell and J. S. Peterson (Boston: Lahaska Press/Houghton Mifflin, 2005), p. 11.

FIGURE 4.1

Model of Excellence in School Counseling

helping others can be amazing. The 12 capabilities can be lumped into three major themes:

1. Grounding the self
2. Realizing a vision
3. Staying the course

The three themes and their corresponding capabilities are sketched out below. For a more detailed explanation, consult *Portrait and Model of a School Counselor* (Littrell & Peterson, 2005).

The first theme we uncovered, *Grounding the Self*, encompasses two capabilities—*Understanding Self* (Capability 1), and *Understanding Change* (Capability 2). School counselors who have an understanding of themselves have visions of how schools can be (e.g., Schools are a place for the development of the whole child/adolescent). They have a solid professional identity that is not buffeted by fads or narrowness (e.g., "I'm only a personal/social counselor/therapist"). Counselors have core beliefs and act on their basic values.

In addition to understanding themselves, counselors understand change. How does change occur? Brief solution-focused counseling is primarily a theory of change, not of personality. As such, its principles are applicable not only to individuals but also to groups, classrooms, schools, and communities. Aligning the theory for all of these entities allows the counselor to have one fundamental framework that is applicable in many contexts.

The capabilities *Understanding Self* and *Understanding Change* form the foundation for the second theme, *Realizing a Vision*, which is composed of eight capabilities. Brief counselors are skilled at *Reading a School Culture* (Capability 3). They know how their school functions, how change is perceived, the rhythms, the morale, the differing perspectives and styles, the implicit rules, roles, and surrounding environment.

While continually reading the school culture, counselors can begin *Acting Contextually* (Capability 4). Different languages are taught in schools. By this, we mean the philosophical language of power/control, responsibility, learning, growth, and problem solving/solution focused. Brief counselors attune themselves to how students, teachers, staff, and administrators use various languages and their effects on the school climate. Schools that are caught in the grip of power/control languages (e.g., "This is the way we do it here") and responsibility languages ("Show some responsibility") are often gripped by fear. Brief counselors move schools toward languages that are more learning, growth, and problem solving/solution focused.

Capacity 5 is *Designing a Developmental Curriculum*. Rather than remaining isolated, brief counselors have a counseling curriculum. Aimed at fulfilling the counselor's vision within the school, the curriculum is implemented as the counselor uses five more capabilities: *Guiding Students in Classrooms* (Capability 6), *Facilitating Groups (*Capability 7), *Counseling Individuals* (Capability 8), *Building Partnerships* (Capability 9), and *Advocating for Children* (Capability 10). As is now obvious, the brief solution-focused counselor is an active, multifaceted professional, capable of exerting his or her influence to change a school in a way that enriches the lives of students and school personnel.

It is not enough to simply do the above, though. Brief counselors must be prepared for *Staying the Course*, the third major theme. Two additional capabilities are needed: *Planning, Organizing, and Persevering* (Capability 11), and *Ensuring Comprehensive Renewal* (Capability 12). Lack of planning, organizing, and persevering will undermine the counselor's good intentions of achieving a vision. Knowing the next steps, organizing efforts to take those steps, and staying on the path are capabilities exhibited by counselors who make a difference. Comprehensive mental, physical, social, emotional, and spiritual renewals are essential if all of the above capabilities are to be realized.

The Process of Change and Stages of the Counseling Process

To guide their thinking about change, brief counselors have two maps: the problem-solving brief counseling model developed at MRI (Fisch et al., 1982; Watzlawick et al., 1974) and the solution-focused brief counseling model (Berg & Steiner, 2003; de Shazer, 1985, 1988).

PROBLEM-SOLVING BRIEF COUNSELING

The staff of the Mental Research Institute (Fisch et al., 1982; Watzlawick et al., 1974) developed the problem-solving model. This model has four recognizable stages (Watzlawick et al., 1974, p. 110):

1. A clear definition of the problem in concrete terms
2. An investigation of the solutions attempted so far
3. A clear definition of the concrete change to be achieved
4. The formation and implementation of a plan to produce this change

The theory underlying the MRI four-step model is simple and relatively easy to learn (Littrell, 1998):

> A person attempts to effectively deal with one of life's problems. Occasionally, the person's attempted solution not only fails to achieve the desired outcome but in fact even exacerbates it. When the problem is not solved by the attempted solution, the person takes a more-of-the-same approach. To extricate the person from the more-of-the-same trap, the counselor

> assists the person in clarifying goals and doing activities that
> are not in the more-of-the-same category. (p 14)

The elementary school counselor mentioned above operated out of the problem-solving brief counseling model. She found that school personnel, and especially students, readily understood the language of problem solving.

SOLUTION-FOCUSED BRIEF COUNSELING

Rather than begin with problems, the solution-focused, brief counseling model emphasizes exceptions to clients' problem situations and builds on those exceptions. Brief counselors using this model ask students questions such as: "When is this problem not a problem?" and "When is the problem less of a problem?" When exceptions to the problem are found, time is spent examining what the student is doing during those times that effectively makes the problem not a problem. The counselor assigns tasks for the student to do more of what is done when there is not a problem.

As an example of exploring exceptions, the counselor might ask the student:

> So, Jim, given that you are really good at procrastinating in exploring colleges to go to, when is it not a problem and you actually take some steps to explore—or when is it less of a problem and you find yourself procrastinating just a bit less?

By helping Jim explore the problem in this way, Jim can experience the "problem" in a different way. It is no longer always the same problem but can be different at various times. This differentiation underscores the idea that if the problem can already be changing at different times, the problem itself can be changed.

CHARACTERISTIC #3: TIME LIMITED

How is "brief" defined? Is it the total number of sessions? The length of sessions? Or the total time that the counselor and client meet? In a school setting, "brief" can be defined as anything between 5 minutes and 6 hours. This recognizes that within schools, counselors encounter time constraints because of the many demands on their time from students, teachers, parents, and administrators. Schools are not designed to accommodate counseling/therapy practices that direct so much time to one student that others are neglected. Referrals to other professionals are necessary if working extensively with one student means that others will continue to suffer.

By setting a limit on time, counselors have found that many people have a way of rising to the occasion and making helpful changes within the limits. Brian Fantana once described the effectiveness of his special cologne in the following manner: "60% of the time it works all the time." Applied to brief counseling—most of the time the brief counseling approach works all the time. But brief counseling is designed specifically to work within limits, and sometimes the situations that students bring are beyond the scope of what school counselors can address.

CHARACTERISTIC #4: SOLUTION FOCUSED

In brief counseling a solution is a temporary answer to a specific difficulty in life. Brief counselors are not engaged in changing people's personalities. Rather, they help clients deal effectively with specific concerns. A useful framework for thinking about concerns was first proposed by Walsh and Osipow (1970), who wrote that people coming to counseling are (1) in need of supportive counseling, (2) frustrated in making a decision, or (3) wanting to do more of or less of some behavior.

In the first concern, brief counseling offers support by providing accurate listening and responding. It provides a caring person. When a student loses a friend, there is not a solution in the sense of changing behavior, but the act of truly listening can be most therapeutic in that "solutions" emerge from having shared with another person. While I believe that being solution focused is a most helpful act, I also believe that sometimes the most therapeutic act we can engage in is to give our undivided attention to others without trying to solve their concern.

In the second concern, brief counseling helps the student make a decision. Decision making involves knowing alternatives, weighing them, and figuring out a course of action. The act of goal setting helps define what students want and consequently assists in decision making.

A third concern of brief counseling is behavior change. Does the student want to be doing more of something (e.g., studying) or less of something (e.g., picking on other kids)? Brief counselors have in their repertoire a wide range of tools, techniques, and strategies to aid students in making the changes that will enhance their lives.

CHARACTERISTIC #5: ACTION BASED

Brief counseling endorses the sentiment in a Chinese proverb: "Talk doesn't cook rice." Even though talk is definitely the currency that drives our talk therapies, its prominent role can obscure the need to translate students' words into action, movement. Alfred Adler demonstrated his understanding of the therapeutic role of action when he said, "Trust only movement. Life happens at the level of events, not of words. Trust movement."

Movement can consist of small steps that help the student move from a Precontemplation stage to the Contemplation stage in the framework of Prochaska, Norcross, and DiClemente (1994). To help the student take small steps, the counselor might say, "Would you be willing to begin looking at the pros and cons of turning in your assignments on time?" Note that the movement here is not turning in the homework on time (Action stage in Prochaska's framework) and not even getting ready to turn in homework on time (Preparation). Rather, the movement is to have the student begin thinking about the behavior. By going only one step beyond the stage where the student is, the counselor ensures more cooperation from the student because the small step makes much more sense in the student's world than the huge step of taking actions to change.

CHARACTERISTIC #6: SOCIALLY INTERACTIVE

Brief counselors assume that the person they work with is part of the fabric of social networks (e.g., parents, friends, teachers, administrators, relatives). They also assume that social networks are conservative in nature and not eager to change familiar patterns. Therefore, the student's current patterns of behavior are continually reinforced. So even if the student's patterns are not helpful, they are at least predictable to others. If the student were to change, others would have to adopt new ways of being with the student.

The brief counseling emphasis on viewing social interaction as a key to change leads counselors to understand problems by concentrating on interactions. Counselors do not restrict their focus to looking for causes within the student. The nature of problems is both intra-actional and inter-actional. What a student thinks, feels, and does, does matter. What the people in the student's world think, feel, and do also matters.

Brief counselors enlist the support of others in effecting change for several reasons. First, to ignore the world around the student is to make the student's job of changing much more difficult. The ancient poet Homer expressed this sentiment in *The Iliad* when he wrote, "Light is the task when many share the toil." Social support has continually been shown to assist people in making the changes they want. Finding even one other person to share the toil is sometimes as simple as asking the student two questions:

1. "As you think about all of the people in this school, who are three you think would be willing to help you with this problem?"
2. "Would you be agreeable to have me ask those three people if they would be willing to work together with you to make the changes you want?"

CHARACTERISTIC #7: DETAIL ORIENTED

The therapist Jay Haley once supervised a therapist who told him that a client was stuck in a symbiotic relationship with her mother. Haley responded, "I would never let that be the problem." What is the meaning of his response? One way to understand this is to see that the therapist had framed the problem at a highly abstract level. The abstractness did not seem to be grounded in the client's thoughts, feelings, or actions. Haley was directing the therapist to be more concrete and specific so the client could do something about the concern.

In a similar manner, brief counselors are dedicated to being detail oriented. Unfortunately, the most prevalent use of detail orientation has been directed to the student's problem state. Historically, counselors have been taught to gather a considerable amount of information before we can really help. While we help students be specific about their problems, we are tenacious in eliciting details and examples of their resources and strengths, their goals, and the many ways by which they might reach their goals.

Often I begin sessions by asking, "What are five of your top strengths, talents, and resources?" After the initial groans of having to identify so many, I say, "Okay, okay—only six." The humor in my increasing rather than decreasing the expectation becomes apparent, and the student begins to name them. Next I explore in detail more information about each one. Often, by the time we finish, the student's physiology has changed: The student is sitting up straighter, is more animated, and indicates some hope. Then we explore the student's concerns in a more resourceful state.

A danger in being detail oriented is missing the bigger picture. We do not want it said that we were too busy mopping the floor to turn off the faucet. Being detail oriented means helping a student move ahead, not collecting scrapbooks of information with little relevance to the student's counseling goals.

Multicultural Applications

CHARACTERISTIC #8: DEVELOPMENTALLY ATTENTIVE

As young people mature, they must deal with issues arising in the realms of physical, social, mental, emotional, and spiritual development. Conflicting norms, values, and expectations from parents, teachers, peers, media, and other sources emphasize making choices, forging an identity, and relating to others. Little wonder that someone once said, "A characteristic of the normal child is that he or she doesn't act that way very often."

Brief counselors tend to view most human problems as arising from attempted solutions to the complexities of life. For example, Rita, a 13-year-old Hispanic growing up in an urban setting, who is not receiving attention at home, seeks sex with older male students. Her attempted solution to the lack of attention increases her risk of becoming pregnant. Temporarily, Rita may become the object of lots of attention, but she adds to her problems by also acquiring labels (e.g., immature, irresponsible), which jeopardizes her opportunities in life (e.g., dropping out of school and thereby decreasing her economic opportunities), and increasing (rather than decreasing) her dependency on others. Rita's attempted solution to the problem of lack of attention backfires. She has the attention, but the attention she receives undermines her attempt to receive attention that enhances her status. Contrarily, she has added to her problems and practically guarantees that the attention she does receive will keep her trapped.

In the example of Rita, brief counselors are aware that the development of children and adolescents is fraught with social traps. Cross and Guyer (1980) defined a social trap as "a situation characterized by multiple but conflicting rewards" (p. 4). These traps "draw their victims into certain patterns of behavior with promises of immediate rewards and then confront them with consequences that the victims would rather avoid" (p. 4). Rita's reaching out for the promise of immediate attention or intimacy will increase the chances of an unintended and potentially stifling future.

Effective counseling with students like Rita demands that brief counselors be knowledgeable about human development. What are the social, intellectual, cultural, sexual, and spiritual expectations for an adolescent like Rita who is growing up in an urban setting? What resources, programs, and opportunities are available in the schools, religious and local communities, and state, to support young girls like Rita? Does she have access to a counselor who speaks Spanish?

In summary, brief counselors are not just skilled at individual counseling. They also look at problems as being primarily developmental in nature. They design programs, facilitate groups, and help students identify and connect with available resources so young people can successfully navigate the tricky, sometimes dangerous, but always challenging pathway to adulthood.

CHARACTERISTIC #9: CULTURALLY RESPONSIVE

A quiet revolution started in the 1960s with the publication of C. Gilbert Wrenn's (1962) *The Counselor in a Changing World.* Wrenn introduced the concept of *culturally encapsulated counselors.* These helpers are said to be limited to perceiving the world through only the eyes of their own culture. They lack the ability to see others through the lenses of assumptions and worldviews that differ from their own. Encapsulated in their own cultural viewpoints, they ignore evidence that their counseling approaches do not necessarily fit the people they are working with, because the counselors simply do not perceive this. Slowly, the helping professions have discovered that the world is incredibly diverse and that clients often share worldviews that are quite dissimilar because of differing cultural assumptions.

Thus born, the field of multicultural counseling has established that the world indeed is a diverse place. People are understood in innumerable ways, through lenses including gender, sexuality, learning styles, socioeconomic status, ability or disability, age, and so on. Human beings often wrap their identities in these garments or assign others to these garments. To assist the maximum number of students, brief counselors conceptualize human beings as being diverse. Counselors seek to be knowledgeable about the many facets of people's lives. To be ethical, counselors must be aware and knowledgeable about their students' lives and conditions and possess the skills to help them. Counselors should hold the view expressed by Franklin Thomas:

> One day our descendants will think it incredible that we paid so
> much attention to things like the amount of melanin in our skin
> or the shape of our eyes or our gender instead of the unique
> identities of each of us as complex human beings.

While diversity is an essential element in counselors' preparation, the complementary concept of *universality* has been neglected. In the current zeitgeist, we have concentrated on diversity to the exclusion of seeing the universals that human beings share. Counselors have assumed erroneously that because there is so much diversity, there is no universality. Brown (1991) made a case for human universals, presenting a list of more than 200 universals found across all cultures. These human universals include, among others,

- childhood fears;
- conflict;
- discrepancies among speech, thought, and action;
- emotions;
- empathy; and
- facial expression of anger, contempt, disgust, fear, happiness, and surprise.

Obviously, culture influences how these universals find expression, but the universals are aspects of what makes us all members of the *Homo sapiens* species.

Brief counselors avoid the extremes of total diversity and total universality by approaching people's desire to solve problems by utilizing people's own cultural frameworks. Rather than being prescriptive of what people should do, brief counselors help students shed light on aspects of their own and others' lives that work and to identify resources that have not yet been tapped.

Interventions

Applying Brief Counseling in Schools

The earlier-cited model of excellence in school counseling provides a blueprint for how the brief counseling theory can be applied in schools.

For example, the counselor's vision may be a school where everyone collaborates to enhance the learning of academic, personal/social, and career skills. In such a school, finding solutions to problems that range from minor to major would be essential. When one thinks about applying brief counseling to systems, it becomes not just an approach to counseling individuals but, rather, a way of thinking about whole systems.

Applying this theory in schools in a systemic manner has several advantages.

1. The approach provides a unifying framework for viewing problems at individual, small-group, classroom, and school levels. No longer do counselors have to jump back and forth between theories—or fly by the seat of their pants—to address concerns at different levels of the system. The counselor is free to master one framework rather than to be a practitioner of many frameworks and master of none. Essentially, this is what the school counselor Claudia Vangstad did when she applied one type of brief counseling—problem solving—to her entire school (Littrell & Peterson, 2005).

2. School personnel can easily understand the language of brief counseling. It is not filled with jargon—with the possible exception of de Shazer's (1988) Miracle Question: "Suppose that one night there is a miracle and while you are sleeping the problem that brought you into [counseling] is solved: How would you know? What would be different? What will your [teachers] notice?" (p. 5).

3. Brief counseling emphasizes people's strengths and resources rather than their deficits. Focusing on what works and the strengths people can use to reach their goals enhances and motivates people.

A potential limitation of applying brief counseling in schools is that it can be perceived of as the next fad. To overcome this limitation, the counselor Claudia Vangstad avoided making brief counseling *the* solution. Rather, she consistently focused on helping kids solve problems. Her consistency was such that eventually we compared her approach to being like water over stone: She slowly but persistently created new channels that supported problem solving (Littrell & Peterson, 2005).

Individual Counseling Applications and Interventions

Problem-solving and solution-focused brief counseling approaches origi-nally were designed to help individuals make changes in their lives. When working with individuals, brief counselors have an array of techniques and strategies from which to choose (Metcalf, 1995).

INTERVENTIONS WITH CHILDREN

A marvelous brief counseling resource for working with children is Berg and Steiner's (2003) book, *Children's Solution Work*. It provides numer-ous examples of how to work with children by asking *scaling questions*, asking the Miracle Question, and *finding exceptions*. Children as young as second graders can use scaling to assess change. The counselor might use a "thermometer" (100 degrees equals "very, very mad"; 0 degrees equals "calm" or "not mad at all") to help the child with incremental responses (Davis & Osborn, 2000, p. 69).

Asking the Miracle Question as a "magic wand question" evokes new possibilities. For example, the counselor might say to the child, "When I wave this magic wand, the problems you have will go away. What is your life like if that happens?" New solutions can emerge when the focus becomes the future rather than the problematic past or present.

Exceptions can be found by asking, "Jim, when do you get your homework done right away even though you're tempted to put it off?" A companion book to Davis and Osborn (2000) is Selekman's (1997) *Solution-focused Therapy With Children: Harnessing Family Strengths for Systemic Change*. Together, these books provide a comprehensive explo-ration of the power of solution-focused brief counseling when helping children.

INTERVENTIONS WITH ADOLESCENTS

Numerous books offer guidance for working with adolescents within a brief counseling framework. Particularly helpful are those by Davis and Osborn (2000), Murphy and Duncan (1997), Selekman (2005), and Sklare (2005). Not overlooked in these sources are cases involving difficult and complex situations, as Fisch and Schlanger (1999) aptly demonstrated in their book *Brief Therapy With Intimidating Cases: Changing the Unchangeable.*

An example of using brief counseling when working with a potentially dangerous situation is described in a chapter by Zinck and Littrell (2002) entitled, "A Peaceful Solution." Two ninth-grade girls were intent on setting fire to a rival girl. The counselor, Kirk Zinck, was brought in to work with the three girls. Upon finding out that the girls had once been friends, he began asking exception questions, such as, "So what was it like when the three of you did things together?" Kirk was persistent in this line of questioning, and by the session's end the rivals had declared a truce and were willing to tell their friends to abandon taking sides. A second meeting solidified the gains made during the first meeting. For Kirk, the exception questions demonstrated the power of focusing on when something is not a problem rather than focusing on what is not working.

Group Counseling Applications and Interventions

A relatively unrealized application of brief counseling theory is in working with groups. Most brief counseling groups have been modeled after the work of individual brief counseling, and group leaders have directed only cursory attention to group dynamics. Often the emphasis has been on working with one individual at a time, with vicarious learning for the rest. A leader-led group is a predominant characteristic of most brief counseling groups. Sources for this type of group work are found in Metcalf's (1998) *Solution Focused Group Therapy: Ideas for Groups in Private Practice, Schools, Agencies, and Treatment Programs.* Sharry's (2001) *Solution-Focused Groupwork* does address group work, but little is directly applicable to school counselors.

GROUP COUNSELING APPLICATIONS WITH CHILDREN

In our portrait of Claudia Vangstad's work as an elementary school counselor, we observe that she used the MRI brief therapy approach consistently in her group work (Littrell & Peterson, 2005). In her Bomb Squad club, she asked group members questions such as, "How is [whatever difficulty is described] a problem for you?" She emphasized "for you" to seed the idea that the motivation to change would come from the student. When assessing a student's motivation, Vangstad often asked a scaling question: "How eager are you to be here?"

GROUP COUNSELING APPLICATIONS WITH ADOLESCENTS

With the exceptions of Davis and Osborn (2000), LaFountain, Garner, and Eliason (1996), and Metcalf (1998), few authors have addressed brief counseling groups for adolescents. The basic principles and techniques of brief counseling are, for the most part, simply woven into the practice of good group counseling.

One issue that arises in brief counseling groups is how much of the process is leader led versus student led. Brief counseling is characterized by its assumption that approaching problems and solutions in a unique way is helpful in promoting change. To the extent that the counselor is trained in the model, the counselor takes the lead in structuring the group experience. To the extent that the ways of approaching problems and solutions are shared with the group, group members have the opportunity to employ the skills with each other.

Classroom Guidance Applications and Interventions

Classroom guidance is a powerful tool for reaching many students. Claudia Vangstad, the elementary school counselor we studied, had four goals as she entered classrooms with her whole-class interventions (Littrell & Peterson, 2005, p. 91):

1. Teachers would be able to take care of classroom problems themselves.
2. Teachers would alter how they interact with students.
3. Children would learn to be problem solvers.
4. Children would feel safe.

These goals are highly compatible with a brief counseling framework. The first and second goals address her goal of changing the behaviors of teachers in the system called a classroom. While she was addressing the students in the class, her more powerful intervention was in changing teachers' ways of dealing with students. To that extent, she was constantly encouraging teachers to stay in their classrooms during the guidance lessons so they would be learning as much about problem solving as the students. At the same time, the third and fourth goals helped to meet the developmental goals of problem solving and safety—two goals that superseded the specific lessons of the guidance curriculum.

Specific to brief counseling, in her classroom guidance lessons Vangstad implicitly taught the four steps of brief counseling (Watzlawick et al., 1974) when she repeatedly asked clear, direct questions to elicit highly specific responses.

- What is the problem?
- How did you try to solve it?
- Did your solution make the problem bigger or smaller?
- What can you do to make the problem smaller?

By asking these questions throughout guidance lessons, as well as in her work with individuals and clubs, she established an overall framework in the school in which teachers, administrators, and students think in a brief, problem-solving way.

Strategies for Working With Teachers and Parents

As mentioned, in presenting guidance lessons, Vangstad was intent on changing teachers' behavior. Helping teachers and parents is a way of assisting in a systemic manner. The danger is that if teachers and parents perceive that they are being counseled, they often resist.

Consultation models that incorporate brief counseling ways of thinking are particularly useful in reaching otherwise reluctant parties. In our way of thinking about consultation, we work with one party to help change another party. The consultation literature does acknowledge that the person being worked with directly is often the first to change his or her behavior, and that change influences the other person's behavior. When we keep the focus on the third party, we ask solution-focused questions of consultees to loosen up their thinking.

Kirk Zinck provides a salient account of the power of helping teachers find exceptions (personal communication, July 10, 2005). Kirk was asked by a high school teacher if he would see Tim, a student who was being disruptive in class. Kirk said to the teacher, "I'd be glad to talk with him. In the meantime, I'd simply like you to observe times when Tim is on-task and behaving himself." The teacher agreed. The next week the teacher complimented Kirk for the effects of counseling on the student because Tim was much better behaved now. Kirk did not have the heart to tell the teacher that he had not yet had a chance to see Tim.

If this type of outcome were rare, we would not mention it, but we consistently find that when we direct teachers and parents to begin looking for positive changes, they discover that it is not always a problem and many times the problem begins to dissolve. Useful questions we ask include the following:

- "When is the situation a bit better?"
- "When is it a bit less of a problem?"
- "Can you see if you can catch [the child] acting like you would like [him or her] to act?"

• •

CASE STUDY: MANUEL

Who Has the Problem?

A hallmark of brief counseling is to ask the question: Who has the problem? In the case of Manuel, the answer is obvious: It is *not* Manuel. Those most concerned about his behavior are his teacher and parents. If Manuel has a problem, it seems to be getting others off his back.

In brief counseling, counselors are inclined to work with those who have a problem versus those who do not. Thus, the primary way to approach this situation may be to reframe it, not as the Case of Manuel but, instead, as the Case of Those Who Are Concerned About Manuel.

If I were the counselor, my first step would be to begin working in a consulting role with the teacher and parents. In our first meeting I would (a) validate their concerns and frustrations, and (b) reframe the situation as a problem they have that I will help them with—even as I acknowledge that the consequences of Manuel's behavior are serious.

Attempted Solutions

As a second step, I would explore the teacher's and parents' attempted solutions. Because these solutions are not working, I would explore how their doing more of the same will most likely result in Manuel doing more of the same. In brief counseling terms—if something is not working, stop doing it. There are indications in the case write-up that those concerned about Manuel have tried numerous solutions—to no avail—to change his behavior. We are aware that the teacher's attempted solutions involve redirecting and reassuring Manuel. The teacher most likely has found that redirecting and reassuring succeed with other children and thus expects these "solutions" to work with Manuel. These solutions do not work with Manuel, and because they do not, we should stop doing them. I would explore other attempted solutions that are not working and cease them as well.

Goals

To date, the goals by the parents and teachers have been stated in what they do *not* want: Manuel's distractibility, discouragement, angry outbursts, and anxiety related to his grades and report cards. These negatively stated goals hinder his achieving them. In my third step, I would work with the teacher and parents to define the goal as what they would like to see happen rather than what they do not want. For example, rather than a goal to "reduce his distractibility," I would try to negotiate, for example, a new goal of "increasing Manuel's ability to focus on academic tasks." I would go through the same process for the other three concerns.

Reaching Goals

As a fourth step, I would brainstorm some fun, interesting, and exciting ways for Manuel to reach the new goals. Helping the teacher and parents have a complete repertoire of options, rather than only one or two, will assist them in not becoming discouraged as they look for signs of progress in Manuel's behavior.

"But we want you to work with Manuel." Understandably, the teacher and parents may expect me to work directly with Manuel. In that case, I would agree, with the understanding that they would also work in the ways stated above.

If I were to work with Manuel, I would first validate his strengths—the most obvious being his athletic ability: "Wow, Manuel, you're really good at soccer, baseball, basketball, gymnastics, and ice skating. I'm curious—how are you able to pay so much attention when you do those sports?"

You can see where I'm going. I want to have Manuel figure out how he can concentrate so well in those sports, because he can apply that skill to his academic work as well.

Second, I would approach Manuel with skepticism rather than reassurance. I might say the following:

> You know, Manuel, I'm not sure you can get the job done with your schoolwork. Maybe it's too hard for you. Maybe you can't figure out how to use your good thinking in sports to figure out how to do good schoolwork. I hope you don't surprise your teacher, your parents, and me by figuring out how to use your brain because if you did, you'd be on the winning team and I don't think you can be on the winning team in schoolwork.

This "skeptic approach" to Manuel avoids the "reassurance approach," which does not work. The new approach provides a challenge in terms of a sports metaphor that seems to make a lot of sense for Manuel. Will this work? I don't know for sure, but in taking a 180-degree swing from an approach that doesn't work, I've at least guaranteed that we will not fall prey to that which clearly doesn't work.

Another approach to Manuel may be to draw on his strength as a young person who seems skilled in approaching the world kinesthetically. Helping Manuel learn in the classroom with a more kinesthetic approach may address how he best learns.

CASE STUDY: AMY

Depression. This word as a label is enough to make one's shoulders sag, spirits sink, and thoughts turn glum. Although the clinical definition of depression suggests specific interventions, brief counselors would first want to rule out alternative explanations, such as (a) life is stressful for a 14-year-old adolescent, (b) she is sleep-deprived, (c) her nutrition is inadequate for a growing body, and (d) she lacks of peer and adult support in that arduous journey called adolescence.

One way to check alternative hypotheses is to have Amy provide a concrete and detailed answer to the directive, "Tell me in some detail about a typical day in your life." My guess is that I would discover that Amy's life is filled with one or more of the following: (a) numerous stressful events, (b) irregular sleep and too little of it, (c) less than nutritional eating habits with far too many empty calories, and (d) counterproductive attempts to elicit social support. Any of these alone could make one feel down or blue—and that is precisely how I would begin talking with Amy. I would substitute the words *feeling down* or *feeling blue* for the word *depression* as a way of beginning to normalize her experience rather than make it a pathological state.

Next I would assess where Amy is in Prochaska's stages of change (Prochaska et al., 1994). Based on the case presentation, my best guess is Contemplation, in which Amy is aware of her feelings but has little confidence about how to proceed. It makes sense to help Amy move to the next step—Preparation. Solution-focused ways to achieve this are to validate concerns, ask the Miracle Question, explore exceptions to the problems, and ask scaling questions.

Amy believes that few people are on her side. I would deliberately arrange the chairs so my chair would be beside hers. Literally, I want to be on her side as we work together. I also would make sure that she has time to tell her story, but as she tells it, I would not let it be a monologue. I would paraphrase, reflect her feelings, and summarize so she also could hear herself as she sounds to another person. Most important, I would validate Amy's concerns by saying, "Amy, you're struggling with lots of things. It's little wonder you're feeling down right now."

Asking the Miracle Question would help Amy move from dwelling on her "problems" to how she would like her life to be. Often, the Miracle Question changes the tone of a session from one of hopelessness to one of hope. In asking the Miracle Question, I might provide the frame by saying,

> Amy, you've talked about relationships with friends and the pressure you put on yourself to be a high achiever. Suppose that one night there is a miracle and while you are sleeping, the problem that brought you into counseling is solved. How would you know?

I would follow up with additional questions:

> What would be different? What would be the first thing you notice that would indicate to you that a miracle had happened? What would your teachers notice? What would your friends notice? What would your parents notice?

Amy is not always feeling down. What are the exceptions? When is it not a problem? When is it a little bit less of a problem? On occasions when it is not a problem, what is she doing differently? I might ask her, "I'm wondering Amy—when is it that you feel a little bit better and have a little more energy?" If exceptions emerge, I would ask for her role in the exception: "How do *you* get that to happen?"

Along with exploring exceptions, I would have Amy indicate where she is on a scale with the endpoints of 1 = *Most Down I've Been,* to 10 = *A Miracle Has Occurred.* Where is the worst she has been? What is the best to date? Where is she currently? What would be a small step she could take to move her up .5 points on the scale? I would tie the small step to the Prochaska stages of change so the small step would be in the direction of Preparation.

Conclusion

Theories are tools that help us in assisting others make the changes they desire in their lives. As a tool, brief counseling inspires hope by emphasizing what works, drawing on strengths and resources, and focusing on the future. Because tools are designed to help in specific ways, brief counseling is yet another tool that may prove helpful in the counselor's repertoire of skills. As with any counseling theory, when a brief counseling approach is employed, it should be used skillfully, with finesse and empathy, and in a warm, genuine, and caring manner.

References

American Psychiatric Association. (2000). *Diagnostic and statistical manual of mental disorders* (DSM-IV-TR). Arlington, VA: Author.

Berg, I. K., & Steiner, T. (2003). *Children's solution work.* New York: W. W. Norton.

Brown, D. E. (1991). *Human universals.* New York: McGraw Hill.

Cross, J. G., & Guyer, M. J. (1980). *Social traps.* Ann Arbor: University of Michigan Press.

Davis, T. E., & Osborn, C. J. (2000). *The solution-focused school counselor: Shaping school practice.* New York: Brunner-Routledge.

de Shazer, S. (1985). *Keys to solution in brief therapy.* New York: W. W. Norton.

de Shazer, S. (1988). *Clues: Investigating solutions in brief therapy.* New York: W. W. Norton.

Fisch, R., Weakland, J. H., & Segal, L. (1982). *The tactics of change: Doing therapy briefly.* San Francisco: Jossey-Bass.

Fisch, R., & Schlanger, K. (1999). *Brief therapy with intimidating cases: Changing the unchangeable.* San Francisco: Jossey-Bass.

LaFountain, R. M., Garner, N. E., & Eliason, G. T. (1996). Solution-focused counseling groups: A key for school counselors. *School Counselor, 43,* 256–267.

Littrell, J. M. (1998). *Brief counseling in action.* New York: W. W. Norton.

Littrell, J. M., & Peterson, J. S. (2005). *Portrait and model of a school counselor.* Boston: Lahaska Press/Houghton Mifflin.

Littrell, J. M., & Zinck, K. (2004). Brief counseling with children and adolescents: Interactive, culturally responsive, and action-based. In A. Vernon (Ed.), *Counseling children and adolescents* (3rd ed., pp. 137–162). Denver: Love.

Metcalf, L. (1995). *Counseling toward solutions: A practical solution-focused program for working with students, teachers, and parents.* Englewood Cliffs, NJ: Center for Applied Research in Education.

Metcalf, L. (1998). *Solution focused group therapy: Ideas for groups in private practice, schools, agencies, and treatment programs.* New York: Free Press.

Murphy, J. J., & Duncan, B. L. (1997). *Brief intervention for school problems: Collaborating for practical solutions.* New York: Guilford Press.

Prochaska, J. O., Norcross, J. C., & DiClemente, C. C. (1994). *Changing for good.* New York: William Morrow.

Selekman, M. D. (2005). *Pathways to change: Brief therapy solutions with difficult adolescents* (2nd ed.). New York: Guilford Press.

Selekman, M. D. (1997). *Solution-focused therapy with children: Harnessing family strengths for systemic change.* New York: Guilford Press.

Sharry, J. (2001). *Solution-focused groupwork.* Thousand Oaks, CA: Sage.

Sklare, G. B. (2005). *Brief counseling that works: A solution-focused approach for school counselors and administrators* (2nd ed.). Thousand Oaks, CA: Corwin Press.

Walsh, W. B., & Osipow, S. H. (1970). *Strategies in counseling for behavior change.* New York: Appleton-Century-Crofts.

Watzlawick, P., Weakland, J., & Fisch, R. (1974). *Change: Principles of problem formation and problem resolution.* New York: W. W. Norton.

Wrenn, C. G. (1962). *The counselor in a changing world.* Washington, DC: American Personnel & Guidance Association.

Zinck, K., & Littrell, J. M. (2002). A peaceful solution. In L. B. Golden (Ed.), *Case studies in child and adolescent counseling* (3rd ed., pp. 108–117). Upper Saddle River, NJ: Merrill Prentice Hall.

CHAPTER 5

RATIONAL EMOTIVE BEHAVIOR THERAPY

· · · · · · · · ·

Ann Vernon

· · · · · · · · ·

Overview

Albert Ellis, the grandfather of cognitive behavior therapy, developed rational emotive behavior therapy (REBT) in 1955 after diligently practicing and subsequently questioning the effectiveness of psychoanalysis (Ellis, 2002). In its more than 50 years of existence, REBT has been applied successfully to individual, marital, group, and family therapy for a wide array of problems, and is a well-established form of counseling that has been used with children as well as adults. In fact, REBT has a long-standing history of applications with children, most notably through the Living School that Ellis established in 1971 to help school-age children learn rational principles (Vernon, 2004a). Although the Living School no longer exists, the principles continue to be introduced throughout the world in educational as well as therapeutic settings to children of all ages for problems such as school phobia, anger, underachievement, depression, anxiety, perfectionism, acting out, procrastination, and typical developmental problems (Bernard, 1991; Ellis & Wilde, 2002; Ellis & Bernard, 2006; Vernon, 2002a; Vernon, 2004a).

Rational emotive behavior theorists stress the interconnectedness of thinking and feeling, as well as behaving (Dryden, DiGiuseppe, & Neenan, 2003). Central to this theory is the notion that emotional distress

153

results from dysfunctional thought processes such as exaggeration, over-simplification, illogic, overgeneralization, unvalidated assumptions, absolutistic thinking, and faulty deductions (DiGiusepe, 1999).

Fundamental to REBT is the concept that these dysfunctional, irrational thoughts emanate from three main categories of demandingness (Dryden et al., 2003):

1. *self-demandingness*, which requires that we must always perform to win others' approval, because if we don't, we are incompetent, unworthy, and inadequate;
2. *other-demandingness*, which implies that people with whom we associate must always treat us fairly and kindly, and if they do not, they are bad and unworthy; and
3. *world-demandingness*, which means that the conditions in which we live must be hassle-free, safe, and enjoyable, and if they are not, it is unbearable and awful.

According to Ellis (2001a, b), the best way to reduce the emotional distress created by irrational thinking is to help people change their thoughts so they can experience less intense negative emotions, behave in more self-enhancing ways that will help them attain personal goals and lead happier and more fulfilling lives, and think more rationally and functionally.

Ellis developed the A-B-C model to conceptualize the major constructs of REBT, as well as the process of change (Dryden, 1999; Dryden & Ellis, 2001; Ellis, 2001b). According to this theory, people erroneously assume that an activating event (A) causes their negative emotions and self-defeating behaviors (C). It is not the event itself, though, as two people could experience the same event but respond differently because of how they think about it. Therefore, emotional and behavioral consequences (Cs) are affected by beliefs (Bs) that may be rational and lead to self-helping consequences, or irrational and result in self-defeating consequences (Ellis, 2001b). To reduce the negative impact of irrational beliefs, these beliefs must be disputed (D), resulting in effective new beliefs (E) and more moderate, healthy emotions (F).

REBT is designed as a self-help, educative therapy that emphasizes the acquisition of skills, thereby distinguishing it from some other forms of therapy (Ellis, 2002; Vernon, 2004a). The primary goal is to teach people how to get better, not just feel better (Ellis, 2001a, b; Vernon, 2002a). This can be accomplished using a variety of emotional, behavioral, and cognitive techniques that can be adapted readily for younger populations (Vernon, 2002a; Vernon, 2004a; Wilde, 1992).

Major Constructs of Rational Emotive Behavior Therapy

Goals of Counseling

The primary goal of REBT is to help clients develop a rational philosophy of life that they can employ with present as well as future problems to reduce emotional stress and self-defeating behavior. Specifically, REBT counselors endeavor to help clients accept themselves as fallible humans who should not equate their self-worth with their performance or expect that they have to win others' approval to be worthwhile. In addition, counselors work with clients to develop high frustration tolerance so they can cope more effectively with everyday hassles and life's conditions and learn that they can withstand things that are uncomfortable or difficult. Finally, REBT counselors strive to help clients become less demanding and intolerant of others and give up the notion that others must treat them fairly (Dryden et al., 2003; Dryden & Ellis, 2001).

Ideally, a major goal for the REBT counselor is to help clients achieve philosophic change—which means that they relinquish irrational beliefs and replace them with rational beliefs. In essence, they adopt a rational philosophy about life (Dryden, 2002a). In reality, this is difficult for some clients, particularly children and adolescents, given their cognitive limitations. Therefore, counselors encourage clients to make behavioral changes and challenge inferences and automatic thoughts so as to correct distorted thinking so they can view situations more accurately.

A key aspect of this theory is helping the client identify constructive goals for change. This stage in the therapeutic process begins after the client has described a specific example of the target problem and has identified the negative emotions (Dryden, 2002a). Having the client agree on the goals for change encourages problem ownership and motivates him or her to work on the targeted issues.

Role of the Counselor

REBT counselors are active and involved, educating clients and helping them develop more effective problem-solving skills. This approach is especially appropriate for children and adolescents because their sense of time is more immediate and they need something to help them *now* (Vernon, 2004b). Throughout the counseling process, REBT counselors promote skill acquisition and help clients develop practical coping skills. Most important, they teach clients how to *think* better, which helps them *feel* better, and also *get* better because they correct the faulty thinking that creates and perpetuates problems.

The REBT counselor assumes a variety of roles throughout the counseling process. First and foremost, he or she is a psychological educator, helping clients see the connection between their thoughts and their feelings and behaviors, helping them understand the distinction between rational and irrational beliefs and how to identify and dispute them, and teaching them about the process of emotional and behavioral change (Dryden, 2002a; Dryden & Neenan, 2004). The counselor is also a coach, helping clients learn and practice new skills by assigning homework between sessions and in vivo practice during the session. In addition, the counselor is an encourager, intervening early in the counseling process to address clients' problems and show them that they can do specific things that will give them hope and encourage them to continue working on the issues (DiGiuseppe, 2002; Dryden & Neenan, 2004). Dryden and Neenan pointed out that counselors encourage clients to complete tasks and attain goals, as well as deal effectively with relapses.

Another role that the REBT counselor assumes is that of a collaborator who works with clients to examine the "empirical and logical validity and pragmatic value of the client's dysfunctional thoughts" (Dryden & Neenan, 2004, p. 49). Dryden and Neenan indicated that collaboration is important because the client knows more about his or her experience than the counselor does, but the counselor knows more about the therapeutic approach. In this regard, the REBT counselor also assumes an authoritative role and is open about his or her theoretical expertise, clearly communicating these concepts to the client. Dryden and Neenan (2004) labeled this type of relationship *realistic egalitarianism*, which implies that the counselor and the client are equal in humanity and worth as people but unequal in expertise or in personal knowledge about the problem.

Nature of the Counseling Relationship

Although REBT counselors have been characterized as being directive and deemphasizing the therapeutic relationship (DiGiuseppe, 2002; Dryden, 2003), Ellis (2001b) noted that "we had better be in psychological contact with our clients; be congruent, genuine, integrated persons; experience accurate, empathic understanding of clients' awareness of their own therapeutic experience" (p. 122). Although Ellis himself prefered a more active, directive therapeutic style with most clients (Ellis, 2002; Ellis & MacClaren, 1998), he acknowledged that the extent to which a person is active and directive is a choice. Dryden (2002a, 2002b) pointed out that the REBT literature has underplayed the importance of the relationship and stressed that counselors must be flexible. According to Dryden (1999),

> effective rational emotive behavioral counselors vary their therapeutic styles and can adopt a variety of therapeutic styles to fit with the therapeutic requirements of different clients. (p. 20)

Especially when working with children and adolescents, establishing a good therapeutic relationship is important, and being patient, flexible, and less directive is essential. Vernon (2002b) developed the C.A.R.E. model, which describes various ways of connecting with young clients, including self-disclosure, having a sense of humor, and being warm and genuine. She discussed the use of games, art techniques, and specific get-acquainted activities as effective ways to build rapport with this population.

REBT counselors adopt many different therapeutic styles with clients, being flexible and varying the style according to the client. They are like "authentic chameleons," a term coined by Arnold Lazarus (as cited in Dryden & Neenan, 2004), "changing style but doing so with authenticity" (p. 51). Counselors may be serious or humorous, formal or informal, encouraging or prompting, self-disclosing or non-self-disclosing, more or less active-directive, and educational (Dryden & Neenan, 2004).

The counselor–client relationship is a working relationship—implying that the two come together to work on an issue, not to socialize, as Dryden and Neenan (2004) pointed out. Within this relationship the client is encouraged to discuss the problem and what he or she hopes to achieve from counseling. The counselor listens attentively, encouraging the client to feel comfortable enough to speak openly about the issue and conveying to the client confidence in his or her ability to help.

The Process of Change and Stages of the Counseling Process

Dryden and colleagues (2003) developed an 18-step treatment sequence that best illustrates the stages of the counseling process and how change occurs. The first step is to ask the client what problem he or she would like to discuss, what is most bothersome or troubling. This immediately communicates to the client that this is "an efficient and focused approach to emotional problem solving" (p. 13) and indicates that the counselor is there to help with this process.

This step may be somewhat different when working with children or adolescents because

1. they may not be able to articulate the problem clearly;
2. they may be referred by someone else and, therefore, don't see the problem as their problem; and
3. they may be reluctant consumers, unsure and hesitant about the counseling process.

Consequently, the counselor may have to spend more time developing rapport and use various developmentally appropriate strategies to elicit the target problem.

If the client discloses more than one problem, the second step is to agree on which problem to work on first. At this point the counselor also helps the client distinguish between emotional and practical problems. For example, an adolescent may have a practical problem—say, not completing homework—but feels anxious and guilty, which is the emotional problem.

Step three involves selecting a goal relative to the problem as it has been defined. This goal should be realistic and healthy, and the counselor should also help the client distinguish between long-term and short-term goals. When working with younger clients in particular, it is often helpful to ask for a specific example of the target problem (e.g., "When is the last time this happened?"). This specificity, step four, helps the client deal more constructively with the problem and helps the counselor more accurately assess the *A, B,* and *C.*

In step 5 the counselor assesses the emotional consequence or the activating event, depending on whether the client first describes an event or a feeling. Typically, children and adolescents present the activating event, and if this is the case, the counselor actively listens to the client's description of the problem. Generally speaking, REBT counselors do not encourage clients to elaborate extensively on the activating event (Dryden, 2002b), but this varies depending on the nature and severity of the problem. During this assessment the counselor determines which part of the activating event triggers the beliefs, remembering that the *A* can be a thought, an inference, a behavior, a sensation, or an event. In assessing the *A*, the counselor may determine that it is a clear distortion of reality. Rather than confronting it at this point, however, the counselor assumes that the client's perception is correct and works on identifying the associated irrational beliefs.

If the activating event was assessed in step 5, step 6 involves assessing the *C*, emotional and behavioral consequences. In this step the client is asked to describe how he or she feels relative to the activating event. This may be somewhat challenging for younger children or even adolescents whose feeling vocabulary may be limited. In this case, the counselor should employ various strategies such as feeling word lists, games, role play, or pantomime to elicit the feelings (Vernon, 2002a). It is also important to assess the frequency, intensity, and duration of the feeling and to distinguish between healthy and unhealthy negative emotions that differ in intensity. Counselors help clients differentiate concern and extreme anxiety, sadness and depression, guilt and remorse, for example. They ask, "How do you feel about the situation?" rather than, "How does that situation make you feel?" (Dryden et al., 2003, p. 25), because the latter reinforces that idea that *A* causes *C*.

In addition to assessing the emotional consequences, in step 7 the counselor asks the client how he or she behaved. This is especially important in working with younger clients because, though they may not label the emotion accurately, the behavioral response provides clues as to what the child may have been feeling. For example, when asked how she felt when her brother hit her, the child may reply that she felt sad but, given that she hit her brother in return, she most likely felt more anger than sadness.

After the activating event and the emotional and behavioral consequences have been assessed, the counselor and client agree upon a goal with regard to the assessed problem in step 8. This may involve helping the client understand the consequences of the unhealthy negative emotion and behavior so he or she has more motivation to identify a goal, which should be realistic and specific.

Next, in step 9, the counselor helps the client understand the link between the problem as the defined goal and the problem as the assessed goal. This is followed by identifying and assessing any relevant meta-emotional problems. For example, clients may feel depressed about being depressed or angry about being anxious, and these meta-emotional problems generally should be addressed first, according to Dryden (2002b).

Step 10 involves teaching the connection between feelings and behaviors (C) and beliefs (B). Using a specific example is often helpful, such as asking the adolescent girl to imagine being stood up for a date. After ascertaining how she would feel in this circumstance, the counselor would explain that the reason the young man did not pick her up was because his mother had just been in a serious car accident. Once again, the counselor asks the client how she feels now, and points out how the feelings most likely changed once the perception about the event changed.

After this link is clear, step 11 involves assessing the irrational beliefs. This can be more difficult with younger clients because they often distort the negative intensity of the emotion. Therefore, the counselor should employ various techniques such as *thought bubbles* to elicit specific beliefs relative to an activating event, eliciting beliefs through puppets with younger children, supplying an inference as a hunch (Vernon, 2002a), and using open-ended questions such as, "What was going through your mind?" or, "Were you aware of any thoughts in your head?" (Walen, DiGiuseppe, & Dryden, 1992).

While assessing beliefs, the counselor searches for the core beliefs: self-demandingness, other-demandingness, and demandingness about world/life conditions (Dryden et al., 2003).When working with younger clients, it is essential to assess inferences and other distorted thinking patterns such as tunnel vision (seeing only a small aspect of the situation), awfulizing and catastrophizing (blowing things out of proportion and emphasizing the negative), overgeneralizing (assuming that things will always be this way), and dichotomous thinking. During the assessment process the counselor should note any of the following specific irrational beliefs common to children (Waters, 1982, p. 57):

- It's awful if others don't like me.
- I'm bad if I make a mistake.

- Everything should always go my way; I should get what I want.
- Things should come easily to me.
- The world should be fair, and bad people must be punished.
- I shouldn't show my feelings.
- Adults should be perfect.
- There's only one right answer.
- I must win.
- I shouldn't have to wait for anything.

Waters (1981, p. 6) also enumerated common irrational beliefs of adolescents:

- It would be awful if my peers didn't like me. It would be awful to be a social loser.
- I shouldn't make mistakes, especially social mistakes.
- It's my parents' fault I'm so miserable.
- I can't help it. That's just the way I am, and I guess I'll always be this way.
- The world should be fair.
- It's awful when things don't go my way.
- It's better to avoid challenges than to risk failure.
- I must conform to my peers.
- I can't stand to be criticized.
- Others should always be responsible.

Having assessed the irrational beliefs, these are connected to the emotional and behavioral consequences in step 12. Eliciting this from the client is preferable to telling the client that the connection exists. With children and adolescents, the counselor uses various approaches to teach this connection. Worksheets such as "I Think, I Feel" (Vernon, 2006a, pp. 103–104) and "Changing Thoughts, Changing Feelings" (Vernon, 2006a, pp. 193–196) or bibliotherapy selections from *Color Us Rational* (Waters, 1979) are effective strategies.

Step 13 is intended to help the client question his or her beliefs.

> The major goal of questioning at this stage of the REBT treatment process is to encourage clients to understand that their irrational belief is unproductive (i.e., it leads to self-defeating

emotions), illogical (i.e., it does not make sense), and unrealis-
tic (i.e., it is inconsistent with reality) and that the alternative to
this belief (i.e., a rational belief) is productive, logical, and realistic. (Dryden et al., 2003, p. 47)

Irrational beliefs are challenged using techniques such as employing
different questioning styles, using humor, asking the client how well the
irrational belief is working for him or her, asking the client for evidence
that the belief is true or how logical that thought is. Children and adolescents benefit from different disputing techniques, such as the "friend dispute" (Dryden et al., 2003, p. 47): Suppose your best friend fails a test.
Would you think she is an all-time stupid idiot? If not, why do you think
you're so stupid and idiotic if you don't perform well?

Other developmentally appropriate disputations include writing rational
endings to stories and creating rational limericks, such as the following:

> There once was a girl named Kate
> Who really loved to roller skate
> So when she fell down
> And her brother called her a clown
> Kate laughed and said she didn't need to be great.

Other age-appropriate disputations include having clients make
"rational posters": on one side they list or illustrate irrational ideas, and on
the other side, rational counterparts (Vernon, 2002a). Additional effective
disputing strategies include using worksheets such as "Erase the
Irrational"(Vernon, 2006b, pp. 247–248), in which the client replaces irrational beliefs with rational counterparts, and introducing an activity such
as "Challenging Irrational Beliefs" (Vernon, 2006c, pp. 53–55) to help
clients learn how to challenge dysfunctional thoughts.

After the irrational beliefs have been challenged, clients deepen their
conviction in rational beliefs by repeatedly questioning the irrational
beliefs in step 14. This can be done through reverse role playing with
younger clients, in which the counselor plays the role of the irrational
client and the client disputes the beliefs (Vernon, 2002a). This step also
can be accomplished through homework assignments such as having the
client convince his or her parents why their rational beliefs are better than
their irrational thoughts or by using a *paradoxical intervention*, in which
the client deliberately voices irrational thoughts for 10 minutes and

records himself or herself, then plays them back to hear how exaggerated these thoughts were.

Step 15 involves checking the validity of the activating event because, after questioning the irrational beliefs, it may be relevant to ask how realistic the *A* was. Would there be another way to view the situation, or were the inferences true? For example, if an adolescent's *A* was that nobody liked her, and after questioning this, she realized that she had lots of friends but that a few peers said they did not like her, the client would come to realize that she had distorted the *A*, which would help her be more realistic about troublesome events in the future.

Homework is an integral part of the therapy process. Step 16 involves negotiating relevant homework assignments that help the client continue to practice questioning the irrational beliefs and strengthening the rational beliefs. Homework assignments can be as creative as the counselor wishes and may include imagery assignments, emotive-evocative assignments, or cognitive assignments (Dryden et al., 2003).With children who attach a negative connotation to the term "homework," asking them to complete projects or experiments may yield more positive results. Examples of age-appropriate projects or experiments could be writing rational verses such as:

> Jack and Jill went up the hill to fetch a pail of water.
> Jack fell down and broke his knee.
> Jill said, "This is bad, but not a catastrophe." (Vernon, 2002b,
> p. 61)

Other suggestions include writing rational stories, making rational bumper stickers or banners, and analyzing television shows for examples of rational thinking and behaving. These homework assignments should be checked at each session—step 17.

Step 18, the last in this process, is to facilitate the working-through process by helping clients challenge and change irrational beliefs repeatedly. This enables them to integrate rational thinking into their emotional and behavioral repertoire.

Multicultural Applications

Given the likelihood that school counselors will be working with school-age children, as well as parents and teachers from diverse cultures, they must address the cultural appropriateness of this theory. REBT is employed throughout the world through Albert Ellis–affiliated training centers where practitioners learn REBT concepts and subsequently employ them with clients of all ages. Robin and DiGiuseppe (1997, p. 46) posited that REBT is an effective theory to use with culturally diverse clients for several reasons.

1. REBT is a proactive, short-term, and goal-directed approach, suitable with culturally diverse clients who expect that when they go to counseling, they will be actively helped and that the help will be directed to the presenting problem.
2. REBT practitioners encourage clients to maintain their own cultural reality and provide a basis for examining or challenging these assumptions only if they are problematic and cause dysfunction.
3. REBT is "value-free" because it helps the client work toward achieving his or her own personal goals within his or her own sociocultural context.

Robin and DiGiuseppe (1997) cautioned practitioners to be aware of the tendency to expect clients to be a stereotype of their particular culture, and recommended that the counselor ask clients about the salient aspects of their experience within that culture. These authors also emphasized that counselors should not dispute the client's cultural reality but, rather, their assumptions about that reality. They also noted that although REBT can be used appropriately with culturally diverse clients, some additions or modifications may be needed, including having a more laid-back style while gathering data to learn more about the client's uniqueness, being willing to admit ignorance, and asking the client what he or she expects from counseling.

Interventions

Albert Ellis pioneered the application of rational emotive behavior therapy to the treatment of children and adolescents in the mid-1950s, and from its inception, REBT has been psychoeducational in nature. This approach is extremely applicable and effective with young people for the following reasons:

1. The concepts are easily understood and can be adapted to children of most ages, cultures, and intelligence levels.

2. This is a short-term problem-solving form of counseling, which makes it particularly applicable in schools, where time for individual counseling is often limited.
3. The teachable concepts that characterize the theory lend themselves readily to skill acquisition.
4. Children learn behavioral and emotional self-control by understanding the connection between thoughts, feelings, and behaviors.
5. This theory helps children deal realistically with what they can change in their lives and teaches them how to cope more effectively with what they cannot change.
6. The cognitive principles empower children to deal with present concerns, as well as give them tools to use for solving future problems.

In addition, REBT is uniquely suited for use with school-age children because it employs a wide array of strategies that can be implemented in individual or small-group counseling, as well as in classroom guidance. Further, it can be used to address normal developmental problems, as well as more serious situational concerns. Most important, there is a strong interface between REBT and development, as indicated by the following points:

1. Between ages 6–11 and beyond, children are concrete thinkers (Vernon & Clemente, 2005). They see things dichotomously, which obviously limits their ability to identify new perspectives, reframe situations, and see alternatives. This, in turn, has a negative impact on their ability to solve problems. One of the cognitive distortions that REBT identifies and addresses is dichotomous thinking.
2. Children's sense of time is immediate. They look at things in the here-and-now and fail to identify long-term consequences or think beyond the moment. If they can't stand something now, they often overgeneralize or awfulize, thinking that things will be bad forever. As a result, they become discouraged and may act impulsively, often engaging in self-defeating behaviors that can have long-term negative consequences. REBT teaches children how to develop a broader perspective and challenge overgeneralizing and awfulizing, as well as look at short-term and long-term consequences.

3. Because of their cognitive limitations, children often fail to distinguish between facts and assumptions (Vernon, 2002a). Acting on
   assumptions without checking facts can trigger a chain reaction
   that creates more problems.

   For example, for two nights in a row, a teenager's girlfriend
   didn't call him when she usually did. After the second night he
   assumed that she was out with someone else and didn't want to
   date him any longer. He didn't stop to consider that there might
   be other reasons she hadn't called. He drove around town and
   joined a group of girls at the coffee shop. Someone saw him with
   this group, reported it to his girlfriend, who was grounded unbe-
   knownst to him, and she threatened to break up with him. All of
   this could have been avoided had he checked out his assumption
   in the first place. REBT utilizes numerous age-appropriate interventions to help children check out facts and verify assumptions.

Individual Counseling Applications and Interventions

Children and adolescents have to deal with normal developmental problems in addition to more serious situational problems stemming from dysfunctional family environments, death, illness, abuse, or other major
issues. These problems manifest themselves in internalizing disorders
such as anxiety, self-downing, depression, guilt, and perfectionism, and in
externalizing disorders such as anger, acting out, procrastination, and
underachievement.

REBT lends itself readily to addressing these problems through individual counseling in school settings because it is generally short-term, it
is a problem-solving approach, and it embraces a wide variety of creative,
developmentally appropriate interventions. The goal in employing this
theory with young people is to teach them the connection between their
beliefs, feelings, and behaviors and to help them learn techniques for identifying and disputing irrational beliefs. Counselors have to be more creative
when working with this population—employing engaging, developmentally appropriate strategies to convey the major constructs of the theory.

INTERVENTIONS WITH CHILDREN

Like it or not, most children do not escape from elementary school without being teased. Ideally, we would want the teaser to desist, but in reality,

this usually is not the case. Therefore, helping children learn to tolerate teasing is far more empowering. One intervention that has been used successfully is to have the child write a specific example of a teasing incident next to the letter A on a sheet of paper (activating event), then ask the child to identify emotional consequences in terms of feelings and behaviors and write them beside the C. Next, the counselor helps the child identify what he or she was thinking when being teased ("They shouldn't do this; I can't stand it; it's not fair," etc.) and write these beside the B (beliefs).

Then the counselor discusses with the child the difference between not liking to be called names and not being able to stand it, and asks the child if what the teaser said is true—and if not, why get upset? The counselor asks the child how likely it is that he or she can change the teaser's behavior and invites the child to discuss what has been tried and how well it worked.

Then the counselor introduces the child a strategy to use to tune out teasing so he or she doesn't have to get as upset. In this technique the child is instructed to cover a shoebox with construction paper and draw dials on it to make it look like a radio. Using the analogy of tuning a radio to a different channel if she doesn't like the music, the counselor and child brainstorm together what she could think or do when someone teases. Ideas such as the following are elicited and written on the box as a reminder of how to tune out teasing:

- Think to yourself: Am I what they say I am? Can words really hurt me if what they are saying about me isn't true? And even if what they say about me is true, that doesn't make me a horrible kid.
- Ask yourself if you want to give them the satisfaction of getting you upset.
- Ask yourself about the likelihood that you can change them, but remember that you can be in control of how you respond.
- Realize that you aren't happy about being teased but you can tolerate it.
- Remember that sticks and stones can break your bones but words can never hurt you *unless you let them.*

After reviewing these concepts, the counselor encourages the child to practice using this approach to deal with teasing (Vernon, 2002b, pp. 222–224).

Another common problem that many children deal with is being shy, especially about performing or presenting in front of others. This intervention (Vernon, 2002b) provides some pointers for children. First, the counselor normalizes that many children feel shy, but that they can overcome it in various ways. The following limerick can be personalized using the child's name (pp. 261–262):

> _____was so shy;
> In front of a group he would usually cry.
> One day his favorite teacher said,
> Being shy is all in your head.
> To which ____replied, "Oh my; oh, my; oh, my."
> So next time you stand in front of a crowd,
> Let your voice ring out, clear and loud.
> There's no need for fears,
> They're just between your ears;
> So hold your head high and act very proud.
> Well, _____did what the teacher said;
> He remembered that being shy was just in his head.
> When it was his turn,
> His stomach did churn,
> But he did just fine—there was no dread.

After reading the limerick, the counselor discusses with the child the meaning of the phrase "being shy is just in your head" and shows the child how thoughts such as how awkward he thinks he is, how nervous he is about performing and how terrible it would be to make a blunder causes him to feel shy in front of a group. The counselor helps him dispute the overgeneralization that he will always make a fool of himself by asking him for evidence that he has always done this. Then the counselor teaches the child to challenge beliefs such as "this is so difficult" by having him identify other difficult things he has done and how he has coped. The counselor invites the child to write his own limerick or advice column about how to overcome shyness.

INTERVENTIONS WITH ADOLESCENTS

Given that adolescents change more during this developmental period than at any other time except infancy (Vernon & Clemente, 2005), these years clearly can be challenging. It is typical for adolescents to have mood swings, and depression is fairly common (Vernon, 2006a). Depressed adolescents often feel powerless to control their feelings. Therefore, the counselor should help them understand that the event, such as breaking up with a significant other or getting a bad grade on an exam or fighting with friends, is not what depresses them but, rather, what they tell themselves about the event.

"When You Need a Helping Hand" (Vernon, 2002b, p. 131) is an empowering strategy that teaches clients to identify and dispute irrational beliefs associated with an event about which they depress themselves. The counselor initiates this intervention by asking the teen to trace his or her hand on a sheet of paper, and on each of the fingers, write what is depressing, including irrational beliefs. Then, on the space between each of the fingers, the teen is helped to identify a dispute for each of the irrational beliefs.

For example, an adolescent girl might write on one finger, "I don't have any friends," and on another, "My boyfriend hates me and I can't stand it." Possible disputes would be: "I have lots of friends, but right now I'm fighting with some of them"; "My boyfriend is mad at me, but where is the evidence he hates me? And even though it's hard, I'm tolerating it." The counselor would help her identify and challenge the overgeneralizations and catastrophizing through the disputes and have her refer to the helping hand as a reminder about how to dispute depressing thoughts.

Another common problem with this age group is anxiety. Many adolescents are anxious about performance, their future after high school, relationships with parents and friends, and how to deal with pressures associated with sexual activity and substance abuse. An intervention that helps them put situations in perspective by identifying and disputing anxiety-provoking beliefs is as follows (Vernon, 2002b, p. 91).

First, elicit from the teen his anxiety-provoking thoughts, such as, "I'll never pass that test" or, "I know I'll get a terrible score on the ACT and never get into college." Explain that the event itself is not what is creating the anxiety but, rather, what he is thinking. Invite him to sit in a chair and verbalize the anxious thoughts specific to the situation. With his permission, record this monologue.

Then ask him to switch to another chair and pretend that he is a friend who is experiencing the same sort of situation but isn't as anxious about it. Ask him to verbalize these thoughts, and record this as well. Play it back and discuss the difference between the two responses. Clarify how overgeneralizations and assumptions such as getting a terrible score and not being admitted to college create anxiety because they are predictions that may well be false. Encourage the adolescent to engage in this sort of mental exercise to challenge future anxiety.

Group Counseling Applications and Interventions

REBT has a long-standing history of applications to group counseling, beginning in 1959 when Albert Ellis started his first group (Ellis, 1997). Ellis cited several advantages of group work. Because most people who enter counseling have interpersonal and relationship problems and the group is a social situation, many problems can be addressed more effectively than they can in individual counseling.

According to Wilde (1992), counselors in educational as well as private settings are utilizing groups because of the increasing number of children and adolescents who require professional assistance. Cognitive, emotive, and behavioral techniques lend themselves well to this approach, and, according to Ellis (1997), these techniques can be adapted readily to almost any type of group process. Ellis also suggested that through a group approach, members have "more opportunity for learning positive and unlearning self-defeating behavior" (p. 157) because they receive feedback and input from other group members in addition to the leader.

Three types of groups are (Vernon, 2004a)

1. open ended, problem centered,
2. topic specific, problem centered, and
3. preventive.

In the open-ended, problem-centered group, members take their current concerns to the group and are taught to apply REBT principles to ameliorate these issues. In this type of group, which is generally more appropriate for adolescents, the group leader uses some didactic methods to teach the ABCs, as well as disputational skills and problem-solving strategies. As group members learn the concepts, they take a more active role in helping the individual who is presenting the problem apply the REBT principles.

In the topic-specific group, members all share the same problem, such as divorce, anger, friendships, eating disorders, or substance abuse. As group members relate a problem about the issue, other members and the leader interact with the participant to help him or her identify and dispute dysfunctional beliefs and learn effective problem-solving strategies.

The preventive type of group is similar to rational emotive education except that the process occurs in small groups of 6–10 members. In this type of group, the focus is on children's normal developmental issues, is usually topic specific, and is something from which all children can benefit. It is not problem focused. For example, groups may be developed around topics such as understanding and expressing feelings, dealing with difficult people, developing self-acceptance, identifying effective stress-management strategies, or making and keeping friends. Unlike problem-centered groups, which are not as structured, the preventive group is typically organized around a specific stimulus activity that introduces the topic and skills and the leader involves members in discussion and application of concepts.

Procedures for screening group members, establishing group rules and building relationships through ice-breaker activities, and all other issues relative to group formation and debriefing apply to REBT groups but will not be addressed in this chapter. Following are (a) an example of a preventive group sequence for elementary-age children and (b) a description of a topic-centered problem-centered group sequence for adolescents.

GROUP COUNSELING APPLICATIONS WITH CHILDREN

Children of all ages can benefit from a proactive, preventive approach that teaches them skills in dealing with friends. In a six-session group sequence, the following topics could be introduced and modified based on age level.

Session 1—Circles of Friendship (Vernon, 1998a, pp. 101–103): In this session group members learn to distinguish between positive and negative friendship behaviors through a stimulus activity that uses hula hoops, beanbags, and a list of positive and negative behaviors that they categorize when their beanbag lands in the hula hoop. Content and personalization questions aim to distinguish between these two types of behaviors, which behaviors facilitate friendships, and which of these behaviors they practice or would like to develop.

Session 2—Find a Friend (Vernon, 1998a, pp. 161–163): This session builds on the previous session, with a focus on enhancing skills in making and keeping friends and practicing friendship behaviors. The stimulus activity involves children milling around the room to find another group member whose "find a friend" statement matches his or her "find a friend" response. After the partners find each other, they talk about how to be a good friend and are encouraged to offer feedback about the friendship behaviors they see in fellow group members.

Session 3—Good Friends Should (Vernon, 2006c, pp. 287–288): The objective of this session is to help members differentiate the concepts of *preferring* and *demanding* in friendships. After reviewing concepts from the previous lessons about positive and negative friendship behaviors, group members discuss the idea of a "perfect friend" and the counselor asks the group to identify characteristics of a perfect friend. Then the counselor introduces the idea that friends can't be perfect. Therefore, it is helpful to develop UAO—unconditional acceptance of others. This means that, although they would prefer perfect friends, there is no such thing, so we have to accept them as they are and not get upset if they do not exhibit perfect friendship qualities. Then group members are asked to make a poster illustrating the concept of UAO and how this might help them in dealing with friends.

Session 4—Face the Facts (Vernon, 2006c, pp. 175–176): One of the most frequent causes of conflict among friends is failing to distinguish between facts and assumptions—the purpose of this session. Through a stimulus activity designed to help students understand the concepts of facts versus assumptions, group members categorize typical statements about friends into "fact" and "assumption" columns. Debriefing focuses on their understanding of how this differentiation is important in dealing with friendship issues, with an emphasis on personalizing the discussion to their own examples and how to use the concepts to improve their relationships.

Session 5—Fights with Friends (Vernon, 2002b, pp. 225–227): In this session group participants learn more about assumptions and how they cause problems in friendships. By playing a game similar to tic-tac-toe, they decide whether a situation represents rational thinking and factual information or assumptions and irrational thinking. They also identify effective and ineffective coping strategies. The leader then invites group members to personalize the information to their own issues and identify goals for change.

Session 6—Solve It (Vernon, 2006c, pp. 283–284). In this session the objective is for group members to learn positive conflict-resolution techniques. After a discussion about typical problems they encounter in interpersonal relationships, the children are divided into pairs and each pair is given a problem card, such as "You shared something in confidence with your friend, then your friend told it to someone else. You try to talk about the situation but end up fighting." The pairs are to discuss a positive solution to the problem and then role-play it for other group members.

After each role play, the problem-solving technique is identified. Content and personalization questions address ways to overcome problems, with specific discussion of which strategies group members have utilized and how effective they were. A good homework assignment is to have group members each select a new strategy to try.

GROUP COUNSELING APPLICATIONS FOR ADOLESCENTS

The leader of an REBT problem-centered group has to decide whether the group will be open ended or if the trust level will be affected negatively if members are allowed to join at any time. In this type of group, the emphasis is on applying REBT concepts to current personal problems. In contrast to the preventive group described for children, this type of group is typically less structured and aims for problem resolution, with more emphasis on utilizing the group process to facilitate this. The following example describes how a group like this might be structured.

Session 1: After some trust-building activities and establishing parameters and purpose for the group, members are invited to share why they joined this group and what types of issues they would like to address. The group leader then provides a detailed explanation of the ABC paradigm for group members to refer to as they help each other develop effective strategies for dealing with the problems that will be introduced in the group meetings. Following this explanation is a discussion about the differences between rational and irrational beliefs, with specific examples relevant to this age group. Examples include overgeneralization ("she will never date me"), exaggeration ("I'm the ugliest girl in this class"), or mind-reading ("I know he hates me").

Session 2: After a go-around in which members identify on a 1–10 (good) scale how their week was, the leader invites any member to initiate a discussion about a problem he or she experienced. During the sharing the group leader can conceptualize the problem by writing on poster paper the A, Bs, and Cs as he or she hears them, as a way of reinforcing the concepts for the participants. The leader encourages dialogue about the specific irrational beliefs and how they cause the emotional and behavioral consequences and engages the group members in helping the adolescent presenting the problem identify effective disputes, ways to reframe the issue, and behavioral changes that would facilitate problem resolution.

Sessions 3–5: The same procedure as described in session 2 is continued, with more emphasis on eliciting input about the A, Bs, and Cs from the participants, as well as with the disputations. The focus is on disputing irrational beliefs and rational approaches to solving individual problems presented by group members.

Session 6: In the final session the group leader may invite participants to share what they have learned about emotional and behavioral self-management and how they will continue to apply what they learned in everyday life. Some or all members might like to continue meeting if they still have significant problems to address.

Classroom Guidance Applications and Interventions

Because of the educational nature of REBT theory, it can be incorporated into classroom guidance easily and systematically. Utilized in this manner, the primary emphasis is on prevention, with the major goal being to help children and adolescents learn the general principles of emotional health and behavioral well-being and how to apply these concepts to help them deal more effectively with the challenges they encounter throughout their school-age years and beyond (Vernon, 2004c).

In a classroom setting at both the elementary and secondary levels, rational emotive behavior education (REBE) is ideally implemented through a series of structured lessons that are experientially based, allowing for student involvement and group interaction. These lessons should be developmentally and culturally appropriate. In addition, the concepts should be presented sequentially so they build on each other.

The major premise is that, through these lessons, children and adolescents learn skills to help them deal with typical developmental problems as well as more serious situational problems. REBE empowers recipients to take charge of their lives, first by understanding the connection between what they think, feel, and do, and then by learning that even though they may not be able to change other people or the events in their lives, they can exercise control over themselves. Vernon (1998a, 1998b, 1998c) developed a lesson plan format with the following components:

- One or two specific objectives for each lesson
- A stimulus activity that corresponds to the objectives, such as games, worksheets, art or music activities, bibliotherapy, movies, role playing, or simulations
- Content questions that address concepts introduced and learned in the stimulus activity
- Personalization/application questions that invite students to talk about how these concepts apply to their own lives and how they can use them

REBE lessons are developed around the core REBT concepts of self-acceptance, the connection between beliefs, feelings, and behaviors, identifying and disputing irrational beliefs, and developing appropriate problem-solving strategies. Within this broad scope, creative lessons can be developed to help students apply REBT principles to typical developmental problems (Vernon, 1998a, 1998b, 1998c), and achievement (see Bernard, 2001).

An example of a classroom guidance lesson on procrastination that can be adapted, depending on grade level, is to have students imagine two clubs—the procrastinators and the nonprocrastinators. The counselor divides students into two groups and designates one group as the procrastinators and the other group as the nonprocrastinators. Each group is to think of all the advantages of being a member of that club and design a poster that would entice others to join their club. The class then can discuss advantages and disadvantages of procrastinating and the irrational beliefs that promote procrastination. For a complete description of this lesson, refer to "Calling All Procrastinators" (Vernon, 2002b, p. 184).

Strategies for Working With Parents and Teachers

As consultants, school counselors will find REBT principles applicable to parents as well as teachers. Parents and teachers fall victim to a number of dysfunctional beliefs, including the following (Vernon, 2004b):

- *Uncertainty* (anxiety). Parents and teachers frequently think they should know exactly what to do in certain situations involving children, and when they don't, they get anxious.
- *Self-condemnation.* Adults often blame themselves when they have problems with children at home or in the classroom, erroneously assuming that if the children misbehave or do poorly on exams, it reflects on the adult.
- *Demanding.* Authoritarian adults demand that children behave in a certain way, and if they don't, it is awful. This type of thinking contributes to negative relationships.
- *Low frustration tolerance.* This relates to the idea that adults should not experience any frustration or discomfort in dealing with children. Further, adults may believe that children should have an easy life, so they rescue and enable, which prevents them from following through with reasonable consequences for misbehavior.

As consultants, counselors may work individually with these adults, or they may conduct workshops for teachers as well as parents on basic REBT principles and how to apply them to their own issues about teaching or parenting, to increase their effectiveness as educators, role models, and nurturers of young people. Because REBT is a comprehensive approach, consultants can teach parents and teachers how their irrational thoughts and negative emotions interfere with their ability to teach or parent.

Consultants also can inform parents and teachers about some practical problem-solving approaches including effective discipline and communication strategies, as well as general practices that will and will not work with children and adolescents. In addition, consultants can educate teachers about how to conduct REE lessons in the classroom and how to employ these principles in managing personal and work-related stress.

For more information about REBT applications with parents and teachers, consult *Managing Parental Anger* (Barrish & Barrish, 1985), *Surviving and Enjoying Your Adolescent* (Barrish & Barrish, 1989), *What Growing Up is All About* (Vernon & Al-Mabuk, 1995), and *Rational Emotive Approaches to the Problems of Childhood* (Ellis & Bernard, 2006).

• •

CASE STUDY: MANUEL

Prior to meeting with Manuel, the REBT counselor consulted with his parents and teachers to find out about more about the nature of the problem, including the frequency, duration, and intensity of his behavior. The counselor also observed Manuel in the classroom setting and at recess to learn more about his behavior in different contexts.

Following the consultations and observations, the counselor arranged a time to meet with Manuel. One of the goals of this initial meeting was to build positive rapport with him, because establishing a good relationship with young people is an important element in REBT. A way to achieve this was to play a get-to-know-you game, "Who Are You" (Vernon, 2002b, p. 21), involving a back-and-forth exchange between the counselor and Manuel, to reduce his anxiety by being personable and approachable.

The counselor said, "I'm a person who likes animals. Who are you?" Manuel responded, "I'm a person who likes sports." This was particularly helpful to the counselor because this information can be integrated into future counseling sessions. If Manuel gets frustrated and wants to give up, the counselor might ask him what he thinks athletes do when they feel like giving up, and so forth.

After the initial get-acquainted period, the counselor shared with Manuel that his parents and teachers wanted her to work with him because they knew he was unhappy at school and worried about his grades. She asked him to tell her more about what it was like for him at school, to learn more about activating events (A). After Manuel explained how hard

With collaboration from Laurie Kirkpatrick

school was for him, the counselor asked him how he felt when the work was too difficult and what he did (emotional and behavioral consequences, C). After spending some time discussing his frustration and anger and his tendency to give up, the counselor moved on to elicit his beliefs (B).

Because children generally respond well to games, the counselor introduced a sentence-completion game, which allowed her to identify any self-downing, awfulizing, overgeneralizing, or low frustration tolerance in Manuel's thinking patterns. In this game the counselor and Manuel took turns rolling dice, moving a token along a gameboard, and drawing unfinished sentences out of a box when they landed on a space. Examples of sentence starters are: "When I'm at school, I feel …" "I can't stand it when …" "My teachers are …" "If I could change something about school, it would be …" and "When something isn't easy for me, I feel …." This game helped the counselor learn more about Manuel's irrational beliefs that perpetuated his negative feelings and behaviors.

Next the counselor asked Manuel for a specific example of when he felt angry or frustrated with his schoolwork. After thinking about it for a minute, he related that when he was trying to do his reading, there were so many hard words that he got mad and gave up. On a sheet of paper the counselor drew a head with a "mad face" and at the top wrote, "When I can't get my reading done because I think it's too hard, I feel angry and frustrated." Then she drew three thought bubbles coming out of the head and asked Manuel to tell her what he was thinking when he felt so angry and frustrated. With the counselor's help, and referring back to his responses on the sentence-completion game, Manuel wrote the following in the three thought bubbles: "I'm stupid," "I'll never learn this," and "I can't stand to do such hard work."

The counselor then moved into disputation (D) and asked Manuel if he would like to help her test his hypothesis that he's stupid. First she asked him to look up the definition of "stupid" in the dictionary, and they discussed the definition of stupid as "lacking in intelligence." The counselor asked him, "How can you be lacking in intelligence if you get Bs and Cs on your report card?" She also disputed the irrational belief that he identified in the sentence-completion game (he is stupid because he never gets anything right) by asking him to list times when he *does* get things right.

The counselor challenged the next belief, "I'll never learn to do this," by asking Manuel to tell her about soccer. When he first started playing, were there things he didn't know how to do? And after he had worked on those skills a while, did he learn them? The counselor explained that school is like that, too, and although it may be harder for him to learn things in school than in soccer, he obviously must be learning things or he wouldn't be getting Bs and Cs.

To help him dispute the last belief, "I can't stand to do such hard work," the counselor jokingly pointed out that he must be able to stand it because he is alive—which made Manuel laugh. Then she read him the story *The Little Engine That Could"* (Piper, 1974) and asked him how the engine got up the hill and how that related to his doing his work at school. Together they discussed that things aren't always easy or fun and that some things require more work than others. Because Manuel likes sports, the counselor suggested a brief homework assignment: Before his next session would he talk with his soccer coach about whether it had always been easy for him to learn things in sports and what he had to think or do to keep trying to improve.

During the next session the counselor and Manuel discussed what he learned from his homework interview assignment, and they talked some more about how some things require hard work and persistence. The counselor wanted to help Manuel understand that all people have strengths and weaknesses—things they do well and things they do not do as well. To illustrate this, the counselor employed an intervention called "I Can, I Can't" (Vernon, 2002b, p. 71), using an empty tin can labeled "I Can" and another labeled "I Can't." Tasks or skills were written on each of several strips of paper, and the counselor asked Manuel to draw a slip of paper and perform the task or skill written on it. Examples included hopping on one foot for one minute, rapidly reading a paragraph from a book, spelling "dictionary," reciting the multiples of 5, and doing 10 sit-ups.

As Manuel performed these tasks, he and the counselor discussed whether they were things he could do or couldn't do, and he put the slip of paper in the corresponding can. The two of them processed the activity by discussing that everyone has things they can and can't do, and that not being able to do something doesn't mean he is a bad kid. The counselor again assigned Manuel some homework before their next session: Keep track of "cans" and "can'ts" for the next week.

In future sessions the counselor will help Manuel learn more about how to handle his frustration when he has difficult tasks to accomplish, by teaching him how to use rational coping self-statements such as, "I can tough this out," initiating a self-reward system when he does tolerate frustration (playing a favorite game when he has completed the frustrating task), and helping him learn to verbalize his feelings of anger instead of acting them out. The counselor also will work with the teacher on some behavior management strategies (cues to help him calm down or get on task).

The goal of REBT counseling is to help Manuel learn to apply these strategies so he can feel and behave better and, more important, have a better school experience by adopting more rational beliefs that will reduce his current self-defeating behavior. The counselor supports him by helping him identify his positive traits, educating him in a developmentally appropriate way, and successfully demonstrating how these skills can translate to anything he may encounter throughout his life.

• •

CASE STUDY: AMY

After some initial rapport building with Amy, the counselor used a brief depression screening tool, which confirmed that Amy was significantly depressed. The counselor discussed the results with Amy and asked her to tell her more about the frequency, intensity, and duration of the depressed feelings. Based on what Amy said, her depression seemed to be manifested at times as anger (specifically toward her parents), but at other times she felt sad and unmotivated. The counselor asked Amy to elaborate more on the times she was the most depressed and angry, and Amy said that she feels worst when her friends don't pay attention to her, when her parents don't understand her needs, and when she looks in the mirror and sees herself as a dumb, fat, ugly slob.

The counselor explained to Amy that the events or things that happen are not what depress her but, rather, what she tells herself about these. If she believes that she is dumb, fat, and ugly, and that she has no friends, no wonder she feels depressed or angry. The counselor further explained the A (activating event), B (beliefs), and C (emotional and behavioral consequences) and asked Amy to mention a recent event in her life that resulted in the depressed or angry feelings. Amy said she gets depressed when she is getting ready for school. The counselor pointed out that an event like this doesn't result in depression for most students and asked Amy what she is thinking about this experience that makes it so negative for her. Amy said that when she is getting dressed, all she can think about is that she looks ugly and fat no matter what she decides to wear, and that because she looks like such a loser, no one will talk to her at school. She also shared that because her grades are dropping, she must be dumb.

The counselor then demonstrated the disputing process to Amy by asking her if she *always* gets bad grades, if she *never* looks good, if she has absolute proof that *no one* in school likes her, and even if they didn't, if that would make her a loser, and so forth. Then the counselor asked Amy to pretend that her best friend came to her with a problem similar to Amy's, to imagine that this friend is sitting across from her, and to verbalize what she would tell her friend. Amy was able to generate effective disputations to help her "friend" put this problem in better perspective.

At the end of the first session, the counselor suggested that Amy keep a "feeling chart," rating the intensity of her depression on a 1–5 scale during the next week, several times each day, to learn more about the depressed feelings. At the next meeting they reviewed the feeling chart together, noting the times when Amy felt less depressed than at other times, and they discussed what she was thinking that contributed to her less depressed emotions.

The counselor pointed out that it wasn't the events that actually changed (she still got ready for school), but that what she was telling herself about the event was what resulted in a less depressed feeling. Once again they reviewed the ABC model, and the counselor introduced a continuum to help Amy learn how to decrease her overgeneralizations, as these seemed to have a direct link to the times she felt more depressed. The counselor drew a line across a sheet of paper, and labeled one end "always" and the other end "never." Then he asked Amy to take several examples—one with her grades, one with her looks, and one with her friends. First she was to put an X on the line relative to her grades. Does she always get bad grades, never get bad grades, or anywhere in between? After doing this with all three issues, Amy saw that nothing was at the "always" end. Sometimes she got bad grades, she usually but not always thought she looked ugly, and she usually had some friends. From this intervention, Amy learned how inaccurate her overgeneralizations were, which in turn helped her to think more rationally.

In subsequent sessions the counselor continued to monitor Amy's depressed feelings, and noted that they decreased in intensity as she began to think more rationally. After a few sessions Amy was able to understand the link between her beliefs and her feelings and could employ effective disputations that allowed her to replace her irrational beliefs with more rational ones.

The counselor had first worked on building positive rapport with Amy, then turned to teaching her rational thinking strategies that should positively impact how Amy feels about herself and her life. The homework is an essential part of the REBT process because it ensures that Amy is practicing and perfecting her new coping skills.

Conclusion

Given that children and adolescents often have little control over some of the major disturbing events in their lives, REBT is a practical theory in that it empowers young people to change their thinking and thereby gain control over their feelings and behaviors. A major strength of this theory with school-age children and adolescents is that cognitive, behavioral, and emotive interventions can be adapted to address developmental and multicultural considerations at the various levels. Readers are encouraged to integrate the basic constructs of REBT into their own counseling style, emphasizing the development of a good relationship by being warm and genuine.

References

Barrish, H. H., & Barrish, I. J. (1985). *Managing parental anger.* Shawnee Mission, KS: Overland Press.

Barrish, I. J., & Barrish, H. H. (1989). *Surviving and enjoying your adolescent.* Kansas City, MO: Westport.

Bernard, M. E. (Ed.). (1991). *Using rational emotive therapy effectively: A practitioner's guide.* New York: Plenum.

Bernard, M. E. (2001). *Program Achieve: A curriculum of lessons for teaching students how to achieve and develop social-emotional-behavioral well being (Vols. 1–6).* Laguana Beach, CA: You Can Do It! Education.

DiGiuseppe, R. (1999). Rational emotive behavior therapy. In H. T. Prout & D. T. Brown, *Counseling and psychotherapy with children and adolescents: Theory and practice for school settings* (pp. 252–293). New York: John Wiley & Sons.

DiGiuseppe, R. (2002). Idiosyncratic REBT. In W. Dryden (Ed.), *Idiosyncratic rational emotive behaviour therapy* (pp. 32–45). Ross-on-Wye, UK: PCCS Books.

Dryden, W. (1999*). Rational emotive behavioural counselling in action* (2nd ed.). London: Sage.

Dryden, W. (2002a). *Fundamentals of rational emotive behaviour therapy: A training handbook.* London: Whurr.

Dryden, W. (2002b). Idiosyncratic REBT. In W. Dryden (Ed.), *Idiosyncratic rational emotive behaviour therapy* (pp. 2–14). Ross-on-Wye, UK: PCCS Books.

Dryden, W. (Ed.). (2003). *Rational emotive behaviour therapy: Theoretical developments.* New York: Brunner-Routledge.

Dryden, W., DiGiuseppe, R., & Neenan, M. (2003). *A primer on rational emotive therapy* (2nd ed.). Champaign, IL: Research Press.

Dryden, W., & Ellis, A. E. (2001). Rational emotive behavior therapy. In K. S. Dobson (Ed.), *Handbook of cognitive behavioral therapies* (pp. 295–348). New York: Guilford Press.

Dryden, W., & Neenan, M. (2004). *The rational emotive behavioural approach to therapeutic change.* London: Sage.

Ellis, A. E. (1997). REBT and its application to group therapy. In J. Yankurs & W. Dryden (Eds.), *Special applications of REBT: A therapist's casebook* (pp. 131–161). New York: Springer.

Ellis, A. E. (2001a). *Feeling better, getting better, staying better.* Atascadero, CA: Impact.

Ellis, A. E. (2001b). *Overcoming destructive beliefs, feelings, and behaviors.* Amherst, NY: Prometheus Books.

Ellis, A. E. (2002). *Overcoming resistance: A rational emotive behavior therapy integrated approach.* New York: Springer.

Ellis, A. E., & Bernard, M. E. (2006). *Rational emotive approaches to the problems of childhood* (2nd ed.). New York: Plenum.

Ellis, A. E., & MacClaren, C. (1998). *Rational emotive behavior therapy: A therapist's guide.* Atascadero, CA: Impact.

Ellis, A. E., & Wilde, J. (2002). *Case studies in rational emotive behavior therapy with children and adolescents.* Upper Saddle River, NJ: Pearson Education.

Robin, M. W., & DiGiuseppe, R. (1997). *"Shoya moya ik baraba": Using REBT with culturally diverse clients.* In J. Yankura & W. Dryden (Eds.), *Special applications of REBT: A therapist's casebook* (pp. 39–67). New York: Springer.

Vernon, A. (1998a). *The passport program: A journey through emotional, social, cognitive, and self-development* (Grades 1–5). Champaign, IL: Research Press.

Vernon, A. (1998b). *The passport program: A journey through emotional, social, cognitive, and self-development* (Grades 6–8). Champaign, IL: Research Press.

Vernon, A. (1998c). *The passport program: A journey through emotional, social, cognitive, and self-development* (Grades 9–12). Champaign, IL: Research Press.

Vernon, A. (2002a). Idiosyncratic REBT. In W. Dryden (Ed.), *Idiosyncratic rational emotive behaviour therapy* (pp. 143–158). Ross-on-Wye: PCCS Books.

Vernon, A. (2002b). *What works when with children and adolescents: A handbook of individual counseling techniques.* Champaign, IL: Research Press.

Vernon, A. (2004a). Applications of rational-emotive behavior therapy with children and adolescents. In A. Vernon (Ed.), *Counseling children and adolescents* (3rd ed.) (pp. 140–157). Denver: Love.

Vernon, A. (2004b). Using cognitive behavioral techniques. In B. Erford (Ed.), *Professional school counseling: A handbook of theories, programs, & practices* (pp. 91–99). Austin, TX: Pro-Ed.

Vernon, A. (2004c). Rational emotive education. *Romanian Journal of Cognitive and Behavioral Psychotherapies, 4,* 23–37.

Vernon, A. (2006a). Depression in children and adolescents: REBT approaches to assessment and treatment. In A. E. Ellis & M. E. Bernard (Eds.), *Rational-emotive approaches to the problems of childhood* (2nd ed.). New York: Plenum.

Vernon, A. (2006b). *Thinking, feeling, behaving: An emotional education curriculum for adolescents* (2nd ed). Champaign, IL: Research Press.

Vernon, A. (2006c). *Thinking, feeling, behaving: An emotional education curriculum for children* (2nd ed.). Champaign, IL: Research Press.

Vernon, A., & Al-Mabuk, R. (1995). *What growing up is all about: A parent's guide to child and adolescent development.* Champaign, IL: Research Press.

Vernon, A., & Clemente, R. (2005). *Assessment and intervention with children and adolescents: Developmental and multicultural approaches.* Alexandria, VA: American Counseling Association.

Walen, S. R., DiGiuseppe, R., & Dryden, W. (1992). *A practitioner's guide to rational-emotive therapy* (2nd ed.). New York: Oxford University Press.

Waters, V. (1979). *Color us rational.* New York: Institute for Rational Emotive Therapy.

Waters, V. (1981). The living school. *RET Work, 1,* 1–6.

Waters, V. (1982). Therapies for children: Rational-emotive therapy. In C. R. Reynolds & T. B. Gutkin (Eds.), *Handbook of school psychology* (pp. 37–57). New York: Wiley.

Wilde, J. (1992). *Rational counseling with school-aged populations: A practical guide.* Muncie, IN: Accelerated Development.

CHAPTER 6

PERCEPTUAL CONTROL THEORY AND SCHOOL COUNSELING

• • • • • • • • • • • • • • • • • • • •

*E. Perry Good, Shelley A. W. Roy,
and Andrea Christopher*

• • • • • • • • • • • • • • • • • •

Overview

Perceptual Control Theory (PCT) was originated by William T. Powers in his seminal book *Behavior: The Control of Perception* (1973). Until PCT came along, behavioral scientists sought to understand and to explain behavior by looking at which outside stimuli produced which responses. These scientists formulated behavioral theories based on statistical information often gathered from experiments with animals conducted in the laboratory under artificial conditions (Runkel, 1990). Rats were rewarded with food once they mastered a certain task, just as workers are rewarded with a paycheck for work completed or good students are rewarded with good grades (Kohn, 1996). The underlying assumption is that the right stimulus will always produce the desired result.

In PCT this linear "do this to get that" approach is replaced by a model that introduces the ideas of *circular causality* and *negative feedback control,* two well-developed principles known to electrical engineers since the mid–nineteenth century (Spong, Lewis, & Abdallah, 1992). With groundbreaking discoveries and rapid advances being made in the physical sciences, William Powers set about gaining a better understanding of the living sciences, specifically how our mental processes work and how those processes might be related to our actions. Essentially, Powers set out to explain what we refer to as *behavior* with the same scientific clarity that has been used to explain physical phenomena. This was a major shift in exploring the complexity of behavior.

In his quest, Powers picked up on a central observation made by William James in his original text introducing the field of psychology, *Principles of Psychology* (1890)—that this new science should focus on the idea of *purpose*. Prior to this publication, the questions driving psychology were largely relegated to abstract and complex areas of study, such as religion and philosophy. Powers believed that purposeful behavior distinguished living organisms from the rest of the physical world. Prior conceptions of behavior depict it in a linear stimulus–response paradigm (behaviorism); PCT, however, proposes that behavior be viewed in terms of relationships.

The nature of these multiple relationships allows living things to always adjust in order to meet environmental changes and challenges. The environment is not imposing purposes *on* the organism from the outside; that is, nothing outside of us directly controls what happens inside of us. When the fire alarm rings, not everyone immediately exits the building. It is the relationship between internal goals and the environment that is the catalyst for behavior, and when environmental conditions are no longer favorable for life, living systems change or cease to exist.

In PCT, an engineering model of circular causality and negative feedback control replaces the linear approach of behaviorism. As it relates to PCT, *control* involves three components:

1. Perception
2. Comparison
3. Action

Behavior is thus understood as a process of perceiving the environment, comparing that perception to a specific predetermined state, and taking action to maintain as little difference between *reference,* what the individual wants, and *perception,* what he or she expects to get. For example, when you get ready for bed you have a "specific state" (reference) that you want your body to experience. You lie down on the bed and begin to roll around until you perceive that you have achieved the "specific state" you originally wanted. When your perceived reality gets close to matching what you want, you stop taking action. When you decide to paint your house white and you act to do it, you are controlling for the perceived color of your house (Marken, 1992).

Behavior is a circular process involving the comparison of environmental input as a ratio of perceptions to internal standards (references) and actions with the goal of reducing the difference between the two. "The PCT loop" is a graphic representation of the basic process of control (see Figure 6.1). Where R (reference) is the specified state the individual desires, P (perception) is the present state the individual is recording, and E (error) is the difference between the two. C (the comparator function) asks what is the difference between P and R, the result of which is E. What comes back into the loop is not the actions (A) the individual takes but the results of the action. For example, if I am watching a TV show and someone walks into the room talking, the volume I *want the TV to be* (R) and the volume I am *hearing* (P) don't match. So I act by pushing the plus sign on my remote control. I don't record how many times I push it; what I record are the results of pushing the button, which adjusts the present volume. Just as when a teacher begins a lesson, he or she has a very specific "outcome" in mind, and while teaching the lesson the teacher is constantly "perceiving" how well the lesson is going. There is a constant interplay between the "outcome" the teacher wants and the teacher's actions based on how closely the teacher's perception of the lesson matches the desired

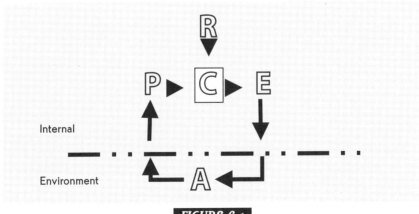

FIGURE 6.1
The PCT Loop

"outcome." The teacher does not record exactly what he or she "did" (action); the teacher records the result. ("Is the lesson getting closer to the intended 'outcome'?")

In the loop no single piece of information gives the total picture: The relationship of the elements explains behavior. All behavior is an attempt to reduce error. Although the process of control has been described as a neat step by step process, all components operate simultaneously. The control process becomes much more complex for humans when you take into account a nested hierarchy of billions of control loops, built over time by experiencing the world around us. According to the PCT model, the linear cause-and-effect explanation that has dominated psychology over the past century is an inadequate explanation of behavior that leads to ineffective short-term practices, which can ultimately be counterproductive to the long-term health of the individual.

Major Constructs of Perceptual Control Therapy

The Goal of Counseling

The goal of counseling in PCT is to get out of the way of the natural process of control and reorganization. *Reorganization* is

- a basic re-wiring of the loops in the hierarchy or
- the creation of a new loop.

This translates to the ability to "control" another variable in the environment, such as learning to tie one's shoes. The PCT counselor believes that the student's distress is over the inability to control for competing "wants." This becomes the focus of therapy. The basic idea is that for every thought the person expresses (foreground thought) there is a higher level thought that has generated the foreground thought. It is the role of the counselor to ask questions so the student may explore the background thought that creates the thoughts expressed aloud. The goal is for the student to move "up a level," to view the situation from a different perspective.

The counselor may teach students the PCT loop and some self-evaluation strategies. This knowledge enables students to look at what they really want and to evaluate what they are currently doing to get what they want (Good, 1992). The primary objective in Applied Perceptual Control Theory is to gain the discipline and ability to focus on internal purposes rather than on external actions. Thus, the content of any particular problem and observable behavior is de-emphasized in favor of helping students understand what they want and what figuratively lies behind their wants.

Applying PCT is somewhat different from other approaches to counseling in that PCT assumes the student has what it takes to solve or resolve his or her own issues; such reorganization is a natural process of growth. PCT shows us that people are in control of their own thinking. The basic role of the counselor is to listen and watch for indicators of the thought *behind* the thought being expressed. At first counselors often find themselves falling into the trap of thinking, "If I could only find the 'right' question, the student would give the 'right' answer." Counselors who have an understanding of PCT know that they can only control themselves and not their students. This leads to a different emphasis in counseling. The goal becomes to help people learn to self-evaluate by modeling and teaching rather than by trying to solve others' problems for them.

Moving away from a focus on a person's action (traditionally called behavior) to the relationship between a person's intentions (references) and his or her perception of the situation is not as easy as it may seem. Traditionally, counselors tend to focus on what they can see (the behavior) and are quick to make assumptions about motivations, which they cannot see. Counselors then give advice or try to coax students into discovering solutions that the counselor thinks are appropriate to solving the students' problems. This approach, while it sometimes yields positive results in the short term, rarely gets at the root of issues and certainly does not help students learn skills to self-evaluate and behave appropriately under new and different circumstances independently. What counselors aim for in teaching PCT and its applications in schools are students who are self-motivated to behave appropriately, even when nobody is monitoring them, rather than motivated by an external consequence or reward imposed by school administrators or teachers.

More often than not, psychological problems or what others view as inappropriate behaviors are results of a failure to fully understand one's own motivations and thinking processes. These are often quite complex and difficult to access. Once counselors understand the PCT model of behavior, they are better able to focus their efforts on peeling off the layers that underlie any specific action or behavior. In this way, they help students evaluate their own behavior based on what they want and perceive rather than based on what they think others might want for them. According to PCT, the better a person is able to clarify his or her underlying intentions and perception, the better that person is able to control for a life that is more satisfying in the long term.

The Role of the Counselor

The counselor's job is to help the student learn the process of self-evaluation. This process begins with the student coming to an understanding of what he or she really wants and an exploration of how he or she perceives what is happening in the environment. It is often difficult to tell another person what one *really* wants. Students share this part of themselves only with someone with whom they are comfortable and to whom they feel a connection. The first step in PCT counseling, therefore, is to establish an authentic connection with the student.

In *Connect* (1999), Harvard Medical School psychiatrist Edward Hallowell wrote,

> What is connection, or what I sometimes call connectedness? It is a feeling of being a part of something larger than yourself. The something may be a friendship, a marriage, a team, a school, a company, an activity that you love, a country, even a set of ideals, like the Bill of Rights or a belief system, like religion.... That feeling of connectedness leads to health and achievement. (p. xvi)

Hallowell found that 80 percent of the students he studied at Exeter felt connected: "In every measure of mental health and happiness that we used, as well as every measure of achievement, the students who did the best were the connected students" (p. 183).

Blum, McNeely, and Rinehart (2002) reported that research on teenagers over the last ten years found:

> When middle and high school students feel cared for by people at their school and when they feel like they are part of school, they are less likely to engage in unhealthy behaviors. When

they feel connected to school they also report higher levels of emotional well-being. In an earlier study, researchers at the University of Minnesota learned that school connectedness is a powerful protective factor. Their research showed that students who feel connected to school:

- are less likely to use alcohol and illegal drugs;
- are less likely to engage in violent or deviant behavior;
- are less likely to become pregnant;
- are less likely to experience emotional distress.

Other researchers have found that students respond better to efforts to improve academic performance when they feel connected to school. (p. 5)

According to researchers Geoffrey Caine and Renate Nummela Caine, "The brain is a social brain and changes in response to engagement with others. Part of our identity depends on establishing community and finding ways to belong. Learning is profoundly influenced by social relationships" (1994, p. 42).

Beyond being genuinely connected to the student, it is important for the PCT counselor to model self-evaluation for students. In order for students to begin looking at their own behavior, it is helpful for them to see the process modeled. In fact, modeling is one of the most powerful teaching tools available. By using personal examples from their own lives, counselors can show students how they have been able to overcome issues that may have troubled them in the past. By being open with the student and admitting that they do not have all the answers, counselors show that they have struggled with similar concerns. By showing students the process of questioning themselves, counselors can teach students the underlying principles that apply to all behavior. PCT counselors hold true to the old adage, "Give a man a fish, you have fed him for today; teach a man to fish, and you have fed him for a lifetime."

The PCT counselor, therefore, acts more like a teacher than a therapist. Our experience has been that students are more receptive to this approach, not only because it teaches them how to problem-solve on their own, but also because it seems less punitive than traditional approaches to counseling. The goal is to aid students to become self-sufficient and to evaluate their actions in all settings.

The Nature of the Counseling Relationship

An effective PCT counseling relationship requires connecting on both a personal and professional level with students. The counselor needs to get to know the student and vice versa. PCT counseling is student led, rather than counselor led. The approach is direct but not directive. The counselor asks questions of the student but does not lead him or her in any way. A core principle in the counseling relationship is "ask, don't tell." The focus is on helping a student realize that the only person one can control is one-self. Often the questioning does not appear to be directly related to the content; a PCT counselor will ask, for example, "As you say that, what are you thinking?"

The Process of Change—Stages of the Counseling Process

PCT proposes that we experience and internalize the world through our perceptions at many levels. Therefore, the process of change occurs at many levels. Powers has tentatively proposed eleven levels of perception starting at the physical or sensory level and becoming increasingly more complex and abstract (1973). The higher levels of perception include program, principles, and systems concepts. The higher levels set the references for the lower levels. This statement has significant implications for PCT counselors engaged in the process of change. Because we have references at all levels of perception, the first stage in the PCT counseling process is to help students become more aware of their higher levels of perception. PCT counselors help students "bump it up" by asking, "What kind of person do you want to be? If you were being that kind of person, what would that look like?" These questions help students set the higher level references, which in turn set the references for the lower levels of perception. For example, "If I were being successful here at school (a higher level reference), what would I do (a lower level reference)?" (Good, 1996).

The emphasis in Applied PCT is on helping students clarify their references rather than focusing on the content of a particular conflict or incident. Also central to the process of change is asking students questions to help them self-evaluate (Good, 1992). The PCT counselor asks questions that are based in part on Glasser's *Reality Therapy* (1967). (Note that these questions are *not* asked until the counselor feels connected to the student and has no intent to seek a specific answer. Sometimes this may take more than one session, but it is imperative that the connection be made *before* the self-evaluation questions are asked.)

- What kind of person do you want to be? (What do you want overall?)
- What do you want (specifically)?
- What are you doing presently to achieve this?
- How is it working?
- What might be your next step?

These questions are asked more than once in a nonlinear way. Note that the questions focus on working *with* the student instead of doing something *to* the student.

The following example illustrates how these questions can help the student become more self-directed. A special needs student was under a cafeteria table barking like a dog. The adults in the cafeteria tried to get him to come out from under the table and stop barking. He would not, and attempts to drag him out failed. One of the counselors got down on her hands and knees and asked, "Sammy, what do you want right now?" Sammy immediately said, "I want some peace and quiet. I tried to tell my teacher that I needed some peace and quiet, but she would not listen. So, I just got under the table and started barking like a dog. Now I can't hear all the noise." The counselor inquired, "So, is what you are doing—barking like a dog under the table—getting you the peace and quiet you wanted?" Sammy replied, "No, not really." The counselor then offered, "If you will come out, I will take you out of the cafeteria and we will go to my office, and I will help you figure out what to do when you need peace and quiet in the cafeteria." Sammy liked that idea and followed the counselor to her office.

Multicultural Applications

Perceptual Control Theory is a scientific theory of how *all* living systems operate. It is not culturally specific. It applies to all cultural and ethnic groups. In the PCT approach, all of the subject matter and self-evaluations are supplied by the students, with their unique backgrounds and cultures as the backdrop.

IAACT faculty member Dr. Jeff Grumley has been working in Canada in the northern provinces with the Inuit. He provides this example of a multicultural application of PCT regarding an Inuk student who knew his elders honored living on the land but did not feel particularly connected to the land himself. This student just wanted to ride his snowmobile and ignore the teachings of his elders. The teaching of elders is a significant part of Inuit culture, and many believe a crisis is occurring in Inuit communities because many students view their cultural values as archaic and irrelevant to their future.

A teacher trained in PCT asked the student what he does when he is on the land riding his snowmobile—a question that was both nondirective and a way to connect to the student. The student thought about what he likes and why he likes doing these things. He said, "I like to be on the land. I test my skills, and I laugh with my friends." Then the teacher asked, "How is that like your grandfather's time out at his winter camp?" The student smiled and remembered what his grandfather said: "When I am out at my camp I listen to the wind, walk on the snow, and watch for caribou tracks; and when I bring my brother out to the camp, we follow the tracks of the caribou, shoot it, and bring it back for a feast with our family and friends."

By approaching it this way, the teacher is helping the student self-evaluate in future situations by looking for similarities between his views and those of his grandfather. With PCT as a cornerstone of counseling and teaching, students learn to self-evaluate what they are doing and to think about their behavior from the perspective of their personal values and beliefs (higher level references). PCT is an understanding that honors each individual's uniqueness. No matter the culture in which people live, connecting references—looking for what is similar instead of what is different—leads to less error and therefore less conflict. Understanding PCT can help mend relationships within families, among communities, and across cultures.

Interventions

Introduction

A key benefit of aligning practices to Perceptual Control Theory in a school setting is that it provides a common framework for all those in the

school (principal, teachers, counselors, students, and parents) to understand that the only people we can control are ourselves. All members of
the school community are encouraged to find common references (beliefs)
for the kind of school they want to have and for what kind of people they
want to be. Individuals and groups then form agreements based on these
beliefs, which lay the groundwork for self-evaluation. Then they are
encouraged to evaluate their behaviors in relationship to what they
believe, who they want to be, and what agreements they have made. This
works best if everyone in the school is exposed to the theory and its
related practices. It is at this point that PCT becomes the foundation for a
common language and understanding.

One of the most difficult obstacles to adopting the PCT approach is
maintaining the principle that one can control only oneself and keeping
that tenet at the forefront of one's interaction with others in the school
community. The belief that one can control others is hard to give up.
Educators have a lot of faith in rewards and punishments. Learning a new
way to be with students is not easy—even when educators recognize that
the punishment and reward system is failing, it is difficult to embrace a
new way of acting.

However, school counselors trained in PCT strategies report that PCT
makes their job easier in that they are not called upon to "fix" students or
create solutions to students' problems. The counselor's job is to empower
students to solve their own problems using PCT and self-evaluation questions. The counselor works with students to better identify and understand
the students' references (what the students want). Only then does the
counselor ask if what the students are currently doing is helping them get
what they want. If not, the students then work to figure out a "next step"
to move toward getting what they want and upholding the agreements they
have made.

Andrea Christopher, a school counselor in Cedar Falls, Iowa, has been
using PCT counseling principles for the past six years. Many educators can
speak about fads and how they cycle through our system. Teachers try out
new programs and systems, and they work for a while and then fade away
when something new comes along. At Lincoln Elementary, where
Christopher works, over half of the staff members have been trained in
Perceptual Control Theory and have been using these ideas for more than
ten years. The momentum behind training the staff is still alive and written

into the school improvement plan each year. PCT applications have allowed Christopher to stay more open, more in balance, more effective, and more connected to her students. PCT is not a fad at Lincoln and other schools; rather, it permeates the entire school culture.

Working with Individuals

PCT provides a variety of interventions for use with individuals. The counselor's first priority is to establish and maintain a connection with students, their parents, and their teachers. Throughout the counseling process the practitioner needs to monitor this connection. When a student says, "I don't know," or "I don't care," this serves as a clue that the counselor needs to deepen the connection to the student. In addition, the practitioner must hold fast to the idea that you can only control yourself. Therefore, questions are directed to the actions, wants, and beliefs of the individual who is speaking and not to the actions, wants, or beliefs of others.

In general, the only difference when working with students of different ages and backgrounds is in the word choice of the counselor. When working with older students the counselor might say, "What type of relationship do you want to have with your parents, even if they never change?" On the other hand, when working with younger children the counselor might say, "What kind of a friend do you want to be with your mommy and daddy?"

Likewise, the counselor encourages the adults in the child's life to focus on what they *want* to see in the child rather than on what they *have been* seeing. One question to ask parents and teachers is, "If this child never changes, how do you want to be within this relationship?" This question encourages them to focus on themselves and their behavior and to become more self-aware of staying in control of themselves, no matter what the child is doing or saying. Once teachers and parents begin to shift their focus to their own behavior, that shift results in a shift in the child's environment. Children then begin to perceive the situation differently and see adults modeling self-evaluation.

Often people are more aware of what they *don't* want than they are of what they *do* want or what they are controlling for. The challenge for the counselor is to allow them time to explore their references and get clearer on what they do want. Sometimes counselors see the biggest shift when students begin to focus on what they want. One sixth-grade student was struggling with friendship issues. On the playground during recess she felt "left out of the group." The counselor sat with her and explored, first, how she perceived the situation. ("So tell me what happened? And when you heard that, what did you think? What was it like to hear that? What did those words you heard mean to you?") Then the counselor explored with her the references or pictures of how she wanted it to be. ("Tell me about being included. What is a friend? How would you know someone is your friend?")

In this student's case, she had been controlling for what her friends were going to do instead of for the resources she had available to her. Her focus had been on how one particular friend was treating her. Once she began focusing on friends who treated her differently—the way she liked to be treated—her body shifted. She sat up and began to smile. When asked, "What just happened for you?" She replied, "I know what I can do to help myself." The counselor responded, "And what's that like to know how to help yourself?" She smiled and said, "It feels really good." This questioning process helps students become more self-reliant.

The counselor would maintain the connection with this particular student by following up after a few days and asking more self evaluation questions: "How have you been helping yourself this past week?" "What's going well for you today?" "How do you see yourself today?" "Where have you been getting a match (i.e., wanting to be included and noticing when you are being included)?"

Some students get fixated on a particular situation and have more difficulty switching their focus to what they want from what is currently happening in their lives. One PCT technique is to evaluate whether a student is "acting in" or "acting out." If a student is likely to "act out," or engaging in what brain research describes as the fight or flight mode, the adult provides an activity that gives him or her time to "act in." Acting-in activities include drawing, journaling, or sitting and looking out the window. The adult is not encouraged to engage with the child verbally before observing a shift in energy. If the student typically "acts in," the adult invites him or her to play a game, take a walk, shoot baskets, or get a puppet out. This helps shift the energy out, so to speak, so the student can process events in a more balanced way.

Misunderstandings can be quickly diffused by asking a few simple questions. The following story illustrates this idea beautifully. A middle school teacher hears a student scream down the hall to one of his friends. She steps out in the hall and asks the student to stop yelling. He tells her that he wasn't yelling. She asks a few more questions to realize his reference perception of yelling is when someone is angry at another person and raises his voice. He just wanted to tell his friend to save him a seat in the lunchroom. The teacher maintained the connection with the student, and both teacher and student were able to really understand each other's perceptions, and the situation was easily fixed. PCT tells us that you can't always tell what a person is doing by simply observing his or her actions.

Group Activities

Experiential activities help kids learn to self-evaluate and internalize these concepts and ideas; therefore, students of all ages would benefit from learning the main concepts of Perceptual Control Theory. Teachers and counselors may use the following group activities to teach them the necessary skills.

"Mind Reader" (Good, 1998) can be used with small groups or large classroom guidance. Children choose something they want (from a group of items) and think about it without telling anyone. Someone in the group then becomes the mind reader and passes out an item to each individual. Many participants do not receive the item they wanted. Children can reflect on feeling a mismatch (error) when they don't get what they want. The facilitator then continues to ask questions to help them explore possible behaviors to help them feel more in balance—ways in which they can reduce error.

The facilitator helps students frame what they want more generally. People who can generalize their wants have better emotional equilibrium. For example, if a student wants a small, colorful ball but was instead given an action figure, the counselor might point out that what the student really wanted was something to play with. Even though the student didn't get the ball, he still got something he could play with. If students understand this, they can generally get back in balance. It is when people are very specific that they run the risk of creating more error and frustration.

Another skill "Mind Reader" teaches is how to reframe disappointment. Questions to explore with the child could include the following:

- What are you giving yourself credit for?
- How can this experience help you become who you want to be?
- What's the good part about what happened?

Other small and large group activities center around understanding human behavior, understanding perception, dealing with conflict, and maintaining connections with oneself and one's peers, teachers, and families.

Optical illusions are effective with upper-grade students. After looking at a series of illusions, students then share what they see. After sharing, students can discuss why people sometimes see things differently. This naturally leads to a discussion on perception. The consecutive lessons would be about "error" and "references."

"Where's Your Error?" demonstrates similar concepts. Students take a small pebble and a small piece of candy. The pebble goes in their socks and the group takes a walk while sucking on a piece of candy. This activity allows students to experience not only their reference of how they want a walk to be, but what is error—in this case pain—in their shoe—and what they are perceiving. This lesson can also be extended for older children with a discussion about shifting awareness by asking, "Were you able to ignore the pebble and focus on the candy?" In this way, they learn that they can view a situation as both positive and negative.

Within a PCT school, teachers have numerous discussions on social contracts, role clarification, and belief statements. This work is sometimes referred to as front-loading. In PCT terms it would be *setting the reference* or *connecting references*. The first priority of the teacher is to establish connections in the classroom. One such connecting activity typically used in a group setting is "3Ps," in which each participant shares, in round-robin fashion, first something personal, then something they are passionate about, and finally a principle they live by. We recommend using connecting activities to start each group session.

When the connections are meaningful to all the students, creating a classroom belief statement becomes an essential collaborative process. The school counselor would work collaboratively with the teacher and students during this process. An example of a class belief statement is "We believe in being kind, being safe, and having fun while we learn."

Although counseling aligned to PCT in its purest sense is individual, some basic principles apply in group settings. Knowing that no two individuals have the same references, the counselor would assist the group in establishing an agreement based on the principles under which the group will operate. Examples include confidentiality, civility, and speaking in turn. It is critical that these agreements are established after the group has become connected and that they come from the group members through a consensus process.

In a group setting, the counselor should weave the basic ideas of PCT into the session, just as in a classroom where the counselor would teach the basic concepts of PCT. As individuals present their issues, the group might then ask questions to help the individual clarify what he or she is controlling for. If the presenting individual asks for ideas, the group should brainstorm ideas, then the counselor should ask the individual, "Will one of these work for you, or have any of these suggestions given you an idea on how you might resolve this issue?"

Often groups end with each individual self-evaluating his or her behavior in terms of the agreement. A typical question might be "In terms of our agreement, on a scale of 1–10, how did you do today?" or "What's one part of our agreement that you think you really focused on today?" or "As you leave here, what's one thing you want to remember that reflects a principle you are trying to live your life by?" There is a parallel between how a PCT counselor and a classroom teacher operate in terms of these agreements. They can be used in managing a group or a classroom (Good et al., 2003).

Overall, in both individual and group settings, counselors provide opportunities for students to tap into their own most incredible resource: themselves. By asking questions within the PCT framework, the student is followed, not led. The counselor focuses on asking questions that will help the student shift his or her awareness. Counselors do not need to label students or believe that they can determine what is going on for a student based on observing his or her actions. Counselors do not necessarily know what is best for the student; they help students explore what is or is not working for them. The beauty of human nature allows some students to arrive at the same conclusion, but each in his or her own unique way. In other words, counselors are a mirror or a safe place for reflection.

• •

CASE STUDY: MANUEL

Introduction

Diagnosis is something to be avoided in PCT counseling. The content of any particular situation is not important for the counselor to know or ana-lyze. In the following examples, the counselor tries to enable the students to gain perspective on their own purposes (references) and their own thinking processes. The focus is on helping the student understand what he or she is controlling for in any particular situation and, in many cases, to "bump it up" —shift the focus to a higher level reference and become "the person he or she really wants to be."

Usually the interventions happen in a few minutes, but they may take up to fifteen or twenty minutes, depending on the complexity of the prob-lem and the extent to which a student wants to learn how to solve his or her own problems. Additional or ongoing counseling seeks to help stu-dents internalize the process and gain an understanding of its underlying principles. It is important that the counselor not set goals for the student and trust in the ability of student to set goals and solve problems inde-pendently. When counseling younger children and adults, little more than word choice requires adjustment. Most often the counselor will use the language of the student as much as possible.

Background

Manuel has been sent to the guidance counselor for the first time for not working on his assigned tasks.

Transcript

Counselor: C'mon in, Manuel. It's good to see you. Do you know what my job is here at school?

Manuel: You're the counselor. You're supposed to solve my problems.

Counselor: That's right, I am the counselor, but I believe that my job is to help you figure out what you want and then help you to solve your own problems. Is that okay with you?

Manuel: I guess so.

Counselor: I'd like to know a little about you before we start, and I wonder if you'd like to know a little about me?

Manuel: Like what?

Counselor: Well, I have a daughter named Jessica who is grown now and lives in Boston. I love the beach, and I like to travel.

Manuel: We went to the beach last summer—and I got a boogie board! My sisters fell down, but I was good at it. I liked the beach. It was my first time there.

Counselor: So, we have something in common. What's going on with you right now? Why did you come in?

Manuel: Ah, man, nothing is going on for me. You know this work is hard. I don't know. I just can't keep up, and they told me to come down here.

Counselor: Well, your teachers and your parents have talked to me. I would certainly like to help you, but most of all I want to know how you see things.

Manuel: Well, I am just not that smart. I am not as smart as my sisters.

Counselor: Do you want to be as smart as your sisters?

Manuel: Well, yeah.

Counselor: So tell me how you know they are smart.

Manuel: Because they do their work and they make all As. And I make like Bs and Cs.

Counselor: So you would be interested in getting As and Bs if that is what it means to be smart.

Manuel: I just told you that I am not smart.

Counselor: I am hearing you, but what I want to know is do you want to be that smart?

Manuel: Well, yeah, I want to be that smart. But if you are not that smart, you are not that smart.

Counselor: Tell me again about your sisters. You want to be smart … and what do they do to be smart?

Manuel: Well, they study. And I guess they pay attention.

Counselor: Do you pay attention?

Manuel:	Not really … You know, I get sort of bored.
Counselor:	Do you think that is helping you?
Manuel:	No, it's not.
Counselor:	So what might be more helpful to you in getting you what you want?
Manuel:	You mean like if I pay attention?
Counselor:	Yeah … so if you were paying attention, would that be getting you what you want?
Manuel:	Well, probably, it would probably be better than what I do now, because what I do now is I don't pay attention, then the teacher gets mad, and then, I don't know, she just wants me to do so much. My parents, too. All the time they are saying, "You have to go to college."
Counselor:	Sounds like a lot of pressure. And what do you want for yourself?
Manuel:	Well, I am really good at sports … you know … I watch sports a lot.…
Counselor:	What kind of sports are you really good at?
Manuel:	Uh, baseball. I love baseball … But now my grades have dropped and I don't even know if I can play baseball this spring. My parents are going to be mad …
Counselor:	Do you want to play baseball? It sounds like you really want to.
Manuel:	Yeah! I want to play baseball … I will be so mad if I don't get to play baseball.
Counselor:	Have they set a boundary for you, like if you don't get good grades, you are not going to play baseball?
Manuel:	Well, sort of … but I hope it's not true.
Counselor:	Will hoping it's not true help you to play baseball?
Manuel:	I guess not, but I'll be mad if I can't play.
Counselor:	Would being mad help?
Manuel:	What do you mean would being mad help?
Counselor:	Would getting mad at not being able to play baseball help you to play baseball?
Manuel:	No, I guess not.
Counselor:	So instead of being mad, what could you believe about yourself in terms of schoolwork?

Manuel: You mean that I could do it?

Counselor: If you believed you could do it, like you believe you are good at baseball, would that make a difference to you?

Manuel: Yeah, if I believed I could do it, and if I believed I was as smart as my sisters.

Counselor: Would believing that you were as smart as your sisters be helpful?

Manuel: Yeah.

Counselor: What's stopping you?

Manuel: From believing that I'm that smart? Because I don't make good grades. Because they make As, and I make Bs and Cs.

Counselor: So I hear you saying that if you can make the shift and start believing you can make As and Bs it might be different for you....

Manuel: Oh … well … do you think I can make As and Bs?

Counselor: I am more interested in what you think.

Manuel: Well, maybe I could … because a B is not that far away from an A. I guess I could try.

Counselor: Do you want to be the kind of person who makes As and Bs? A smart person?

Manuel: Yes, I want to be smart like my sisters.

Counselor: So if you were trying … what would that look like?

Manuel: Well, I guess I would sit there and do my work instead of trying to find other stuff to do. Because when she gives our work out … it's boring … it's so boring. And then, you know, I think I don't want to do it, and then I don't do it.

Counselor: Does that help you be the smart person you want to be?

Manuel: Well, no, and if I don't get to play baseball I am going to be so mad.

Counselor: So what will you be doing instead that will help you get As and Bs and help you to play baseball?

Manuel: Well, I guess I could say if I just pay attention, I could probably make As. I am thinking I could play baseball if I just made Bs. I think my parents would let me play if I made Bs. I don't think they would let me play if I made Cs.

Counselor: Are you willing to try to make As and Bs? Is it important to you?

Manuel: Yeah, it's important to me. I want to be as smart as my sisters.

Counselor: So, at the end of the quarter if you got the As and Bs you wanted, what would that say about you?

Manuel: That I am smart.

Counselor: And what else?

Manuel: That I did it, that I could play baseball.

Counselor: Do you see yourself doing that? Can you picture the report card? Do you see yourself playing baseball?

Manuel: Yes, but I guess the hardest part is going to be having to pay attention in class.

Counselor: How do you pay attention in baseball?

Manuel: Because I know I am good at baseball.

Counselor: And if you knew you were good at school, would that help you in the classroom?

Manuel: Yeah.

Counselor: When you said, "I KNOW I am good at baseball!" your eyes lit up. If you had that same kind of feeling about school, would that be helpful?

Manuel: Yeah, that would be great.

Counselor: So how are you going to get that same kind of feeling about schoolwork? Do you want to figure out a way to get that?

Manuel: Um, well, I didn't get good at baseball all at once.

Counselor: How did you get good at baseball?

Manuel: By practicing.

Counselor: Anything else?

Manuel: I concentrated.

Counselor: See any correlation here?

Manuel: And the thing about baseball is ... I really, really wanted to be good at baseball because my grandpa and my dad are really proud of me.

Counselor: And what about you?

Manuel: Yeah, I am really proud.

Counselor: So in the classroom if you really, really wanted to concentrate and do your work, would that get you what you want?

Manuel: I think it would.

Counselor: And what would that mean to you?

Manuel:	Well, it would mean that I am smart, and it would mean that I could play baseball, and I would be proud of myself.
Counselor:	Well, it seems to me that you know what you want. Let's get together next week and see how you think things are going.

Key Points

1. The counselor immediately tries to make a personal connection with Manuel.
2. The counselor focuses on what Manuel wants, not what his teachers and parents want. The counselor does this by asking questions and exploring in depth what Manuel says about his internal purposes.
3. The counselor does *not* focus immediately (if ever) or specifically on Manuel being off task in the classroom. Instead, the counselor asks Manuel what kind of person he wants to be.
4. The counselor asks Manuel to self-evaluate.
5. The counselor does not make a detailed, specific plan with Manuel.

• •

CASE STUDY: AMY

Background

Amy has been sent to the guidance counselor after a teacher expresses concern about her recent behaviors.

Transcript

Counselor:	Hi, Amy, how are you?
Amy:	Oh, all right.
Counselor:	Do you know why you are here?
Amy:	Yeah, I have been really stressed out and depressed.
Counselor:	And that's my job, actually, to help people who are depressed—that is, if they want help. Do you want help?
Amy:	Yeah, I do.
Counselor:	You do?
Amy:	Yeah.
Counselor:	Okay, then, hopefully you are in the right place.

Amy:	I hope so.
Counselor:	What I always say is that when people are depressed, there is something in their lives that they want that they're not getting.... So what is it in your life that you are not getting?
Amy:	I don't have any friends ... too much work.
Counselor:	Is that right? You don't have any friends?
Amy:	Nope.
Counselor:	No friends?
Amy:	Well, some people hang out with me, but it doesn't feel like it.
Counselor:	It doesn't feel like they're real friends, like you really want to have?
Amy:	They don't call me or anything.
Counselor:	They don't call you up? Well, not having friends is a really good reason to be depressed. Did you know that?
Amy:	No.
Counselor:	Did you know that it's really healthy?
Amy:	No.
Counselor:	You see, if you weren't depressed, you'd be sort of crazy. People need to be connected. So the fact that you are depressed because you don't have friends lets me know that you are a really healthy person. Now our job is to figure out how to get you some of the kind of friends that you want. Is that something you'd be interested in?
Amy:	Yeah.
Counselor:	Okay. So that is one thing we can work on when we meet together. And what was the other thing you said?
Amy:	Just that work is too hard, and I just feel stressed out with homework and stuff.
Counselor:	But you make really good grades right?
Amy:	I don't think so.
Counselor:	Well, I thought I looked at your transcript and you had all As.
Amy:	Well, I still miss problems sometimes.
Counselor:	Oh, that's terrible, Amy ... that is so terrible. You mean you miss a problem, and you still make As? How many kids would like to be in your position?

Amy:	I don't know.
Counselor:	Well, what do you think?
Amy:	I suppose a lot.
Counselor:	Right. So you just don't ever feel like you are good enough?
Amy:	I don't know. I can't get a date, and I'm gaining weight.
Counselor:	You don't look fat to me.
Amy:	My pants are getting tight.
Counselor:	You haven't popped out of them yet, right? But, okay, is that what you want? To be gaining weight, popping out of your pants, and not dating?
Amy:	No.
Counselor:	Let me ask you this question: Who is putting stress on you?
Amy:	Well, maybe I'm putting it on myself, but I just want to do my best.
Counselor:	I think it's great that you want to do your best. But if you want to do your best, and you are making yourself sick and miserable, is that helping you have the kind of life that you want?
Amy:	No.
Counselor:	Do you want to be the kind of person who does her best and essentially kills herself in the process of doing it? Do you think there are people like that?
Amy:	Yeah.
Counselor:	I do, too. So is that what you want?
Amy:	No.
Counselor:	Do you want to know what I think?
Amy:	Yes.
Counselor:	I think that right now is the time to stop this, because if you keep it up, do you think you might end up being that kind of an adult?
Amy:	There's a good chance.
Counselor:	Is that what you want?
Amy:	No.
Counselor:	So you don't want to be miserable?
Amy:	No.
Counselor:	So where do you think the misery is coming from?
Amy:	Inside.

Counselor:	Okay, so if it is coming from inside, then who is essentially making you miserable?
Amy:	Myself.
Counselor:	Right. So is that what you want?
Amy:	No, but I don't know how to help myself.
Counselor:	That's fair, but I do know how to help you. So once again, do you want help?
Amy:	Yes.
Counselor:	Do you want to know a really quick way to get rid of the stress you've been having?
Amy:	Yes, that would be awesome.
Counselor:	Tell me what you are thinking when you put stress on yourself?
Amy:	I am going to fail. I am not good at this. Why hasn't she called me?
Counselor:	So if the next time you are doing your work and you don't want to put stress on yourself, what could you think instead of what you just said to me?
Amy:	I can do this…
Counselor:	I am plenty smart; it's not a big deal.
Amy:	It is a big deal. If I get As and I get the scholarships that I want, I go to college for free!
Counselor:	Is it a big enough deal for you to set yourself up to have a miserable life?
Amy:	No.
Counselor:	One of the things I would like you to be thinking about, because you are old enough to be thinking about this now, is what kind of life do you want? What kind of person do you want to be? I believe you are setting patterns in your thinking that are going to last you your whole adult life. Are the patterns you are setting right now leading to misery?
Amy:	Yeah, I am pretty miserable.
Counselor:	Is that what you want?
Amy:	No.
Counselor:	So if you keep saying that making all As and getting scholarships is really important … is that helping?
Amy:	Um, no.

Counselor:	Are you sure?
Amy:	It's hard for me to let go, even if it's not important.
Counselor:	Maybe we don't have to say it's totally unimportant. One of the things we can say right now is that figuring out how you can be less miserable is the most important thing.
Counselor:	Do you think that if you went to college and you were as miserable as you are right now that you would last in college?
Amy:	I don't think I could handle all the stress.
Counselor:	So even if you got the grades you wanted and all the scholarships you wanted, there's a good chance of what?
Amy:	Not making it in college.
Counselor:	Yes, and does that happen to a lot of kids?
Amy:	Yeah, I know someone who didn't make it.
Counselor:	And I bet he was plenty smart, right? Okay. So my job is to help you figure out how to get some patterns going so you won't be miserable and so you can get some friends. Okay?
Amy:	Yeah.

Key Points

1. The counselor immediately establishes a connection with Amy by telling her that it is the counselor's job to help people who are depressed and that it is healthy for her to be depressed when she does not have friends. (This challenges the way Amy thinks about depression and also about counseling.)
2. The counselor focuses on two of Amy's references, or who she wants to be in those situations: finding the kind of friends she wants and not being stressed out about her grades.
3. The counselor frequently asks Amy questions that lead to her self-evaluation of her current behavior. The counselor does not evaluate the behavior—Amy does.

Conclusion

This chapter presents a more complete and verifiable model of human behavior. The PCT model explains the observation that all living organisms constantly control environmental conditions to meet varying internal standards. We do not simply react to outside stimuli, nor do we behave to meet a set of needs, goals, or desires. By taking into account the fact that people have internally generated purposes, PCT proposes the idea that what is important about behavior is the nature of the relationship between us and the environments in which we find ourselves. The defining feature of this relationship is the comparison of our perception of the information we receive from our environment to what we want—that is, to our internal standards for any particular environmental condition at any given moment. Understanding PCT changes the focus of counseling from diagnosis and advice to helping students solve their own problems. The counselor's role is to get out of the way of the natural process of change and problem solving by helping the student reflect. Teaching students the principles and processes underlying all human behavior is entirely consistent with the true purpose of schooling: to teach students how to think for themselves.

References

Blum, R. W., McNeely, C. A., & Rinehart, P. M. (2002). *Improving the odds: The untapped power of schools to improve the health of teens.* Minneapolis: Center for Adolescent Health and Development.

Caine, G., & Caine, R. N. (1994). *Mindshifts.* Tucson, AZ: Zephyr Press.

Glasser, W. (1967). *Reality therapy.* New York: HarperCollins.

Good, E. P. (1987). *In pursuit of happiness.* Chapel Hill, NC: New View Publications.

Good, E. P. (1992). *Helping kids help themselves.* Chapel Hill, NC: New View Publications.

Good, E. P. (1996). *Overall direction.* Chapel Hill, NC: New View Publications.

Good, E. P. (1998). *The happy hour guide.* Chapel Hill, NC: New View Publications.

Good, E. P., Grumley, J., & Roy, S. (2003). *A connected school.* Chapel Hill, NC: New View Publications.

Hallowell, E. (1999). *Connect.* New York: Pocket Books.

James, W. (1890). *Principles of psychology.* Mineola, NY: Dover Publications.

Kohn, A. (1996). *Beyond discipline: From compliance to community.* Alexandria, VA: ASCD.

Marken, R. (1992). *Mind readings.* Los Angeles, CA: Control Systems Group.

Powers, W. T. (1973). *Behavior: The control of perception.* Chicago: Aldine.

Runkel, Philip J. (2003). *People as living things: The psychology of perceptual control theory.* Hayward, CA: Living Control Systems.

Spong, M. W., Lewis, F. L., & Abdallah, C. T., (Eds.). (1992). *Robot control: Dynamics, motion planning, and analysis.* New York: IEEE Press.

INDEX